My wife and I are entering our third year of marriage, and kids could potentially be in the near future. Because of this, we've begun to talk about how we want to raise our children. To be honest, the thought is terrifying! We want to raise kids who grow up knowing they're loved and who know how to love well. Mostly, we hope they follow Jesus. *Raising Passionate Jesus Followers* teaches a way of parenting and raising children that does just that. In this book, Dad and Mom have shared not simply good ideas, but practical methods that actually work. This isn't a guide to being the perfect parent—that's impossible—but if you share our desire to do parenting well, then I encourage you to read this book.

Matthew Comer

Wise parenting requires the eyes of our hearts be enlightened by godly, experienced, reflective mentors who combine biblical insight and sage application. Phil and Diane Comer have given us this in *Raising Passionate Jesus Followers*. Their success with their own children, plus their pastoral guidance of thousands of others, is the foundation for this treasured resource.

Gerry Breshears, PhD, Professor of Theology, Western Seminary, Portland, Oregon

Phil and Diane Comer have proven themselves to be an invaluable resource for the church. It is a rare thing to find people who have sustained their integrity throughout a life of fruitful ministry and have raised children who are all followers of Jesus. Thankfully, by offering their wisdom through the *Intentional Parenting* materials and conferences, the Comers are providing a much-needed voice in the church!

Chuck Bomar, pastor of Colossae Church in Portland, Oregon and author of *Better Off without Jesus* and *Losing Your Religion*

Phil and Diane's heart for raising children who passionately follow Jesus is evident in the wisdom and content they share with parents around the world. The encouragement and instruction that they provide for parents through their teaching points directly back to the Bible, providing a solid foundation for their practical parenting tools!

Erica Nargizian, children's ministries director, Redemption Church, Costa Mesa

Diane and Phil teach us through very simple principles and practical ways that nation-building starts at our dining tables, playgrounds, and in our children's bedrooms through a very simple exercise: teaching our children to love God and to love their neighbor. We believe that their secret to such a successful legacy of parenting is being truthful and loving against all odds.

Edi Gogu, executive director, Profamilia, and Toni Gogu,
Vice Minister of Justice, Republic of Albania

There is a myth that if you are spiritual you are no fun, and to raise followers of Jesus is boring and dull. This couldn't be further from the truth. Following Jesus is the greatest adventure life can offer, and *Raising Passionate Jesus Followers* will help you lead your family on this grand adventure. Phil and Diane have put together an incredible book that needs to be on every parent's shelf and utilized as an ongoing resource throughout the stages of parenting.

Ryan Ingram, lead pastor, Awakening Church

If the deepest longing of your heart is to leave a legacy of faith to your children, then this book will guide you in your journey. You will be encouraged and challenged by Phil and Diane's transparency and authenticity. They write from the perspective of looking back at what worked. They have lived this out! And their four adult children are their biggest cheerleaders. You need to read to find out why.

Sarah Eggerichs, vice president, Love and Respect Ministries

Phil and Diane share their journey offering biblical, practical, and effective tools to raise passionate followers of Jesus. Being an intentional parent has not only made me a better parent; it's also made me a better husband.

Tarik El-Ansary, executive pastor, Reality San Francisco

The Intentional Parenting Conference was one of the most notable events that has happened at our church since we began five years ago. Phil and Diane's biblically-rooted wisdom gave hope and encouragement to parents and caregivers who are trying to raise children to become Jesus followers in a culture that rejects His truths.

Morgan Antonell, Reality Boston children's ministry director

With their genuine humility, integrity, and love for God and for others, Phil and Diane Comer have already impacted thousands of families in countries around the world. Our prayer is that through this Intentional Parenting book, many more parents and the supporting network of family and friends will embrace the vision to raise children who love Jesus above all else.

The elders of Westside: A Jesus Church

The greatest gift to our children that we can give is to invest our time in learning how to raise them as Jesus followers. This book is an amazing summary of biblical and practical wisdom of how to do this. If you are a parent or soon-to-be parent, I can't imagine not reading every page to learn from those who have gone before us like Phil and Diane.

Dan Kimball, Vintage Faith Church and Western Seminary

Phil and Diane are passionate about equipping parents to inspire their children to walk in the way of love and helping families thrive. They openly share their failures, learnings, and successes with readers with the true aim of inspiring children to love and walk with God.

Scott Harrison

Our church leaders have been blown away by the practical, biblical, and encouraging content that Phil and Diane share during the Intentional Conference. It's exactly what the families with young children in our community need. There's something for everyone to learn as we all seek to raise the next generation of passionate Jesus followers.

Jose Zayas, evangelist and lead pastor, 26 West Church, Portland, Oregon

One thing I love about the Intentional Parents ministry and conference is that the goal isn't to create perfect, well-behaved children; actually, we just want our children to know Jesus. I walked away from their conference filled with hope and faith that this is actually possible. I am sure this book is going to be powerful in the hands of many families.

Ruth Weller, lead pastor, Re:Hope Church, Glasgow, Scotland

This book is a vital read for parents. It not only radiates years of wisdom but tangible, doable ways to steward our most precious calling of all: raising our kids.

Dominic Done, lead pastor, Westside: A Jesus Church

Raising Passionate Jesus Followers

The Power of
Intentional Parenting

**Phil and
Diane Comer**

ZONDERVAN

Raising Passionate Jesus Followers
Copyright © 2018 by Diane Comer

Requests for information should be addressed to:
Zondervan, *3900 Sparks Dr. SE, Grand Rapids, Michigan 49546*

ISBN 978-0-310-34778-1 (ebook)

Names: Comer, Phil, author. | Comer, Diane, author.

Title: Raising passionate Jesus followers : the power of intentional parenting / Phil and Diane Comer.
Description: Grand Rapids, Michigan : Zondervan, 2018.
Identifiers: LCCN 2017045445 | ISBN 9780310347774 (softcover)
Subjects: LCSH: Parenting--Religious aspects--Christianity. | Child rearing--Religious
    aspects--Christianity.
Classification: LCC BV4529 .C597 2018 | DDC 248.8/45--dc23 LC record available at https://lccn.
    loc.gov/2017045445

Published in association with William K. Jensen Literary Agency, 119 Bampton Court, Eugene, Oregon 97404.

Cover design: Studio Gearbox
Cover illustration: © Oleksandr Yuhlchek / Shutterstock
Interior design: Kait Lamphere

First printing January 2018 / Printed in the United States of America

To
John Mark and Tammy
Rebekah and Steve
Elizabeth and Brook
Matthew and Simona
And to your children . . . and your children's children

May the God of wisdom give you all you need to raise up
the next generation of passionate Jesus followers.

Contents

Foreword

John Mark Comer is an extraordinary Bible teacher, pastor, leader, and Christian father. So, when I heard that he asked his parents to teach a parenting class at church, that got my attention. But chills went up my spine when I learned that he sat in the front row, along with his wife Tammy, to take copious notes on what his mom and dad taught on parenting!

"What?" you say. "You said what? He sat at their feet with pencil and notebook? Are you kidding me?"

It was no joke.

In hearing that, I knew I was hearing something special if not astonishing.

What adult child, with children of his own, not only requests his parents to teach on parenting but then signs up for the class and reserves seats up front?

John Mark Comer did!

He knew his parents did something right, something intentional. He recognized that they understood what to do to guide and motivate a child to have a passion for Jesus Christ.

Now, as a new father, he yearned to do the same for his offspring. He had heard the melody, so-to-speak, through his parents parenting and now had a longing to learn the words to that parenting melody. He was ready to understand the what, the why, and the how. He was cognizant that they had built something in him, and his heart craved to use the same blueprint and tools.

I think you'd agree that if your adult children who now have children asked you to lecture them on parenting, it would be evidence that you did something right! Put it this way: bald men do not sell hair restoration oil!

Phil and Diane Comer did it right. They are the real deal. We have seen them up close. They raised four children who have centered their entire lives on Christ and married spouses with the same convictions. Thus, when Phil and Diane talk about parenting, I listen.

By the way, John Mark would never claim that his mom and dad parented him perfectly, but he would claim that the principles they used were biblical, practical, and effective. Look at his notebook.

Oh, and did I tell you that John Mark persuaded the congregation to attend his parents' conference? Did I mention that the leadership of the church persuaded his mom and dad that they must take this message to the masses and would help make that happen?

Everyone who knows Phil and Diane believe in who they are and what they espouse. Truly, people want to take notes on what they present.

Need I say that they feel very uncomfortable when they hear anyone say such things? Of course, that's why I wanted to write this introduction. Somebody needs to say it!

Bottom line: the message of this book is based on scriptural truth and the life experiences of two parents who faithfully applied those truths to their children. There is no promise in the Bible that children will follow Christ with a deep passionate love for Him, given that their parents abide by the principles set forth in this book. However, it leaves one with a question: why wouldn't they?

When a father and mother humbly love Christ and create the most loving environment a child knows, why would a child not choose the faith and values of their parents? Kids are looking for authenticity. Eventually they discern who is for real. This book will inspire you to be that person and parent. Then, maybe one day, your children—as adults with their own kids—will come to you and ask, "Mom and Dad, tell me what you did to parent me. I want to follow your lead."

As for Phil and Diane, who are they? Phil is a godly and wise leader. He has led worship services around the world for Luis Palau, and founded Westside: A Jesus Church in Portland, Oregon, which is part of the megachurch movement. Thousands came week after week to hear his heart on the Bible. To know Phil is to love him. Everyone does. Trust me. Phil models 1 Timothy 3:2–5, the qualifications of a pastor who oversees a local church:

> "An overseer, then, must be above reproach, the husband of one wife, temperate, prudent, respectable, hospitable, able to teach, not addicted to wine or pugnacious, but gentle, peaceable, free from the love of money. He must be one who manages his own household well, keeping his children under control with all dignity (but if a man does not know how to manage his own household, how will he take care of the church of God?).

Based on this passage, Phil managed his household well, which explains why he took care of the church of God and why he and Diane can write this book. Few have lived this out the way Phil has. Everyone who personally knows him would say "Amen" to my comments.

As for Diane, God created her with a plethora of talents, not the least of which is writing. But most impressive is her character. My wife, Sarah, and I have been deeply touched by Diane's heart and deep love for Christ. You see, Diane has suffered, as she wrote in her book *He Speaks in the Silence*:

> "When I was twenty-six, I was diagnosed with a progressive hearing loss—I was going deaf. Doctors gave me little hope for a cure, instead urging me to get fitted for hearing aids and warning me that at the current rate of loss, I would be completely deaf within just a few years. I had three young children, a godly husband, and a custom-created pop theology that could not support the concept that God would allow me

to lose my hearing. My faith began to disintegrate as rapidly as my hearing."

This book will reveal what she did in response. I can tell you one thing, though. When Diane sits in silence, she hears from the Lord. Like few people, she hears the inaudible voice of Jesus. This book is part of the wisdom He imparted to her in the silences. Thank you, Diane, for telling us what He said to you in the quietness.

Are you ready to build your house into a home of passionate Jesus followers? This book sets forth the plan, the foundation, the framing, and the rest. What Phil and Diane did, you can do.

Ok, let's begin. Let's learn what John Mark learned at the feet of his parents.

A Note to Parents

Your children are your greatest treasure. Even when they're bickering and being belligerent, even when their messes mess up your plans and their struggles stress you out. Yes, even then.

In those first awe-filled moments after the agony of birth, you hold your infant close and your breath catches. The truth presses on your shoulders like the weight of the world.

This is a person, a human.

Not an embryo, not a fetus—a real live being with a personality, with a purpose, with potential!

That's when the doubts break through your awe and bring you to your knees. Every fear, every failure, every inadvisable, foolish thing you've ever done washes through the crevices of your vulnerability like a flash flood. All your unspoken fears collide with the hurts you've borne from mistakes your parents made. Like a rising river that will not be contained, this truth rushes you inexorably into the staggering realization:

This is *your child*.

You hold in your hands the potential to hurt her, to damage him, to turn him away from God. A dawning terror screams in your ear: *Don't mess this up!*

What should we do? How should we do it? What if we make a mistake and this child we love with such unexpected ferociousness grows up and decides not to follow Jesus?

This book contains the answers we sought when we clasped hands to pray, when we fasted, when we searched for wisdom time and again. We raided the journals Diane filled, sorted through Phil's bulging files. Then we studied and added more: all those things we wished we'd known. More than three decades of asking and digging, studying and teaching; truths we have gleaned and gathered, learned and implemented. This book is as close to a flow chart for the step-by-step nurturing of your child's soul as is realistically possible.

Harnessing decades of intensive study of the Scriptures with nearly forty years of pastoring people and a bookshelf groaning with the weight of many generations of wisdom, we have compiled what we learned so that you may have what we so desperately wanted when we were raising our children: a guide for the spiritual training of your child.

What you will not find in this book are guarantees. Nor will you come away with the sense that perfect parents raise perfect kids. But we also promise not to give you bumper sticker platitudes that leave you unaware and ill equipped.

Instead we invite you into our imperfect, messy, broken story so that you can catch glimpses of our Redeemer and the amazing grace He delights in bringing into your own less-than-ideal family.

The Jesus we wanted our kids to fall in love with is the One who, when challenged about how much time He was spending with notorious "sinners," declared emphatically that His heart was for those who know their desperate inadequacy and recognize their need for Him.[1]

We have taken great pains to note the mistakes we made and the things we wish we had done differently. It is our hope that you will learn from our mistakes as well as from these truths we share.

For two people who started off with so little to offer, we are now reaping the rewards of having raised four children who center their lives entirely on our Lord and married spouses who live to honor Jesus.

Now our job has changed: we are doing all we can to help our children bring up the next generation of Jesus followers.

It is first and foremost for them that this book is written—John Mark and Tammy, Matt and Simona, Rebekah and Steve, and Elizabeth and Brook—and for the generations of followers of Jesus to come.

In this book, we walk with you through every stage of your child's life, starting at birth. We offer practical, doable, "this is how it looked in our home" examples for you to adjust to your unique circumstances.

At the same time, we lay out the theological basis of raising your children to love and follow after God, giving you an in-depth understanding of how God fathers us. We unpack key passages of Scripture, checked and rechecked by scholars in the disciplines of theology and the original languages.

Finally, we help you create your own plan to intentionally bring your children into a close, personal connection with Christ that will endure and grow for the rest of their lives.

To that end we include:

1. How to draw out of your child a heart that actually wants to obey
2. A surprising key we stumbled upon for guiding especially strong-willed children
3. How husbands and wives are urged in the Scriptures to work together as the lamp and the light of the home
4. Help for parents doing it alone
5. The difference between punishment and discipline
6. A toolbox of time-tested, biblically-based discipline tools along with advice on how and when to use each one
7. The Box—an incredibly effective paradigm for building a secure frame around your child in which he or she will grow and thrive
8. Retrofitting—what if I've done it all wrong? What now?

This is the book we looked for in vain all those years ago. The whys and the how-tos that will give you the hope and help you so desperately need. It's a resource to come back to again and again as your child grows from infancy, through the early years, into the much-maligned teenage years, and on through the day when you hand him the key to build a spiritual house of his own.

Raising Passionate Jesus Followers is a guide for creating in your child a heart that beats for God.

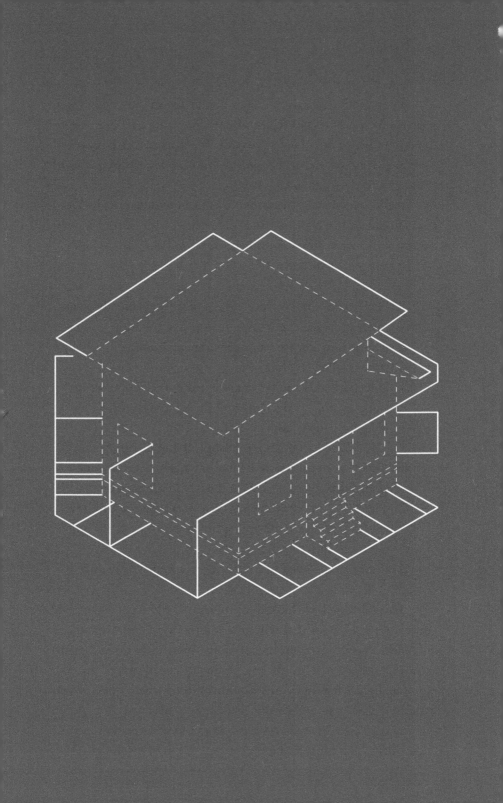

Part 1

Formulating the Plan

Raising a child is like building a house.
~OLD ALBANIAN PROVERB

Chapter 1

Our Story

> I have no greater joy than to hear that my children are
> walking in the truth.
>
> 3 JOHN 4

Neither of us was raised in a Jesus-centered home.

We had good homes—healthy, two-parent homes—but none of our parents would have considered themselves to be followers of Jesus when they were raising us.

Sure, our families went to church from time to time, and certainly we would have filled in the blank for religious affiliation with *Protestant*. Both of our homes had a Bible on the bookshelf, and Phil even went through confirmation, while my parents signed me up for VBS at a Baptist church one summer.

But following Jesus? Neither of our families would have had a clue what that meant.

Phil was in college and playing in a rock band when a friend shared the gospel with him. As he gradually put the pieces together and gave his heart to Jesus, his life was radically and permanently transformed.

Diane, having just returned from living overseas, was an insecure high school student trying to fit in when she stumbled upon a group of churchgoing kids who embraced her right where she was. Experiencing the genuine love of these teenagers brought her to Jesus. She wanted Jesus because she wanted *them*.

By the time we married, Phil was already on staff as the worship pastor of the large church where we met. We had both grown to the point where we were determined to make Jesus the center of our lives and our home. And to our great delight, both sets of our parents were on their way to cultivating a genuine faith for themselves.

As first-generation followers of Jesus, we felt keenly our lack of models in the quest to bring our children into an authentic, life-giving relationship with God, so we looked around at the families of leaders in our church to see what we could learn. We were shocked to see that some of their children were seemingly indifferent to God or even outright rebellious.

How could that be?

How could kids raised in these good Christian homes by godly parents not want Jesus? Why would they deliberately choose to turn their backs on the One who had so radically changed our lives?

We watched the teenagers in our church who went to public schools and saw that many of them acted no differently from their non-believing friends. When Phil taught a retreat for a Christian high school, we were dismayed at the apathy and flippant attitudes that seemed to pervade that group.

The truth began to dawn on us that *Christian parents do not automatically spawn Christian kids!*

Frankly, that incited sheer terror in us.

A few years later, when we were expecting our first child, we found ourselves handicapped by our shared lack of faith background, our lack of models to follow, and worse, the simple fact that we had no clue how to raise up children who would become passionate, all-in followers of Jesus.

We had no idea what we were doing—and we knew it!

So we began asking questions. We looked around at the few families whose teenage or young adult children seemed to be walking close to God, families whose kids we admired. We hoped our kids would turn out to be like theirs, and we invited them to our home so we could ply them with questions—lots and lots of questions! We scribbled down what we learned, filling folders with their wisdom.

We discovered that most often, when kids were all-out following Jesus, their parents were as well, and they had *intentionally* set out to do whatever it took to nurture and train and teach and love their children toward God. The strong faith of those kids was no accident!

THE VISION

A few months after our son, John Mark, was born, we moved to Portland, Oregon, so Phil could go to seminary. We were renting an old, moldy house near the campus of Multnomah University, scraping by with no extra money, no friends, and no family nearby. Yet we both look back on those years now and remember them as one of the best seasons of our lives.

One rainy day we wandered into a Christian bookstore, making our way down the stairs into the basement where the used books were stored. Diane pulled a book off the shelf that would quite literally change the trajectory of our lives, sending us on a quest to piece together an intentional plan to raise up children who would become passionate, wise disciples of Jesus Christ.

The book, however, had an unfortunate title: *Marriage to a Difficult Man!*[1]

It wasn't actually a book about difficult husbands, but rather a biography of Jonathan Edwards, America's first famous theologian. He swept through New England in 1734, his fiery sermons spawning what historians call the Great Awakening. The biographer wrote about Edwards through the lens of his family: his wife, Sarah, and their eleven children. Becoming more and more intrigued, Diane kept interrupting Phil's studies to tell him about this remarkable family.

From the Edwards clan came generation after generation of godly, high-achieving, world-impacting leaders: doctors, lawyers, judges, giants in American industry. There were university presidents, governors, senators, and ambassadors—even a vice president of the United States, as well as over three hundred pastors, missionaries, and theological professors.

As we read, a hope began to form in our hearts. With timid faith, we dared to say, a *vision*.

Could God do something like that in our family? Could He take what we had dedicated to Him and grow it into a lasting legacy? Might He use us to change the course of history—to impact the church?

What began as a wild hope grew into the conviction that, *yes*, God could and would use what we offered to Him to make a difference. Furthermore, we believed He was asking us to nurture and train and teach: to *make disciples* of our children so that they would grow up to impact His kingdom in ways we might never be able to ourselves.

Right then and there, we dedicated ourselves to pouring every bit of wisdom, teaching, energy, and effort into each of the children God would give us. We would make *them* our life calling, putting them before ministry and careers, before personal comfort, before our own agendas—before anything.

With audacious faith, we asked God to use us to become the matriarch and patriarch of generations of Comers who would follow hard after Jesus. We prayed that He would pour His wisdom into us so that we could in turn guide our children to follow Him whole-heartedly, compelling and equipping them to lead their own children to do the same someday.

It was an exhilarating vision for two fresh young believers. We knew beyond a shadow of doubt that this was *exactly* what He had called us to do.

This vision of generations of passionate Jesus followers has haunted our dreams and informed our everydays. It has guided every decision we made: every move, every sacrifice, our vacations, the way we spent our money, where we went to church, where we worked, and how we lived.

Should we watch that sarcastic sitcom? What books should we read our children? Is Santa Claus a good idea or might the myth shadow the real story? Is this church really all about Jesus or might the message cause our children to miss the real thing?

From schools to careers to the church we chose to make our own—everything came under the scrutiny of the question: *Will this help them draw closer to the Redeemer or possibly push them away? Will this make disciples or create disinterested rebels?*

In the pages to come you will read our stories. Let us just state unequivocally that we are not the ideal parents! You will read not only about the things we're glad we did, but also about our mistakes, the things we did that we wish we hadn't done, and why. We also share the things we wish we'd understood while we were raising our children, because we believe those mistakes are not wasted when you can learn from them. You will read about how we worked out the truths and treasures we discovered in the Scriptures for our own family—the practices that effectively captured the hearts of our kids on their way to knowing Jesus.

If that's what you want—for yourself and for your children—read on.

Chapter 2

The Cost

The second chapter of Judges tells a frightening story:

> "The people served the LORD all the days of Joshua, and all
> the days of the elders who survived Joshua, who had seen all
> the great work of the LORD which He had done for Israel.
> Then Joshua the son of Nun, the servant of the LORD, died . . .
> All that generation also were gathered to their fathers; and
> there arose another generation after them who did not know
> the LORD, nor yet the work which He had done for Israel."
> (Judges 2:7–8,10 NASB)

Now, let's look at what happened next:

> "Then the sons of Israel did evil in the sight of the LORD . . .
> and they forsook the LORD, the God of their fathers, who had
> brought them out of the land of Egypt, and followed other gods
> from among the gods of the peoples who were around them."
> (Judges 2:11–12 NASB)

This is exactly what we *didn't* want to see happen to our
children—and what you don't want to see happen to yours!

After dramatically setting His people free from the oppression of
Egypt, then seeing them through the terrible wilderness of their own
rebellion, all the while faithfully feeding them, guiding them, and
giving them good, steady, heroic leaders like Moses and Joshua—a

story of God faithfully fulfilling every undeserved promise of protection—*a whole generation chose to follow other gods.*

Can you sense God's heart breaking in these words? Ironically, in all
our years of walking alongside other families in God's church, we have
seen this pattern replay itself over and over like a rerun that won't quit.

The first generation *experiences* God. Deep repentance gives
way to a whole new, magnificent story of a life redeemed—the result
of an authentic encounter with Jesus Christ, the Savior. This leads to
the radical decision to turn away from the old lifestyle that left them
empty and aching. In his second letter to the Corinthians, Paul called
this the coming of a *new creation*[1] with all the old now passed away.

That's us: first generation Christians. We both have big stories of
a God big enough to change us down to our very core. But if we're not
careful—if we aren't *intentional* about making disciples of our own
children—they are liable to miss their own soul-changing experience
with a God who redeems. They will lack the passionate worship that
follows such an experience.

If that happens, then . . .

**The second generation *knows* God but doesn't *experience*
Him.** If we don't model and pass down to our kids this radically
transforming experience—if we fail to show them what a passionate
Jesus follower looks and feels and sounds and acts like—they may
grow up to simply know *about* God. They may know about what He
expects and how they should live. They may be good people with
strong morals and an admirable lifestyle. They might even go to
church, as they've been taught. But they may never become passionate,
all-out, surrendered followers of Jesus.

This second generation in turn tends to raise their children with
a whole lot of tolerance and goodwill but without a lot of conviction
or direction.

If that happens, then . . .

The third generation doesn't know God *or* experience Him.
The flame flickers and dies a slow, oblivious death. All that radical

passion of the first generation with their pulsing faith and miraculous transformation—*gone*.

That ought to scare each and every one of us right to our knees!

Evangelist Luis Palau says, "God has no grandchildren, only children." Each and every one of our sons or daughters must make their *own* decision to follow Jesus.

For real faith to thrive, *each generation must become the first generation.*

Just in case you're still not fired up to learn how to intentionally raise passionate Jesus followers, note this statistic, which shows how the story of Judges repeats itself in our twenty-first century world:

A 2009 study concluded that 90 percent of youth active in high school church programs drop out of church by the time they are sophomores in college, with only about 34 percent ever returning.[2]

Sobering, isn't it? If you fail to intentionally focus on raising a passionate Jesus follower, that little boy or girl you now hold on your lap may very well be one of the 90 percent. And yet there's hope.

A 2010 study showed a *remnant of homes* where faith stood strong all the way into adulthood. This study showed that parents of college students who did not leave the church emphasized "religion" twice as much as those whose young adult children left the church. And students who stayed in church through college said that the first thing they do when they have doubts or questions is talk to their parents and read their Bibles.[3]

DO WE UNDERSTAND THE STAKES?

God loved each and every one of us so passionately that He chose to do the hardest thing a father could possibly do: He sacrificed His Son.

The Father led His own son to excruciating pain *on purpose*. Not to make us good. Not to make us happy, as so many in our generation seem to think. He did it as part of His plan to bring the world—one person at a time—back to Himself.

Before we even get going on what the Scriptures teach about raising children whose faith will become their own, we are compelled to pause and ask: *Are you a passionate Jesus follower?*

Is Jesus at the very center of your decision-making, your vocation, your relationships? Are you learning and growing and falling more in love with Jesus? Can you honestly say He is your Master? Would you consider yourself part of what A. W. Tozer termed "the fellowship of the burning hearts"?[4]

Or are you like that second generation recorded in the book of Judges—you know a lot about God, even go to church most of the time, but do not know Him in an intimate, life-altering way. Does your faith look more like a moral compass than a passionate pursuit of the living God?

In George Barna's extensive research into families that raise children he calls "Revolutionary Spiritual Champions,"[5] he notes,

> "Many of the parents in our research did not have an upbringing that prepared them to be spiritual champions . . . however, having evaluated the options based on their life experiences, they had concluded that the greatest gift they could give their offspring was a sound upbringing based on biblical principle. That mindset was a reflection of their personal campaign to integrate their faith in Christ into every dimension of their lives."[6]

Your children have an uncanny ability to see right through to your heart. They know the difference between a dad whose interest in God is perfunctory and one whose soul craves what only He can give. They can tell when their parents are on "a personal campaign to integrate faith in Christ into every dimension of their lives."[7] Can you see why we were so afraid all those years ago? We were just beginning to integrate our newfound faith into those broken places in our lives that ran counter to what we were learning about God. We knew with humiliating clarity that we had a long, long way to go.

At the same time, children whose parents are imperfectly but passionately following Jesus have a front row seat to what the Savior meant when He said, "Seek the Kingdom of God above all else, and live righteously, and he will give you everything you need."[8]

We all want our children to hear Jesus saying what we long to hear Him say ourselves: "Well done, good and faithful servant . . . enter into the joy of your master" (Matthew 6:33 ESV).

We wanted that joy for our children—and so do you. As Jesus-following parents, we long to know that each of our kids will spend the rest of eternity with us in the presence of God.

We want our kids not only to *profess* a faith, but to actually *possess* a real faith. We want to see them become passionate Jesus followers.

Chapter 3

Your Story

As a parent who has given your life to Jesus, your top priority is that your kids will not only *know about* God, but actually *experience* Him. Your greatest joy will be seeing them walk with the Lord, and your greatest fear will be that they might walk away from God—neither knowing Him nor caring that they don't know Him.

Just like you, we were haunted by the fear that we might fail. At the same time, we were spurred on by the realization of the immeasurable impact two parents—or even just one—could have if they are willing to pour the best years of their lives into their kids.

Do the math: Phil and I had four children. Let's say you have three kids, and then somewhere along the line you intentionally bring a fourth into your circle, a child who needs your attention and is integrated into your family.

If each of those four, with your urging and training and encouragement, do the same thing—if they pour into four children, making disciples who in turn make disciples, that's sixteen Jesus-following men and women.

Keep that pattern going for a total of twelve generations. A generation is measured by about twenty-five years,[1] so that's a span of three hundred years.

In twelve generations there would be *16,777,216 passionate, Jesus-following disciples who go on to make disciples.*

That is more than the total city population of all of Portland and New York City and Los Angeles and Atlanta and Boston and San Francisco and Seattle and San Diego *combined!*

And it starts with just one person.

What if you decided to start with your family? What if you committed the best of all you have and all you are to this one goal?

This is a quest, an adventure of a lifetime that can only reap the richest rewards. Dare we say this is our duty—God's plan A for evangelism? Each mom and dad making disciples of their own children is God's original, primary way of bringing the world back to Himself. This is the way He commanded the Israelites to live out their faith.

But they didn't. Somewhere along the line they segued into a lackadaisical attitude about their children's training. They assumed all was well in their protected world, that no enemies lurked on the sidelines, wishing to woo their kids away from God. They stopped telling stories about God. They quit the no-compromise stance that Joshua courageously modeled.

Little by little, they failed.

And why were we given this story in the Scriptures? The apostle Paul wrote, "These things happened to them as examples and were written down as warnings for us . . ." (1 Corinthians 10:11).

Fast forward a few millennia, to the twenty-first century—our day. The pattern persists.

DIANE:

Not long ago a good friend of mine poured out her heart to me.

"None of my kids are really walking with the Lord," she said. "They're good people. We have a good relationship. But they just are not interested in following Jesus."

I heard all the grief of a really good mom echo in her words.

She and her husband were good parents—the kind who were at every game, who coached and cared and made every effort to give their children a good home. They even made significant sacrifices to put their kids in Christian school for a time. Without a doubt, both parents were involved and present in the lives of their three children.

Here's the question that kept them awake at night: "We were good parents. We took them to church. What went wrong?"

Bringing your kids to church is great—do it! But it's not enough.

Cooperating with God in the formation of their character, then teaching and training and exhorting and loving them to Jesus—these things must become your top priority.

You must become *intentional* about it.

The truth is, we are intentional about a lot of things: the career we choose, the college we go to, the person we marry. Bookstore shelves are stuffed with bestsellers about living a focused, purposeful, *intentional* life. Yet when it comes to raising children who will love God with their whole hearts and walk with Him for the rest of their lives, many parents—*most parents*—don't really have a plan. We certainly didn't! There were a couple of things we definitely didn't want to do because of mistakes we watched our parents make, but for the most part, even committed Christian parents have no real, well-thought-out plan they're determined to implement.

Someone once said, "Everybody ends up somewhere, but only a few get there on purpose!" The few who get there on purpose are the ones who know where they want to go, then get busy doing what they need to do in order to get there.

Lest we sound like we have a method or a formula that will lock your kids into growing up to walk with God, let us say this: You can do everything right (at least theoretically), and your children still have to make *their own choice* to follow Jesus. As Ruth Bell Graham so poignantly put it, "God has trouble with His kids too!"[2]

Even with the best intentions, there are no guarantees. However, there *are* guidelines. The old saying "You can lead a horse to water, but you can't make him drink" may be true. Yet it's also true that there is much a loving parent can do to incite a thirst for God in their kids.

We believe that if you are intentional in the spiritual training of your children, if you know where you're headed and what you need to do to get there, and (this is important!) if you don't let go too soon, then by the time they become teenagers you will have become good friends. You will have established obedience and gained their respect, and your children will be growing in strength and wisdom, following God wholeheartedly.

Your joy, just like the apostle John's, will be great.

To that end, let's begin formulating the plan.

Chapter 4

The Great Shema

In order to create a practical blueprint for this task of raising children who love and walk with Jesus, let's use the analogy of building a house. The Bible uses this metaphor in Psalm 127:1.

"Unless the LORD builds the house, they labor in vain who build it" (Psalm 127:1 NASB).

Or, as another translation puts it,

". . . the work of the builders is wasted" (Psalm 127:1 NLT).

The same psalm goes on to say, "Children are a gift of the LORD . . . like arrows in the hand of a warrior, so are the children of one's youth. How blessed is the man whose quiver is full of them" (Psalm 127:3–5 NASB).

Jesus loves your children. He longs to bring them close, to redeem them and make them his own.

In Colossians 1:27 Paul says, "This is the secret: Christ lives in you. This gives you assurance of sharing his glory" (NLT). You want this assurance for your children as well! This means the most important people you are to lead to Jesus are your own children.

God is inviting you to join Him in this most hallowed of all assignments. The Father—the One who created your child—desires to use you as a tool to guide your child into the joy of becoming a fully devoted follower of Jesus—one who is a temple of the living God,[1] a house where Jesus lives and is at home.

"Every child must find his or her way to faith," said Wayne Rice, "but God has appointed you to serve as a means of grace through which he draws his children to himself."[2]

BUILDING A HOUSE

Many years ago when we moved to the Pacific Northwest, we had the fun of building a home. Now we live in a small cottage in the woods that we are remodeling from top to bottom.

Sage counselors wisely warn against embarking on such a project, noting that the conflict inherent in making so many decisions might bring undue stress to your relationship. But honestly, we had a blast!

Before beginning construction of a building, before grading the lot or pouring the foundation or tearing down a wall, you must formulate the plan.

How many bedrooms do you want? What square footage seems best? The floor plan has to be finalized, a cost analysis carefully configured, the budget penciled out. Also, when you build a house, it has to be completed in a certain timeframe.

In the same way, when your goal is to help build children into godly men and women, you have a set amount of time to do the job. There is a completion date. Biblically, that would be about twenty years, which is approximately how long it takes for a child to become a full-fledged, responsible-for-himself adult.

While there is no step-by-step set of instructions on how to raise godly kids, the Bible is filled with wisdom for parents from start to finish.

In particular, there are two go-to passages that lay out God's plan for the task: Deuteronomy 6 and Ephesians 6. These Scriptures sketch out God's blueprint for building a spiritual house. First we'll unpack God's plan for families in Deuteronomy, and in the next section, we'll look closely at Ephesians.

Why? Because the place to begin is where God begins. While we may have a measure of success in coming up with a plan to influence our children to become accelerated students, skilled athletes, or good people, the only way to raise passionately committed followers of Jesus is by searching the Scriptures to find out how, and then asking the Spirit to give us wisdom to apply the Scriptures to our own situations.

Let's go back to the beginning of God's story of redemption, to a section of Scripture scholars call the great Shema. These words were recorded at a time when God was issuing urgent orders to His people.

> "Hear, O Israel: The LORD our God, the LORD is one. Love the LORD your God with all your heart and with all your soul and with all your strength." (Deuteronomy 6:4–5)

This was God's all-inclusive, all-encompassing command to the children of Israel: dive into the depths of God with every fiber of your being. No half measures, no passive acceptance. God was looking for all-out committed followers. His intent was to show the world what could happen when a whole nation of people chose to worship the one true God and do life the way He designed it.

But before these bedraggled ex-slaves could catch their collective breath, He turned to the parents and made another sweeping statement:

> "These commandments that I give you today are to be on your hearts. Impress them on your children. Talk about them when you sit at home and when you walk along the road, when you lie down and when you get up. Tie them as symbols on your hands and bind them on your foreheads. Write them on the doorframes of your houses and on your gates." (Deuteronomy 6:6–9)

God gives the Ten Commandments to His people, then He turns to the parents and says, "Now *you* teach these commandments to your children!"

God is not talking to youth pastors here, nor to spiritual leaders in the church. He is not laying out a Sunday school curriculum or a Christian school mandate.

God places responsibility for the spiritual development of children onto the shoulders of their mothers and fathers, and He tells them to do the teaching in the midst of real, in-the-moment life. This may well be why one researcher noted that parents of kids who choose to follow Jesus "intentionally identify their children as their main earthly focus in life during their parenting years."[3]

Someone once said, "The problem with parenting is it's so daily!" Indeed, raising children who love God with passion is a daily thing. This God-centered training happens when you greet your children, groggy-eyed and big-hearted, every morning, and when you tuck them into bed at night, and all the moments in between.

As Mark and Jan Foreman[4] wrote, "Imbedded in this passage is a winning strategy for explaining God to our kids: It's on-the-job training. We use the show-and-tell of everyday moments to transmit spiritual life."[5]

Not long ago the children's pastor of our church told us a story of how he encountered a family doing just this. The couple had a five-year-old daughter. They were visiting our church one Sunday, hoping to find a church home that worked well for them. Sitting through the worship and then the teaching, sensing the presence of the Spirit, both the mom and the dad felt right at home. As they walked to pick up their daughter from her Sunday school class, they hoped their precocious little girl had liked it as much as they had.

Her vehemence startled them both. "I don't ever want to go to that church again!" she said, hands fisted on her hips.

"What? Why in the world would you say that?" Her parents looked at each other, utterly perplexed. The children's ministry seemed so vibrant and appealing.

Mystified, they continued to probe their daughter gently. Finally, the little girl blurted out, "Because of what they did to Jesus!"

It gradually dawned on the little girl's dad that she was talking about the crucifixion. That morning she'd heard, at her five-year-old level, the story of Jesus' death. She'd so empathized with the unfairness of it all that she wanted nothing to do with anyone associated with such deeds!

These two wise parents spent the next week talking to their daughter at her level, explaining to her about the cross, sharing with her about Jesus' choice to allow Himself to be crucified for the truest kind of love. By the time the little girl marched into her Sunday school class the next week, she was all in.

"I have decided to follow Jesus," she declared, "because Jesus loves me sooo much!"

That's exactly what Deuteronomy 6 is describing: a faith passed on by passing it through the every-day-ness of life.

But how? Where is a parent to begin this high-impact but often intimidating way of teaching? Let us give you three foundational truths you'll need to get started.

THREE ESSENTIAL COMPONENTS

Loving God with passion is something that first has to happen in your own life

Of course! God is not simply laying out a moral code of conduct to see if you pass or fail. He longs for a loving relationship with each of us. He wants to speak to us and guide us and counsel us. His aim is always to bring us back to His heart. And He takes us right where we are—no prerequisites of perfection! He takes note of our feeble steps toward Him and infuses our souls with spiritual passion.

Then that passionate, entrusting reliance on God gets modeled in your home, right where daily life happens

Your children get a front row seat to watch what it looks like when a mom or dad loves God with every ounce of their being. They watch you fail, they see you forgive, they observe the freedom that comes from confession. Then they see the tension in your shoulders relax, and they know who it is that gives you peace.

William Booth (founder of the Salvation Army) said this in 1902:

"Don't expect your children to be so naïve that they won't see beneath the cloak of a false Christianity, especially if they find it in their own home. And don't think that after they discover its unreality, they won't despise it. Don't be surprised if when they see such hypocrisy, they make it an excuse for neglecting, if not positively disbelieving, in Christ altogether."[6]

Strong words. But Booth is not talking about perfection here. He's pointing out pretense. When a parent says he's following Jesus, loves God, is a leader in the church, but then fails to live out at home what he claims to believe—that's the "unreality" children come to despise.

Dallas Willard wrote, "Jesus does not call us to do what he did, but to be as he was, permeated with love. Then the doing of what he did and said becomes the natural expression of who we are in him."[7]

Yes! And your children are watching this natural expression. As you live a life of growing love—God's love radiating from your face and words and attitudes—your children will want that same love for themselves. When a parent both gives and receives grace in the home, it's more powerful than the best church or school in the world!

But it's still not enough. For your child to confidently follow Jesus into adulthood, you'll want to practice an oft-overlooked aspect of raising children who follow Jesus . . .

Faith that is alive and real must be intentionally taught to your children

Charles Spurgeon, a preacher from the 1800s, insisted on assigning the task of spiritual training to parents:

". . . Ministers and Sabbath-school teachers were never meant to be substitutes for mothers and fathers . . . What happy hours and pleasant evenings have children had at their parent's knees as they have listened to some 'sweet story of old.'"[8]

Intentionally teaching our children in the every-day-ness of our lives, on "pleasant evenings" as well as in the midst of stressful circumstances, is the way to open their hearts to Jesus.

All three of these truths are necessary to create a home in which children flourish in their love for God: the authenticity of your faith, showing your children what that looks like daily, and purposefully teaching your children all you have learned of God's character and ways.

If you're feeling thoroughly intimidated, take heart! When God commands us to do something, He pours out His Spirit on us, enabling and equipping us to be more than we are. He gives us all we need to carry out our calling.

The implication, then, is that the passing of your faith to the next generation—to *your children*—can be done! God is willing and wants to use us, even in all our own desperate need for transformation. We want you to see that it is possible to raise children who love God with all their hearts and all their souls and all their strength.

You can do this! God has shown us how in His Word. He promises to be with us, giving us wisdom and whispering insight as we walk with Him.

ABOVE ALL ELSE

Fast forward hundreds of years later, to when Jesus was asked, "What's the most important commandment in all the Scriptures?" he quoted the great Shema, saying, "This is the first and greatest commandment" (Matthew 22:38).

And then He added a quote from Leviticus 19:18:

"And the second [commandment] is like it: 'Love your neighbor as yourself.' All the Law and the Prophets hang on these two commandments." (Matthew 22:38–40)

The beauty of these words lies in their simplicity. Instead of 1001 spiritual truths to teach your children, there are just two essentials on which every other truth hangs, truths more vital than teaching them to floss their teeth or do their homework, more important even than training them in responsibility and high standards of morality.

When it's all said and done, Jesus said, *what matters most is loving God with passion and loving people on purpose.*

Sweet relief! No seminary degrees required. No super spirituality called for.

No matter what your story, no matter where you are in your journey, these are the two essentials you are called to pass on to the children you love more than life itself.

Chapter 5

The Lamp and the Light

M ake no mistake, the quest you are about to embark on is not an easy one. As the actor Ed Asner said, "Raising kids is part joy and part guerilla warfare!"

To train up children who *love God with passion* and *love people on purpose* will take every ounce of your creativity and energy and dependence on God. You will need to work together to make it happen. Mothers and fathers will need to use their unique roles and blend their God-given strengths in a way that brings courage and honor to each other and to their children.

As we look back at that time of building a house together, we realize the main reason we had so much fun was because by that time in our relationship, we knew each other's strengths and weaknesses. We knew what to expect of each other, what to avoid, and how to bring out the best in each other.

In other words, *we knew our roles.*

Phil handled the finances: the budget, the loans, the contracts and calls. That's what he's good at; details and management energize him. Staying within that budget (mostly!), Diane handled the design: paint colors, trim work, counter tops and floors. She loves envisioning a concept and creating a home.

Then, together, we did a lot of talking back and forth. We negotiated and compromised, valuing each other's contributions. We listened to each other.

We want to talk to you about how we worked together in the same way to raise children who love God. We want to share truths we discovered in the Scriptures as well as things we put into practice in our own home.

Early on, we stumbled upon a passage in Proverbs that laid out a pattern for blending the strengths and wisdom of both parents in order to train and instruct their children. It sounded sort of strange and mysterious to us, yet we kept coming back to it to try to make sense of what God was saying. It starts with a statement:

"My son, keep your father's command and do not forsake your mother's teaching." (Proverbs 6:20)

The Hebrew word translated "command" here is *mitsvah*. It is a word used to connote the instruction of a teacher to his pupil or of a parent to their child. It is also used in reference to God's commands. In the first five books of the Bible, often referred to as the Pentateuch, this word is used exclusively for God's commands, including the Ten Commandments.

The *mitsvah* of a father is intended to highlight what the psalmist called "the instructions of the Lord":

"The instructions of the Lord are perfect, reviving the soul. The decrees of the Lord are trustworthy, making wise the simple. The commandments of the Lord are right, bringing joy to the heart. The commands of the Lord are clear, giving insight for living." (Psalm 19:7–8 NLT)

He goes on to say, "By them your servant is warned; in keeping them there is great reward" (Psalm 19:11).

God has clearly revealed His commandments. They are available to anybody and everybody who desires to know them. No one has to spend their life searching for them, because they're close at hand—and you don't have to have a seminary education to find them, either.

The father's job, alongside his wife, is to teach the Lord's commands to his children. Dad, you are meant to be far more than a cheerleader on the sidelines saying, "Good job!" to your wife. The Father is inviting you to father the way He does, teaching His ways to your kids.

The word translated "teaching" of the mother is the Hebrew word *torah*, or law. It comes from the verb *yarah*, which means "to teach and instruct."

Just as the priests were to teach the Torah to Israel, in the same way mothers are to teach their children God's laws, God's ways, and basic wisdom for living life skillfully.[1]

This means both fathers and mothers would do well to know the Scriptures! It is said of Ezra that he "devoted himself to the study and observance (practice) of the law of the Lord, and to teaching its decrees and laws in Israel" (Ezra 7:10). He was a man known for his skill in explaining the Scriptures.[2] Every follower of Jesus—and every parent—is invited to do the same.

Proverbs 6 verse 23 goes on, "For this command is a *lamp*, this teaching is a *light*, and correction and instruction are the way to life" (emphasis ours).

What's that all about?

The word translated "lamp" is *niyr* (/neer/). The Hebrews would have heard these words and instantly understood this metaphor from their everyday lives. The lamp was a small, bowl-like piece of pottery containing oil and a wick. Lamps were used to light the tabernacle— the place where the people came to meet God. The lampstands were placed in strategic areas in order to light that holy place.

Your home should be a holy place!

The father's presence is meant to be like the lamp in the tabernacle, shining the light and love of Jesus into every corner of the home.

Light, or *'owr* (/ore/), is an extremely important concept found throughout the Scriptures as a symbol of life, happiness, and joy. In John 8:12 Jesus said, "I am the light of the world. Whoever follows me will never walk in darkness, but will have the light of life."

Light is also used metaphorically in the Scriptures to paint a picture of how God's Word enlightens us, enabling us to walk confidently on His path. In Psalm 119:105 we read, "Your word is a lamp for my feet, a light on my path."

Here, in Proverbs 6, the teaching of a mother offers light: life, happiness, joy, and learning. "When you walk, they will guide you; when you sleep, they will watch over you; when you awake, they will speak to you" (Proverbs 6:22).

In a very real sense, parents are pictured working together as partners in the training of their children. We are called by God to teach our kids, giving them insight and instruction and integrating God's truth into everyday life. The father is to stand straight and strong as the lamp while the mother's clear teaching from Scripture brings light.

This use of metaphorical poetry is not only beautiful but filled with practical wisdom as well. You may work out this concept somewhat differently than we did, but in the interest of practicality, we want to give you a glimpse into how we carried out this principle from Proverbs.

At the same time, we urge you to think this through with a clear assessment of who you are and how you best work together. There is much ambiguity in this passage—no precise 3-step plan to follow. And that, no doubt, is on purpose! Because God made each of us unique, no two families work out the metaphor of the lamp and the light the same way.

That said, here is how this concept looked in our home:

FIRST, THE FATHER ESTABLISHES THE VISION

The Bible clearly depicts the husband as the one who is to lead his wife. Not to dominate her or boss her around, but to take initiative in seeking to understand what God wants for your family. The husband's initiative is to be melded with a humble attitude of servanthood towards his wife and children. *How can I best serve my family and my Lord by initiating a Jesus-oriented way of living?*

In our case, Phil's slide into immorality during his years as a drummer in a rock band led him to want better for his children. He set a tone of godly standards without compromise. This led us to reserve our home as a place of refuge from the immorality found in the world. We wanted to create a holy place, which meant blocking out movies, TV, and music that didn't honor God.

It also meant practicing the instruction laid out in Ephesians 4 to speak truthfully and gracefully to each other. No shouting, no biting sarcasm, no sassing, lots of clearly expressed humility and asking forgiveness when needed.

Our son John Mark has worked out the concept differently. He and his wife share a burden to open their home to people who need desperately to see the love of God in action. This has led them to initiate relationships with the people who live around them. As the father in his home, John Mark has established a vision of community and mission, and that informs the way they do life together.

Another family we know set a vision for servanthood early on. Their two boys grew up learning to serve others as a family, serving people in the church as well as people alienated from the church. In their case it was the mother's burden to serve hurting people that propelled the parents.

More than anything else, Phil established a vision for honoring God in our home. We wanted a family who loved God with passion and loved people on purpose.

NEXT, THE MOTHER CARRIES OUT THE VISION

It was largely Diane who made our family vision happen. She was with the children all day and every night. She was the one who dealt with temper tantrums at the grocery store. She was largely the one who had to handle disputes and disrespect. It was Diane who had to decide in the moment if an outburst was a bad attitude that had to be corrected or just a bad day that needed to be overlooked.

Phil was busy providing for us, working long hours so Diane

could stay home in those early years. When Phil came home in the evenings and on days off, he tried to keep the consistency of purpose in effect, spending intentional time with our children.

This required lots and lots of talking back and forth, redefining what we wanted to see happen in our individual children's lives. We were on mission *together* for our children even though Diane was often the chief disciplinarian in the early years. Phil did discipline the children when they were young, just less often than Diane did. It was primarily up to Diane to carry out what we decided together.

We made significant sacrifices so Diane could focus her full attention on our four young children. Our retirement portfolio is not what it would have or could have been if Diane had gone to work in those years. And yet here we are, nearing the end of our working years and not one bit regretful about how we spent that season of our lives.

Other parents do a masterful job of juggling schedules so that their children receive as much of their direct attention and teaching as is feasible while they carry out their callings in the workplace. Many families we know, burdened with school loans, the rising costs of medical insurance, and an economy that often requires a dual income, have found creative ways to give their best to their young children even with both parents working.

Be aware that we are not promoting a *Leave It to Beaver*[3] ideal of parenting as the ultimate biblical model. Women have always worked. For us, the decision to allow Diane to concentrate primarily on teaching and training our children while they were growing up was a researched decision we believed was best for us but is not necessarily attainable for everyone.

THIRD, THE FATHER DEALS WITH PATTERNS

Instead of meeting Phil at the end of his long day at work with a blow-by-blow account of every misdeed and all her frustrations, Diane mostly just reported patterns.

"Matthew argued over and over again today, what are we going to do?"

or

"Bekah and little Beth fought and bickered all day today. Will those two ever be friends?"

Each of our children showed tendencies, what the King James Bible calls *besetting sins* and the NIV calls "the sin that so easily entangles" (Hebrews 12:1). These are areas of weakness that have to be dealt with over and over again in order to help our children be who God wants them to be: not perfect but free of unhealthy patterns that could entangle them throughout their lives.

Phil made sure Diane didn't wear out and give up. We had two strong-willed boys and two equally strong, emotionally complex daughters. They are all leaders now, but as young children they were often challenging. There's not a single pushover or phlegmatic person in our family!

Phil kept the vision in front of us when we grew weary and tempted to ignore the challenges.

FINALLY, THE MOTHER AND FATHER SEEK WISDOM TOGETHER

When something totally out of character came up, Diane brought the incident to Phil's attention, and together we figured out what was going on.

> **DIANE:**
>
> One time I got a phone call from an irate mother who threatened to report eight-year-old John Mark to who-knows-who because he'd accepted the dare of her oh-so-innocent son and mooned the lady at the Jack in the Box drive-thru on Ocean Avenue in Santa Cruz, California.

I, of course, freaked out, as any self-respecting mother would! I couldn't decide who I was angrier with—the mother on the other side of the phone whose son had obviously enticed John Mark to do it, or my son, who knew he'd crossed way over the line!

Phil calmed me down, reminding me that this was out of character for our son. Then he simply talked to his son, knowing what it's like as a man to be challenged and tempted. He asked questions like, "What's going on, son?" without a whole lot of shame or recrimination.

Finally, he assured me that John Mark was a good kid who still needed lots of supervision, not a criminal in the making.

Often Phil would remind me of our goal: not to raise perfect little mommy-glorifying people, but to train up leaders of the next generation who would dare to break the mold, Daniels and Nehemiahs who would be willing to buck the trend and follow after Jesus fearlessly.

He'd say things like "Don't discipline the man right out of him," reminding me over and over again what we were really after.

Often it is the father who sees the big picture while the mother is down in the trenches doing the "guerilla warfare" that needs to be done on a daily basis. Yet sometimes it is the mom who inspires her husband by envisioning what God is inviting their family to be.

Both parents are tasked with the privilege of teaching God's commands and instructions to their children, weaving His ways into every aspect of life. Why? So that these children you love will grow up with the understanding of what it means to live wisely.

When King Solomon wrote to his son of the wisdom of following God, he urged him, "Never forget the things I have taught you. Store my commands in your heart. If you do this, you will live many years, and your life will be satisfying" (Proverbs 3:1–2 NLT).

If the prospect of all this teaching feels impossible in the midst of your stress-filled lives, we urge you to consider the outcome, to count the cost. In fact, the Bible is filled with stories of kings who were great leaders but failed as fathers.

Clearly God measures success differently than our world does. He has placed the mantle of spiritual leadership firmly on the shoulders of parents, reminding us over and over again that His wisdom is the way to the life that is truly life.[4]

Chapter 6

Goals versus Values

No one can,

without renouncing the world in the most literal sense,

observe my method; and there are few, if any,

that would entirely devote about twenty years of the prime of life

in hopes to save the souls of their children,

when they think they may be saved without so much ado;

for that was my principal intention.

SUSANNA WESLEY

Susanna Wesley's words impacted us deeply. We were living in Santa Cruz where Phil was a worship pastor in a vibrantly growing church, when Diane—searching for wisdom in raising our children—read the biography of the mother of John and Charles Wesley.[1] Our kids were six, four, and one when her words infused a new sense of urgency in us—a renewed call to examine everything in our lives, a charge to renounce anything that might get in the way of "saving the souls of our children," and a willingness to devote the prime of our lives to this quest of raising passionate Jesus followers.

If you're still reading, you've undoubtedly decided the same. You're realizing the immenseness of this calling and are willing to do whatever it takes to tackle the "so much ado" that Susanna poured into her children. To help you accomplish this great task, you'll need to be able to understand the difference between a goal and a value.

Webster's dictionary defines a goal as "the end toward which effort is directed . . . the terminal point of a race."

We are suggesting that as your child grows up, you focus on only one goal: to raise sons and daughters who are passionate Jesus followers.

By "passionate Jesus followers" we mean kids who grow up to truly love and walk with the Lord, who follow Him and serve Him, and who understand their calling to bring others into His kingdom.

We are not talking about perfect paragons of virtue but about followers of Jesus who are being transformed into disciples. Men and women whose life quest is to know Him intimately and please Him continuously. That's the goal! Because when Jesus is first, everything else falls into place. Even when trials, temptations, and difficulties come, your children will never walk in darkness.

Jesus said, "I am the light of the world. Whoever follows me will never walk in darkness, but will have the light of life" (John 8:12).

It is this life-enlightening relationship with Jesus that is our ultimate goal in our children's lives, and to that end you commit yourself to do whatever you need to do in order to see that one goal come to fruition.

A *value* is different from a goal. For the purposes of this book, a value can be defined as something very important to you. Something you prize and admire; something you really want your kids to make a part of their lives.

In order to attain your goal, you will need to take a close and continual look at your values. Are they are helping or hindering you in achieving your goal?

We all have values we want to pass on—qualities, habits, and standards we hope our children will adopt as they grow up to establish their own patterns for living.

We aren't just talking about moral values here, either. Our values will be mostly good, biblical qualities mixed with some cultural standards and life habits that we want to see our kids adopt as their own.

Some values will help, and some will be neutral, but the danger is this: that sometimes *good* things can get in the way of the *best* thing.

One value we have seen over and over is competitive youth sports—a good thing! Sports teach teamwork, discipline, submission to authority, preparing for deadlines, and staying in shape.

But what if it takes your child out of church on Sundays? What if you unintentionally communicate that consistently worshipping Jesus in community is optional? That when push comes to shove, commitment to the team comes first? What if you end up with a son or daughter who gets that college scholarship (which statistics show to be a measly one percent chance) but quits going to church (remember those stats?) and isn't interested in walking with Jesus?

What then?

In that situation, a *value* would have displaced your *goal*.

DIFFERING VALUES

No two families will have an identical list of values. For that matter, no two parents will have an identical list of values.

DIANE:

High on my list of values when I was raising our children were cleanliness, neatness, and order—a place for everything, and everything in its place, as they say. I wanted a well-kept house that sparkled with welcome. That's how I was raised, and that's how I wanted my home to run.

Cleanliness is next to godliness—it's in the Bible, right? Well, no. It's not, but it's in *my* bible!

But Phil didn't—and still doesn't—rate a clean house as one of his top five values. He doesn't want to live in a messy, dirty dump, but neither would he make significant sacrifices to make sure the house is perfect.

On the other hand, having fun is high on Phil's value list—having fun as a family, watching fun movies, planning fun trips and vacations and holidays.

In my family when I was growing up, we worked on Labor Day. We worked because both my parents placed high value on (you guessed it) cleanliness, neatness, and order.

Most of my holiday memories revolve around working together in the yard or painting the deck or some sort of project that required we all pitch in. Phil thinks it's appalling! He can't reconcile his value of having fun as a family with spending our free time working on home maintenance projects. He'd rather take a drive to the beach or go see a movie.

Can you see the collision ahead?

Two different parents with two different sets of values that sometimes clash. This is normal!

As Emerson Eggerichs says, "[It's] not wrong, just different."[2]

GOALS VERSUS VALUES EXERCISE

We want to help you to work out your differences together, so we've compiled a list of values in order to help you identify what you "prize and admire"—what is very important to *you*. Values you feel driven to cultivate in your children's lives. Values you hope your kids adopt and emulate as their own.

Remember, a value is not simply something you prefer, but something you are willing to make *significant sacrifices* to ensure. Phil enjoys a clean house—but will he make significant sacrifices to keep it that way? Not necessarily. Diane enjoys fun—sometimes—but she's not lying awake at night dreaming up the next fun adventure.

Our son John Mark has a beautiful value of his own. He wants his sons to grow up to be best friends. Even now when they get in a disagreement, he asks them, "Why are you fighting? You two are best friends!" What a God-honoring value to instill in our children.

Before you read on, take some time to circle your top five values. Here's a list to help you get started, but feel free to add to it. Once you and your spouse are done, take a few minutes to acknowledge each other's differing values.

Remember to be kind and respectful to each other. A sense of humor is useful at times like these. We are convinced that identifying these important (not wrong!) differences will help you keep the goal in sight as you work together in raising children whose hearts beat for God.

Once you've identified your top five values, ask yourselves this important question: *Are our values helping or hindering us in achieving our one and only goal?*

What *is* your one and only goal? To raise children who love God with passion and love people on purpose.

VALUES

Fun	Tolerance
Organization	Gratitude
Efficiency	Peace-loving
Creativity	Generosity
Respect	Compassion
Healthy diet	Friendliness
Strong work ethic	Respect for authority
Resourcefulness	Care for animals
Success	Good communication skills
Independence	Love of reading
Optimism	Initiative
Athleticism	Ability and willingness to
Protectiveness	resolve conflicts
Physical fitness	Interest in theology
Kindness	Boldness
Honesty	Leadership
Education	Sense of humor

Stylishness

Frugality

Cross-cultural adeptness

Desire for justice

Sexual purity

Confidence

Safety

Spontaneity

Discipline

Punctuality

Hospitality

Concern for creation

Family closeness

Musical skill or interest

Adventurousness

Affection

Friendship among siblings

Responsibility

Artistic skill or interest

Learning

Intellectualism

Competitiveness

Political activism

Management skills

Neatness

Analytical thinking

Strategic thinking

Imaginativeness

Empathy

Positivity

Adaptability

Productivity

Patience

Presence

Deliberateness

Nostalgia

Harmony

Critical thinking

Loyalty

Enthusiasm

⌃ Raising Passionate Jesus Followers

GOAL To partner with God in intentionally raising sons and daughters who grow up to become passionate Jesus followers.

Loving God with passion and loving people on purpose.
Deut. 6v4-9, Mt. 22v36-40

Part 2

Laying the Foundation

Birth through Age 5

Therefore everyone who hears these words of mine
and puts them into practice is like a wise man who
built his house on the rock. The rain came down,
the streams rose, and the winds blew and beat
against that house; yet it did not fall, because
it had its foundation on the rock.
MATTHEW 7:24–25

Chapter 7

A Heart of Obedience

PHIL:

I was driving my regular route to the office, down a steep hill through a neighborhood of large, expensive homes. I glanced to my right, and what I saw caused me to slam on my brakes. A three-story home that had been there the day before was gone! Vanished!

The night before, a storm had brought about a catastrophic mudslide, causing the entire house to slide down the hill in pieces. Fortunately the family was away, so no one was hurt.

The house looked great the day before, with its gleaming front door and brick façade. But something was wrong, very wrong: its foundation was faulty.

When it comes to constructing a well-built home, the foundation is of utmost importance. If you don't get the foundation right, the entire building will suffer. The same is true in parenting. When it comes to raising godly kids, the foundation you lay is critical.

In this section we are going to cover the stage of a child's training from birth to about age five. That said, these are stages, not ages. Every child develops at a different pace intellectually, emotionally, physically, and spiritually. For some reason, girls seem to be light-years ahead of boys!

These are general guidelines for what to expect regarding the spiritual formation of a child during this stage of his life. By the end of this stage, there are two primary things you want to see developing in your child:

1. A heart of obedience
2. A heart of self-control

We aren't suggesting that by the age of five, your child will automatically and without fuss obey your every command. Nor are we intimating that by the end of this stage you will be finished disciplining lapses of self-control. Instead, these are qualities that you want to see *emerging*.

You are beginning to see your child making definite strides in the areas of obedience and self-control. She is understanding her need to control her attitudes, and becoming equipped to master her meltdowns.

Remember, we said there are two go-to passages for parents when it comes to raising their kids. Here is the second one.

In the book of Ephesians God speaks directly to children, giving them these instructions:

"Children, obey your parents in the Lord, for this is right. 'Honor your father and mother'—which is the first command-ment with a promise—'so that it may go well with you and that you may enjoy long life on the earth.'" (Ephesians 6:1–3)

We like this part!

In this passage of Scripture, God commands children to obey their parents. But moms and dads, it's your job to teach them to obey! And we need to begin early, while they are moldable, because before you can teach your child the ways of the Lord, you need to partner with God to create in him a heart that is teachable, or the teaching will fall on deaf ears.

Just as God is after *your* heart, so you are after the heart of your son or daughter. King Solomon understood this concept when he wrote, "My son, do not forget my teaching, but let your *heart* keep my commandments" (Proverbs 3:1 NASB, emphasis ours).

There is a sense of urgency in these words. Why? He goes on to say, "For length of days and years of life and peace they will add to you" (Proverbs 3:2 NASB).

These are instructions from a father who longs to show his son the way to a long and satisfying life! Now, exactly *what* you teach, and *when* you teach, and *how* you teach it, will vary from stage to stage.

In this first, foundational stage, your end goal is to create in your child a heart of obedience. Not *perfect, no-matter-what compliance*, but a heart that actually, honestly *wants* to obey.

WHAT'S THE BIG DEAL ABOUT OBEDIENCE?

The reason we train our children to obey us is not because we are egomaniacs or dictators, nor is it so we can show off our exemplary children like trophies.

We train our children to obey us so they will grow up with the inherent, reflexive ability to choose to obey God rather than their own impulses.

When God spoke about David, a far from perfect man, He called him "a man after my own heart; he will do everything I want him to do" (Acts 13:22).

When we teach our children to obey us, we give them an increased capacity to obey God. What an incredible gift! The kids who never learn to obey their parents (whether they feel like it or not!) have a really tough time as adults.

They don't know *how* to obey God. Many struggle and fail for the rest of their lives, seemingly unable to submit their will to the One they call their Lord.

Andrew Murray, an influential South African preacher in the 1800's, wrote:

". . . a *wayward will* is a curse; but a *will that masters itself* by obedience is the truly strong will."[1]

In other words, we train our children to master their wills in obedience so that they will grow up to be men and women of true strength.

It will cost you to train your child in obedience: it will take focus and work and determination and diligence.

In this early stage of your child's life, you may have to limit opportunities and slow down the pace of your life. You will probably have to stay home a lot. Before you had kids, you could be out every night, but now you've got bedtimes and routines, a schedule to keep.

For many children, being away from home during the intense training required at this stage may precipitate a big step backwards. The boundaries change when you go out to the store with them, or take them someplace where discipline must ease up for a while. Somehow children just know that, and many kids will take advantage of the freedom!

But be encouraged! This stage doesn't last forever. It may *seem* like it lasts forever, but trust us, this period of intensive training will be over before you know it. If you do your job well—custom-creating a strategy for training your child in obedience—and if he grasps the imperative need to obey you with an urgency that overcomes his own craving for control—then this stage will soon be a distant memory.

What happens in these foundational years may well affect how every other stage of his life will go.

The Bible implies that parents have disciplinary windows of effectiveness in this task of child raising. Proverbs 19:18 puts it this way:

"Discipline your children while there is hope. Otherwise you will ruin their lives." (NLT)

This early time in the home is like boot camp: they will fall back on their training later, when you have no control over their choices.

This is a period of time in which there is hope, a time when the training and discipline of and the loving and caring for your child result in a heart eager to come close and obey.

Remember, you are a trainer, not a dictator. A top-quality trainer is strict and aware, with a wisdom that comes from understanding his goal. Paul understood this when he advised Timothy to "discipline yourself for the purpose of godliness; for bodily discipline is only of little profit, but godliness . . . holds promise for the present life and *also* for the *life* to come" (1 Timothy 4:7–8 NASB).

As parents, we discipline our children for the purpose of godliness, instilling in them an ability to choose to obey God. By doing this, someday—when the choice is entirely theirs as to whether or not to follow the way of Jesus—they will possess the innate strength to fall back on the training you gave them rather than give in to their peers or their own unchecked willfulness.

The writer of Hebrews put it this way: "There will be a peaceful harvest of right living for those who are trained in this way" (Hebrews 12:11 NLT).

Chapter 8

Tools for Discipline

I t's great to talk about the *concept* of obedience, but we know what you're thinking because it's what frustrated us when we were raising our children:

How do I do this? How do I create in my child this heart of obedience?

We didn't have it all figured out when our kids were little. We knew we wanted to teach our children to obey us—we were certain of that. We didn't want to raise defiant little tyrants! But we didn't know what means to use; we didn't know *how*.

So we did two things.

First we looked around for parents who had children we admired, and we asked questions. A lot of questions! We invited these families to teach us, to give us insight we didn't have, then we took them out for lunch or coffee and *we paid for it!* Because we read in Proverbs,

"Buy truth and do not sell *it*, *get* wisdom and instruction and understanding." (Proverbs 23:23 NASB)

And then the writer follows with:

"The father of a righteous child has great joy; a man who fathers a wise son rejoices in him. May your father and mother rejoice; may she who gave you birth be joyful!" (Proverbs 23:24–25)

One time Diane asked a mother who lived around the corner if she would meet with her to teach her how to raise godly children. We admired this family's four teenaged kids, who followed Jesus with evident joy. The woman replied by inviting Diane to join her during her early morning runs.

While they ran, Diane asked her questions and Laurie spilled her wisdom. After a few months, Laurie summed up our struggles with our firstborn by saying, "The issue with that boy is control."

A light went on! Of course, yes, that's it!

Her insight guided the way we approached discipline with our son from then on and shined a light on our own tendencies to control people and circumstances. Phil especially noticed his struggle with the desire to manage and control things. He saw this same struggle in his little boy.

Someone once said, "It's a painful thing to see your faults walking around on two little legs!"

A parent's life is a child's guidebook. Your kids are copying you. Think about that for a moment: they are mimicking your tone of voice, the expressions on your face, the way you communicate displeasure. If I don't have a heart of obedience—an open-hearted, non-negotiating, *I-will-do-anything-God-says* attitude towards the Father, how can I possibly expect my children to have a heart of obedience towards me?

Second, we kept searching the Scriptures and praying for wisdom. Time after time, we held hands and prayed, asking God to honor His promise in James 1:5:

> "If any of you lacks wisdom, you should ask God, who gives generously to all without finding fault, and it will be given to you."

We also echoed the prayer of Solomon, which thrilled the heart of God so thoroughly that He gave the fledgling king not only great wisdom, but great riches as well:

"'Your servant is here among the people you have chosen, a great people, too numerous to count or number. So give your servant a discerning heart to govern your people and to distinguish between right and wrong. For who is able to govern this great people of yours?' The Lord was pleased that Solomon had asked for this." (1 Kings 3:8–10)[1]

We got up early to have time alone with God, reading through the Scriptures with eager expectation of receiving wisdom to help us do what we could not figure out on our own.

What we discovered was this: The best way to raise kids who genuinely love and follow God is to copy the way God disciplines and raises *us* as His children!

In our search for wisdom through the Scriptures, we discovered five ways, or five *tools* for discipline that God uses with us. These aren't the only tools of discipline used in the Bible, but they are five of the most important, the ones we found ourselves using over and over again.

These are five tools that can actually change the *heart* of your child. They are not behavioral modification tactics, but God-breathed methods that, when applied to parenting, bring about a softening of the spirit of a child towards his parents.

The first four tools are found in Paul's letter to young Timothy. Paul considered himself like a father to Timothy, calling him "my true son in the faith" (1 Timothy 1:2). When instructing Timothy in how to lead the church he was pastoring, Paul wrote this:

"Preach the word; be prepared in season and out of season; correct, rebuke, and encourage—with great patience and careful instruction." (2 Timothy 4:2)

You may be thinking, *But that verse is written to a pastor about his church, not to a father or mother about their children.* And you'd be right. But now, after forty years as a pastor, Phil is often asked by young pastors how he led and pastored the churches he served in. He tells them, "The same way I lead my family, because the church *is* a family!" A healthy, maturing church functions like a family, with all the conflicts and complexities that every family encounters.

These tools are not listed in any order of importance. Nor should they be used in a sort of graduating intensity. Instead, they are to be used interchangeably as the situation warrants. Like tools in a toolbox, when you need a hammer, that's what you reach for, and when a screwdriver is the most appropriate tool, that's the one you choose.

There will be times when a quiet correction is all that is needed. At other times, a stern but loving rebuke will be the most appropriate tool of discipline. You are not using anger to control your child's behavior, but simply utilizing an effective tool to wake up and tenderize your child's heart towards obedience.

TOOL #1: CORRECTION

The Greek word *elégchō,* translated as *correct,* means to reprimand, show fault, expose, or convict. It can also be translated "reprove." This is the same Greek word found in John 16:8 where Jesus says His Father will send the Holy Spirit, who will "convict (*elégchō*) the world concerning sin and righteousness and judgment" (NASB).

This is the tool we so often sense the gentle Holy Spirit using in our own lives to initiate a needed course correction. When we sit in church listening to a sermon and something the pastor says causes our hearts to leap in recognition. Or we're meditating on Scripture and it's as if a light suddenly illuminates a still-rough area of our lives. Or when we're sitting in church and we sense the tender voice of the Spirit saying, "Forgive that one who hurt you." Our response when something like this happens can be immediate:

Oh! Yes, Lord, please forgive me and align my heart to beat with Yours. Help me!

And He does.

Four mistakes parents often make

1. Ignoring the behavior or attitude

   Rather than being fully present with our children, we are distracted and therefore miss opportunities to nip a behavior in the bud before it gets out of hand. How many meltdowns could be avoided if we were simply more alert to our children?

2. Thinking they'll grow out of it

   This is a common myth that prevents parents from seeing the gravity of their child's behavior. What seems kind of cute when they are two or three may be downright obnoxious as they get a little older unless we step in to gently teach them a better way.

3. Making excuses for your child's attitude or actions

   We act as if our child gets a free pass because "he's just tired" or "she's too shy" but is this realistic? Sometimes our children are genuinely tired and shy, but we need to help them recognize their own vulnerability. By giving them tools to cope rather than making excuses, we enable our children to grow and change.

4. Raising your voice in anger and pressure

   This is perhaps the most pervasive mistake young parents make in order to control their child. It is what many of us resort to when we face the consequences of our having neglected to pay attention and use gentle correction before the child's behavior is out of control.

Every parent makes these mistakes from time to time. We sure did! But recognizing that these tactics are *not* part of your plan to raise children whose hearts are inclined to obedience allows you to pay attention and recalibrate your responses.

The ten-year rule

What about those times when you just don't know if something your child is doing even warrants discipline? This can lead to confusion and inconsistency, and it is why we came up with what we call the Ten-Year Rule. Just ask yourself, *What will this behavior or attitude look like in ten years?*

If your child is slamming the door in anger now, will he squeal off in a three-thousand-pound car when he's seventeen?

If your toddler is kicking you when she doesn't like something or running away from you when you call her, ask yourself, *What will she be doing ten years from now?*

What will his temper tantrum look like when he is eighteen? Or twenty-eight? Or thirty-eight? Who will be the victim of all that uncontrolled anger?

The truth is, children do not grow out of anything except their clothes! If they don't learn to control their attitudes and actions now, there can be more serious implications to them later in life.

In the Pacific Northwest where we live, blackberry bushes grow wild. When we first moved here, Diane was enamored with the idea of sweet, juicy berries ripe and ready to be plucked and popped right into her mouth—and they were growing right outside our back door for free! During our first summer, she clipped errant blackberry shoots at the soil level when she saw them growing where we didn't want them. That was a mistake! That very same runner showed up way on the other side of our yard. We soon learned that the only way to keep blackberry bushes from overwhelming our house was to dig deep and pull up the entire root system.

It's the same with your children's misbehaviors and bad attitudes. Unless you get to the root, they will keep popping up. And it will get harder and harder to root them out.

Now, this doesn't mean you should pounce on your son or daughter every time their attitude or behavior is less than ideal. Who could live with that kind of censorship? We are just trying to emphasize the importance of staying alert to your children and watching for patterns that may need to be gently addressed before they become firmly entrenched, like those pesky blackberry bushes.

If you *love* your child, there will be times when you will correct him. God says about disciplining the people He calls His own, "Those whom I *love*, I reprove (also translated *correct*) and discipline" (Revelation 3:19 NASB, emphasis ours).

When you gently correct your child, as the Spirit does with us, he will not only feel your love, but he will eventually love you for the time you put in correcting and reproving him as needed. As it says in Proverbs, "Reprove a wise man and he will love you" (Proverbs 9:8 NASB).

You will often find that correcting a behavior early, before it gets out of hand, is enough to stem the tide. Sometimes all your child needs is a reminder of what you expect of him. A wise parent doesn't wait until their child is out of control, but *watches closely* and *steps in early* with this gentle correction.

Don't miss this important truth! Catching behavior early—not laughing at it, thinking it's cute or harmless—will save you from having to issue heavy-handed and far less effective discipline in the future.

Notice the wisdom in Proverbs 29:17 that urges you to:

"Correct your son, and he will give you comfort. He will also delight your soul." (NASB)

Use correction when it is the appropriate tool to use. In very young children, it is often the first step of discipline.

As your child matures and looks to you for approval, sometimes correction means a friendly raising of the eyebrows to subtly draw attention to his behavior. Or a simple question such as, *Are you sure you want to be doing that?* He knows exactly what you mean and can choose to stop himself before further discipline is needed. For a toddler who is just beginning to reach for objects you don't want him to handle, you might gently hold his hand before he can grab it, and with a loving voice say, "No, no!" Or if she's squirming uncontrollably on the changing table, laying your warm hand on her belly and saying, "No! Hold still," and then distracting her with a colorful toy. You're introducing her to the concept of controlling her behavior well before she fully understands obedience.

Of course, we have to be careful not to nitpick our kids for every little childlike response to life! Jesus loves children so much, he even rebuked his disciples for keeping kids from climbing into His lap. Be careful to strike a livable balance lest you cause your child to draw away from what seems like a crabby, impossible-to-please mom or dad who is constantly correcting inconsequential behaviors.

There are times, however, when a slightly stronger tool is needed to stop unwanted behavior or a spiraling attitude. For those times, consider this second tool—similar to a correction, but a little more intense.

TOOL #2: REBUKE

The Greek word *epitimáō*, translated *rebuke*, means "to warn or sternly tell, to admonish strongly." It's that look in your eye that says, "You had better stop right now!"

When a gentle correction hasn't been enough to change your child's behavior, this tool may be what is needed in order to make a course correction. Your tone of voice is growing firmer and more intense, but you are not yelling or communicating anger.

The writer of Proverbs has this to say about the son or daughter who does not listen:

"You will say, 'How I hated discipline! How my heart spurned correction! I would not obey my teachers or turn my ear to my instructors. And I was soon in serious trouble'." (Proverbs 5:12–14)

We rebuke our children because we love them enough to help them avoid serious trouble. But take note, your voice will need to be measurably stronger in order to warn your child that you are most definitely not going to ignore his behavior. This gives him a chance to consider whether or not it's worth it to continue.

Proverbs 9:8–9 says, "Do not rebuke mockers or they will hate you; rebuke the wise and they will love you. Instruct the wise and they will be wiser still; teach the righteous and they will add to their learning."

No one enjoys having to rebuke someone. Yet when you take the time to rebuke someone you care about, *in love* and *with grace,* you are actually loving them. Proverbs 27:5–6 assures us that, "Better is open rebuke than love that is concealed. Faithful are the wounds of a friend" (NASB).

Notice the emphasis on love. This is not a tool to use when you are stressed and impatient and at the end of your rope. Your irritation will taint your words. Instead, wait until you are calmer, and then have a firm conversation about how inappropriate the behavior or attitude was.

When you lovingly rebuke your child, and he responds with obedience, your intervention prevents him from getting into even more trouble!

Rebuking, however, is not yelling across the room at your child, "Hey! Knock it off right now!" Nor is it a harsh, humiliating scolding.

A biblically practiced rebuke is a private, stern warning used to prevent your child from needing further discipline. You've upped the intensity, but you're not yelling. You are not using anger to control your child.

DIANE:

Need an example? A few weeks ago, I was helping my daughter get the kids settled into their respective Sunday school classes so she could keep the baby, who was sick, away from the throngs of children. One of my grandkids balked at having to go into his class. First, I put my arm around his shoulders and asked a few questions to find out what concerned him about the situation. I reminded him that his parents wanted him to go into his class. That's a correction.

When he still wouldn't go in, I took his hand, led him to a quiet place, got down on his level, and let him know that if he didn't go in I would have no choice but to tell his parents about his refusal. I was friendly, warm, and very firm. No shame, no emotional manipulation, just a brief, logical explanation with a note of urgency.

This is what a rebuke looks like: a little bit of intensity without anger or a shame-laced scolding. Obviously, this was a pretty simple situation. Breaking up a fight between siblings or stopping a toddler from toppling a bookcase would warrant a firmer voice and immediate intervention.

He still refused to go to class. Now, I'm his Amma (the nickname given to me by my grandkids) so I have no real authority, nor do I want it. Therefore, I took him to his mom and explained the situation.

Now you're wondering what she did, aren't you?

This is where the wisdom I see in my grown children just astounds me sometimes. She had the Spirit-given insight to recognize that this child, in this particular situation, was not being defiant. A perfect storm of events was colliding in his heart, leaving him loath to participate in an hour or more of loud, rollicking group activities. She gave him the choice of staying in church with her or going to class. When they got home a few hours later, she spent some time helping her son to recognize, process, and articulate his raw emotions in a healthy way.

A loving rebuke is simply a chance for your child to stop and think about his behavior or attitude and correct it on his own if he can. It is a suspended moment when his head and his heart can grapple with the consequences that are sure to follow if he continues down the path of disobedience. Thus, a rebuke ignored should be followed by action on the part of the parent, not just a louder voice.

In fact, a published study comparing *authoritative* parents with *authoritarian* parents concludes that "a combination of reasoning and power assertive consequences is more effective than either one alone."[2] In other words, most children need to know that their parents' correction and rebuke will be backed up with action.

Yet in the case of our grandson, a "power assertive consequence" would have been inappropriate, which is why it is so very important that we parent in Christ. By listening to our children and being alert to the nudges of the Spirit, we know when to make exceptions to the usual progression of discipline.

Remember, parenting is not an exact science! We discipline out of relationship. By knowing and being alert to our child's heart, we have the discernment we need to guide and teach our children well.

The third tool you have available to use as you fashion a heart of obedience in your child is the tool of *encouragement*, also called *exhortation* in some translations of the Scriptures.

TOOL #3: ENCOURAGEMENT

The Greek word *paráklētos*, translated *encourage*, comes from two Greek words: *para*, which means *by the side of*, and *kaleo*, which means *to call*. To enourage means to come alongside someone in order to help, to bring aid, to comfort, and to bring courage.

This is the same word Jesus used when He said, "But the Helper, the Holy Spirit, whom the Father will send in My name, He will teach you all things, and bring to your remembrance all that I said to you" (John 14:26 NASB).

Parents, more than anything, you are called alongside to help your kids—twenty-four hours a day! Just as God never abandons us, so you need to be there for your kids, helping them develop into the people God wants them to become. Our own kids are all married and walking with Jesus, but they still need us to come alongside and help, especially when they need free babysitting!

Encouraging your child includes telling her "Good job!" when she does what is right.

It was former first lady Lady Bird Johnson who reminded a generation of parents that "Children are likely to live up to what you believe of them." If all they ever hear from you is *corrective*, many children will eventually come to the conclusion that there's something wrong with them—that they're difficult or bad or too much trouble—or even that the gospel doesn't work for them.

Which is why for every rebuke there ought to be ten "well dones."

DIANE:

This is a tool I underused in my own home. The one complaint I have heard more or less from each of my four children is that I was quick to correct and rebuke and so slow to exhort and encourage. I expected a lot of my kids, which in itself is not a bad thing! But that next step of encouraging and cheering them on when they got it right—don't miss that!

Exhortation, or encouragement, is one of the most powerful tools for actually changing the heart of a child.

I remember when my oldest son was three years old. Every other month I got a publication in the mail that covered the developmental milestones for children his age. I studied it every time it came. All the latest scientific studies about brain development, what sounds they should be forming or feats they normally conquer at that age.

One month, I read these words: "By this age your child wants to please you."

I started to cry! My strong-willed three-year-old son did not show the least desire to please me!

But here is what I've found: You can actually influence your strong-willed child to have a heart to obey you by using the tool of encouragement. It works wonders!

The minute he obeys even a little, make a big deal about it. Be his cheerleader. Let him overhear you tell his dad how incredibly obedient he was. Watch for even an inclination to do what he is told and capitalize on that, saying, "Good job, son! I see you aren't going to pull your little sister's hair! I'm so proud of you!"

To become an encouraging parent, I had to learn a whole new language—the language of encouragement. It was Phil who coached me and became my example as I noticed the lack of encouraging words in my vocabulary. I had to choose to push past my natural reserve and shove aside my tendency toward perfectionism in order to master this language. Over time, with practice and humility, as God has grown my spirit to love like Him, I have become fluent in the language of encouragement. But oh, how I wish I had learned this earlier!

The character chart

One thing we did to help us heap encouragement on our kids was create a character chart. Diane started it because she'd begun to feel like a policeman all day long, correcting and nagging, breaking up arguments, and generally sensing an increasing crabbiness in her interactions with the kids.

Now, this may sound hokey to you, and it kind of was. But remember, this was pre-iPhone, pre-iPad days. You can make this work in a much cooler way—in fact, we hold out hope that one of these days a computer genius will read this and make an app for it!

We taped a simple sheet of construction paper to the front of the refrigerator. At the top we wrote, "Character Chart." On it we wrote what we wanted to see develop in our children's lives, character qualities like gentleness and generosity, humility and servanthood.

Then, we put a star sticker next to their names each time we noticed them exhibiting one of these character qualities. And because our kids were as competitive as yours, we told them that the first one who got one hundred stars next to their name got to go out to dinner with the whole family *and* choose the restaurant. Lucky for us, Carl's Jr. seemed the height of culinary ambition for our kids at this age!

Exhortation is verbally affirming your children for who they are, for the choices they make, for their godly responses and their success in difficult situations.

Long after our children had outgrown character charts and star stickers, the practice of encouragement worked wonders to influence them to *want* to obey. Why? Because your children will become who you tell them you see them becoming. Have you grasped that? It's worth reading again:

Your children will become who you tell them you see them becoming.

Use this tool generously, and you will be amazed at the results as your children begin to *want* to obey you for the recognition and affirmation they know they will receive.

Paul urged Timothy, his "true child in *the* faith" (1 Timothy 1:2 NASB) to correct, rebuke, and encourage those God had called him to shepherd. But he didn't stop there. He went on to say, "with great patience and careful instruction" (2 Timothy 4:2).

TOOL #4: PATIENT INSTRUCTION

Instruction means to actively teach, not just passively show.

Paul uses the word *patience* (Greek: *didaché*) as a way of explaining the best approach to this tool of instruction. Just as God lovingly and patiently instructs us—often needing to teach us the same things over and over again—so we ought to patiently and lovingly instruct our kids.

You didn't arrive at the masterpiece of perfection that you are overnight! And we shouldn't expect our kids to either. Maturity takes time to develop—it's a process, not an event.

Instruction is when you take a negative behavior and patiently instruct your child in how he *could* have and *should* have behaved. It is when we say to our children, "Not that way; this way."

We've all experienced the annoyance of our child interrupting a conversation to make a request that, to him, is urgent. If we were to take Paul's advice to patiently instruct, we might take that child aside later and say something like this:

"Honey, don't interrupt me to get my attention; just come up to me and put your hand on my side if I'm talking to someone else. I'll grab your hand to let you know I've noticed you, and then you should wait patiently until I can speak to you."

Can you see the beauty in this gracious response to our children? Instead of embarrassing them with a frustrated scolding, we offer a better way.

Sometimes, especially in public, we expect far too much maturity from our children during toddlerhood and the preschool years. We somehow expect them to instinctively know how to conduct themselves, as if by the time they are four years old they should know what is appropriate and inappropriate.

Then we act appalled at their misbehavior when all along, all they needed was patient instruction—over and over again.

St. Theophan the Recluse, a Russian bishop from the seventeenth century, wrote "Doing good must be taught just like everything else . . . it is not difficult to train them to do these things. Opportunities for them occur every minute. One has only to use them."[3]

This kind of careful instruction is really a form of *training*. Webster's dictionary defines training as "teaching a particular skill or type of behavior through practice and instruction over a period of time." *Training* our children to do good. *Training* our sons and daughters to love well. *Training* our kids to work through conflict in a calm and peaceable way.

One Greek word translated "train" in the New Testament is *gumnázō*. This is where we get our word "gymnasium". A gym is a place to practice. It is also where we go to get in shape and stay in shape. Metaphorically this word refers to training for the purpose of godliness.

Remember our goal? To raise *godly* children.

The writer of Hebrews used *gumnázō* to describe the spiritual maturity of those "who, because of practice, have their senses *trained* to discern good and evil" (Hebrews 5:14 NASB, emphasis ours).

Proverbs 22:6 gives sage advice to parents: *"Train* up a child in the way he should go, even when he is old he will not depart from it" (NASB, emphasis ours).

This is not a promise; it's a principle. It doesn't mean that if you take your child to church, VBS, or AWANA when he's young, he'll always love and walk with Jesus.

What it *does* mean is this: Children who are patiently instructed day after day, week after week, year after year in how to love God and walk in His ways, until it becomes second nature to them, will likely not deviate from their training when they're older.

This does not negate our God-given freedom of will; it is simply a wise observation of the consequences and rewards of patient instruction.

This kind of instruction takes a tremendous amount of time and attention—you've got to be on it!

We have often seen our daughter-in-law, Tammy, use this tool of patient instruction. Tammy's values spill over from her warm Italian/Spanish-Cuban heritage, cultures which place a high value on people skills. She is training her children to express thankfulness to people, and she is training them how to be affectionate, regardless of their natural inclinations.

For many years, the kids came to our house on Thursday nights for "date night." (Up until our grandson Jude was about five, he thought date night was his date with us!) Every time the kids arrived at our front door, Tammy insisted that they greet us with a hug and a kiss and "How are you, Amma?" or "How are you, Pops?" while looking us fully in the face. If they didn't—if they ran past us straight to the toy closet—she made them come back, and she patiently reminded them that a warm and personal greeting was imperative.

Then she'd watch carefully until they got it right, sending them on their way with words of encouragement. Her training has been relentless! And all three kids have become naturally grateful and loving.

Now that the kids are older, whenever they see us, they literally run and jump into our arms! We have to ready ourselves for their enthusiastic greetings or we get knocked over by their great hugs. What a blessing that is to us! And it's all because Tammy is training them how to love people on purpose.

We patiently instruct our children in life skills like good manners: how to say please and thank you, how to treat people with respect and dignity. And we train our children in appropriate behavior like using soft voices in certain places or not barging past people in lines.

Even more, we use patient instruction to train our children to respond to God with love and worship and gratitude. Over and over, we help them to notice God in creation, to thank Him for good food, good days, and good friends.

In the next stages of their lives, you will use these same four tools to train your kids to instinctively run to the Word for comfort from the Spirit. You will patiently instruct them in the art of listening to God and learning to see Him in the midst of the everyday, training them to center their very lives around Him.

A lot of talking

You can't help but notice by now that these first four tools all involve talking—no drastic consequences or long involved punishments, just different forms of communication. In a culture that seems bent on shaming anyone who steps out of line, all this use of words may seem ineffective, but studies show otherwise.

In a pioneering study of non-Jews who risked their lives to save Jews during the Holocaust, researchers found that what differentiated rescuers from those who stood by and did nothing as their neighbors were being persecuted was how their parents disciplined bad behavior and praised good behavior. Parents of rescuers talked and taught and explained. "It is in their reliance on reasoning, explanations, suggestions of ways to remedy harm done, persuasion, and advice that the parents of rescuers differed most . . . Reasoning communicates a message of respect . . . it implies that had children but known . . . they would not have acted in an unfavorable manner."[4]

Patient instruction is also the way God brings *us* along, strengthening us as well as inviting us into His presence, patiently urging us to live courageously according to His design—for His glory and for our good.

By now we suspect some of you want to shoot your hand up in the air like impatient students, insisting, "But I've tried all those things and my toddler still defies me! No amount of correcting, rebuking, encouraging, or instructing seems to get through to my preschooler's heart!"

What then?

What will your response be if, after using all four of these biblical tools, your child continues to resist, defiantly disobeying you? What will you do when your four-year-old, whom you've tried to convince over and over again not to dash out into the busy street, continues to do just that?

Nearly all children will at times defy their mother or father. Every parent knows they will face these situations where a line is drawn in the sand. When your sweet little girl looks you in the eye, and says, "Make me!"or your darling little blue-eyed boy says, "I don't like you! You're stupid!"

For situations like these, the Bible speaks of a fifth tool which, when used with wisdom and discernment, may be just the reinforcement you need to guide your son or daughter into self-control and obedience. In the Scriptures, that tool is named the *rod of discipline*.

TOOL #5: THE ROD OF DISCIPLINE

The "rod of discipline" is the biblical term for what we commonly call a spanking. *Strong's Hebrew Lexicon* defines *shebet* as a "rod, staff, branch, offshoot", while *musar* refers to "discipline, chastening, or correction".

In America and other parts of the world, controversy rages over what some call "corporal punishment." The idea of striking a child in anger in order to intimidate him into compliance is indeed appalling. Lashing out in a fit of parental fury is so against the heart of God as to be rightly considered outrageous. Violence is not the way of the kingdom that Jesus taught about so prolifically, and neither is *punishment* for our failures.

The biblical **rod of discipline** is neither punitive nor violent, but rather a loving tool parents are invited to use in the training of their children to bring about obedience and self-control. The incongruities between a beating and a humble, careful spanking are as vast as the difference between yelling at your child in anger and giving a loving but firm rebuke. One is training, the other is simply an adult temper tantrum.

Many young Christian parents today are choosing to raise their children without using this tool. Every parent who is a follower of Jesus needs to decide what they believe the Bible teaches on this subject and how they will implement this tool, should they choose to use it.

Because of the amount of misunderstanding surrounding the rod of discipline (which we will call a spanking for the sake of clarity), we are going to take some time to look at what the Scriptures teach on this subject.

Although *spanking* is not a biblical word, it is a biblical concept. Consider these verses from the book of Proverbs:

"The rod and reproof give wisdom, but a child who gets his own way brings shame to his mother." (Proverbs 29:15 NASB)

"Whoever spares the rod hates their children, but the one who loves their children is careful to discipline them." (Proverbs 13:24)

"Folly is bound up in the heart of a child, but the rod of discipline will drive it far away." (Proverbs 22:15)

"Do not withhold discipline from a child; if you punish them with the rod, they will not die. Punish them with the rod and save them from death."[5] (Proverbs 23:13–14)

The writer of Proverbs set out to emphasize the effectiveness of using this tool *in love*. By *properly* utilizing this tool of discipline, parents can save their children from foolishness that results in either metaphorical or actual death.

Now let's unpack Hebrews 12:5–11 in order to hear God's heart on the matter. And remember: keep this passage in the context in which it was written. The previous chapter (Hebrews 11) contains a list of history's bravest and most faithful men and women. This remarkable passage is often called the Hall of Faith—exactly the kind of faith we hope our children will someday cling to. No sooner do we read their stories than God begins a conversation about our own stories and how *He* fathers *us*:

My son, do not regard lightly the discipline of the Lord, nor faint when you are reproved by Him;

For those whom the Lord loves He disciplines, and He scourges every son whom He receives.[6] It is for discipline that you endure; God deals with you as with sons; for what son is there whom his father does not discipline? But if you are without discipline, of which all have become partakers, then you are illegitimate children and not sons. Furthermore we had earthly fathers to discipline us, and we respected them; shall we not much rather be subject to the Father of spirits, and live? For they disciplined us for a short time as seemed best to them, but He *disciplines us* for *our* good, that we may share His holiness. All discipline for the moment seems not to be joyful, but sorrowful; yet to those who have been trained by it, afterwards it yields the peaceful fruit of righteousness. (NASB)

The Greek word here translated as "chastens" (NIV), or "scourges" (NASB), is *mastigóō*. It refers to what was then the common Jewish practice (both legal and domestic)[7] of striking with the rod.[8] Here in Hebrews, it is used figuratively of God, meaning to chastise or correct.[9]

The word translated "punish" in Proverbs 23:13–14 is the Hebrew word *nakah*, which refers to the physical discipline with the use of the "rod."

Both the writer of Proverbs and the writer of the book of Hebrews, under the inspiration of the Spirit, remind us that in His love, God sometimes spanks us.

When God spanks us, it is not because He is mad at us, but because He longs for us to experience His holiness, to share in the beauty of His goodness.

Sometimes that spanking spares us from death—death of relationships, death of intimacy with God, and even physical death.

Even though it is painful. Even though we don't like it. Even at the risk of being misunderstood and rejected, He "scourges" us as a means of training us.

And the anticipated result? A life overflowing with a rich harvest of righteousness and peace. These are the benefits the psalmist spoke of when he wrote, "Your *rod* (*shebet*) and your staff, they comfort me" (Psalm 23:4).

The fact that God uses the rod in our lives is actually proof of our belonging to Him and of His deep love for us.

Although the Bible does not prescribe when or how often to use the rod of discipline, it does offer it is a loving tool available to parents to use in the training of their children.

Therefore, be cautiously leery of anyone who urges you to use spanking as the *only* or even the *primary* tool of discipline. The purposeful vagueness of God's instructions about spanking imply that for some it may be a one-time disciplinary experience. For others, perhaps, this will be a tool used effectively a great deal more often. And let's be honest—there are some children who should never be spanked and some parents who may find it the better part of wisdom to abstain from spanking.

Spanking is a tool, not a cure-all. Used carefully along with the other tools, it can be a marvelous means of softening the heart of your child.[10] But used indiscriminately and harshly, it can be a means of wounding and alienating your child, not only from you but ultimately from God.[11]

It is up to the two of you *together*, mom and dad, to decide how and when spanking will be used in your home.

We find ourselves reluctant to write about this; some who are reading may take what we write and be far too severe as a result, even abusive or oppressive, which is never God's heart! Others need to be given permission to properly use this tool so they can bring their children under control without losing their self-control in the process.

That said, spanking must be handled prayerfully and carefully, and in some cases rarely.

While preparing the material to teach this section for a conference, we received a sad email from a woman who was worried about what we were planning to teach in regard to spanking. This young woman had watched her well-meaning but unwise parents spank her strong-willed younger brother over and over again for everything and for way too long. Her heart ached for her brother, who wound up wounded in his spirit and convinced that he was a hopeless case, unredeemable and worthless.

What that boy may have needed was to be told, "You're a good boy, made in the image of a good God," to be encouraged and taught and guided when his behavior tripped him up. By misusing and overusing the tool of spanking, his parents left him defeated, destroying his trust in God's no-matter-what love for him. How the heart of the Father must ache for that wounded boy!

There are some parents who may choose never to spank for legitimate reasons. If you have a quick temper and are prone to violent rages, you may be better off forgoing this tool. Dr. Dobson warns, "Give children maximum reason to want to comply to your wishes. Your anger is the least effective alternative."[12]

Or if your child is unusually fearful, as many adopted children can be, this tool may not be effective or wise. If you are the guardian of a foster child, you must abide by the agency's rule of never spanking that child. This is a tool you may need to take out of your toolbox. Many abused and abandoned children are not receptive to spanking as a means of loving discipline. Too much pain has shadowed their tender lives, infusing a spanking (no matter how well-intended) with meanings no loving parent or guardian wishes to convey.

As for us, we did choose to use the rod of discipline with all four of our children. Now our children are grown, and they too have chosen to include this tool in the raising of their children. Like us, they are using it prayerfully and carefully but also confidently. Each of our children have assured us that they have no bad memories from the times we chose to lovingly and calmly spank them. In fact, most often hurtful memories come from times when parents strike out with their words in a frustrated moment of not knowing what else to do. It is our conviction that a God-honoring use of the rod of discipline is a much kinder, less shaming, less manipulative means of discipline that may even prevent lasting pain.

For those of you desiring an even more practical and in-depth look at the use of this tool, please visit IntentionalParents.org. There we lay out for you when we chose to use this tool, how we went about it (the process), and what never to do when using the rod of correction.

TOOLS TO CONSIDER *NOT* USING

Notice what tools we didn't mention: time-outs (in a punitive sense), loss of privileges (in the early years), and so-called "creative discipline." These commonly employed means of discipline may be effective in the short term, but can create confusion in tender hearts in the long run. We urge parents to think and pray about *how* or *when* or *if* ever to use these forms of discipline.

Time-Outs

We didn't send our children to their rooms or make them sit in a corner as some parents do, thereby using time-outs as a means of punishment.

Here's why: God doesn't send us to our room in anger when we disobey. He lovingly deals with us with extreme tenderness and grace. By sending your children away from you when they've annoyed you, you may be inadvertently teaching them that God may get so mad at them that He doesn't even want them in His presence.

You want to teach them the opposite: that they are invited to run *to* God when they are overcome by sin.

What we did do, however, is give them what we called breaks. A friend of ours called them "fill-ups." Dr. Karyn Purvis in *The Connected Child* called them "time-ins." A time-in is an intentional time you create to help your child settle down and gain perspective. Often, one of us would cozy up on the sofa with an overwrought child and read a story, or feed him a healthy snack, or go for a walk in the fresh air.

Do you see what we mean about this sort of intentional training taking lots of time? It's easier to send our children to their rooms or have a little one sit in isolation than it is to utilize a time-in.

Here's the thing: **When our aim is to tenderize the hearts of our children so they will *want* to obey, sending them out of our presence in frustration sends the wrong message.**

Dr. Purvis says, "A version of a time-out, this involves having the child spend time in a designated location that is near to the family and offers few distractions. This becomes a 'time-in,' where instead of being sent away, the child is brought closer. The child doesn't go there alone but is accompanied by an adult who stays nearby."[13]

Breaks or *fill-ups* or *time-ins* are an effective means of training our children to practice healthy personal habits when they are older. When life gets overwhelming, rather than lashing out at everyone around them, they know how to take a moment to settle themselves down and regain control over their raging feelings.

Taking Away Privileges

Very young children simply cannot understand this form of discipline, especially when it is dished out by an utterly frustrated parent. They are incapable of connecting the dots between what they did wrong and not being able to do something they enjoy. This often leads to sullenness, exacerbating the problem rather than teaching a better way of behaving. Again, it is *heart change* that you are after.

Although this will be an effective way of training older children (more on that later), we want to caution you to make sure your younger child is mature enough to grasp cause and effect before you take away privileges.

Watch your child and listen to him to make sure the discipline makes sense to his developing mind. Also, it is important that the privilege you take away is somehow related to the purpose of the disciplinary action. For instance, taking away a toy that your toddler used to smack his older brother in the face will instantly make sense to him.

"Creative Discipline"

Proverbs 26:4–5 contains an apt warning for parents of young children: "Do not answer a fool according to his folly or you will also be like him. Answer a fool as his folly *deserves,* that he not be wise in his own eyes" (NASB).

Any trainer worth his billable hours must learn to incorporate creativity into the routines he prescribes. A client who has no anticipated goals soon loses steam, and a would-be athlete who is bored with the tried-and-true exercises often loses motivation. We all get that.

Once, a young mother proudly told me she had discovered the cure for the common dilemma of toddlers who bite. When her little boy bit her in frustration, she bit him back! A prime example of answering a fool according to his folly.

Instead, we are to "Answer a fool as his folly *deserves,* that he not be wise in his own eyes." For parents to avoid this kind of tit-for-tat randomness, they must think through and pray about using appropriate, biblical tools to train the "foolishness" out of their children's unwise actions.

Sometimes, otherwise good parenting books suggest "creative" consequences that are borderline bizarre, like the book that told the story of a mother who was driving with her four children in rush hour traffic when the kids began to squabble. After warning them repeatedly, she ascertained that her grade-school-aged son was pushing his sisters' buttons, thereby exacerbating the bickering.

In a burst of annoyance, this mother ordered the offender to bend over with his head in his lap for the rest of the twenty-minute drive home. Then she told his sisters not to talk to him—he was to be completely shut out of the conversation.

Why? To teach him a lesson.

What kind of lesson does that teach?

We need to examine these books (including our own) on the basis of Scripture, not the other way around. Those of us who have chosen to follow Jesus look to the Word of God as the ultimate guide by which to align our lives with the way of Jesus. And there are clues everywhere! If you are consistently spending time with God in the Scriptures, listening to the Spirit, inviting God to give you specific wisdom for your specific child, He promises to give you the wisdom you need.

As a representative of the father heart of God to our children, dare we cobble together vindictive methods of child training in our moments of frustration in order to "teach a lesson" that is unidentifiable?

We should be disciplining, not punishing.

Godly discipline is different from punishment, although we often use the words interchangeably. Webster's dictionary defines the verb *punish* as "to inflict a penalty or sanction as retribution for an offense." Is this our goal in training our children? Or are we focusing on cultivating a longing and a love for God in their hearts?

Godly discipline is formative, not punitive.

The Greek words translated as discipline in Ephesians 6:4 and Hebrews 12:5–11 are *paideía* and *paideuo*. These words mean "to instruct, chasten, correction, to educate."[14]

Paideía is to be distinguished from the words translated as "punish": *kólasis*, which is best defined as penal infliction or punishment, and *timōría*, which denotes penal retribution.[15]

Punishment says, "You get what you deserve," or "Shame on you!" The intent is to penalize. Thus, it is characterized by rejection and humiliation.

Discipline says, "Let me help you change," or "This way, not that way." The intent is to teach and train. Discipline is imposing and enforcing self-control and obedience. The intent of godly discipline is not to penalize, but to equip your child to obey God and to one day be capable of controlling his selfish impulses.

In the twenty-third psalm, the Shepherd's discipline is described: "Your rod[16] and your staff, they comfort me."

Godly discipline brings a sense of comfort and assurance to your child, just as God's discipline of us leads us to a better place, a place of safety and security.

Thus, although the English word *punishment* is commonly used as a synonym for *discipline*, parents need to keep in mind the difference between the two. Even more, we need to be careful to discipline our children with the same kind of lovingkindness with which the Father trains and corrects us.

BE CONSISTENT

One of the most important ways to render discipline as effective as possible is consistency. Your child thinks in black and white. She is not yet able to reason abstractly. For a strong-willed child especially, one failure to follow through can lead to more and more testing of boundaries to see if you really mean what you say.

PHIL:

I remember the day Diane called me at work, crying, "I've tried correcting and encouraging—I've even spanked him! And I still feel like he's won! What do I do now?"

It wasn't long after that day, at the age of four-and-a-half, that our son gave his life to Jesus and we saw a real change occur. His heart began to soften, yielding to our instruction. That very real event, combined with consistent, persistent training, led to the breaking of our son's willfulness to disobey without breaking his spirit.

However, it is not always possible or advisable to be 100 percent consistent.

DIANE:

As a recovering perfectionist, my perceived need to be consistent just about drove me crazy! I heard the advice to "Be Consistent!' as a rule set in stone.

What could I do when extenuating circumstances prevented me from disciplining properly? What about when a child was sick? Or when I was in a public place that did not leave room for disciplinary action? What should I do when her meltdown had more to do with my own poor judgment in keeping her out too long and what she really needed was a nap?

I could see that sometimes my children lost all semblance of control because their brains could no longer reason normally due to fatigue or over-stimulation. What then?

EXTENUATING CIRCUMSTANCES

Here is a short list of circumstances that may warrant backing off from anything but the lightest discipline:

- When your child is sick
- When you have kept your child out too long or up too late, and he's melting down because his brain can no longer reason
- When your child is overstimulated
- When there is no way to get to a private place
- When you know there is something else going on that needs to be handled with tender care[17]
- When your child is not developmentally able to fully grasp the loving but firm meaning behind the disciplinary tool you've chosen

Around the time we were beginning to ask ourselves and others these questions, we came up with our own unapologetically unscientific guideline: *Aim for 80%.*

THE 80 PERCENT RULE

If you are consistently disciplining your child 80 percent of the time he needs it, you are doing great! Fabulous! Better than almost anybody!

Remember, you are aiming to influence the *heart* of your child, not create automated machines. Be as consistent as you reasonably can be, but know that letting discipline slide occasionally is not going to ruin your child forever. Give both you and your child a little credit for all the hours you are putting into teaching and learning. And give the Spirit room to work His beauty in both you and your child—after all, isn't that what grace is about? With God's help, wisdom, and insight, you are building a foundation for your child one brick at a time. The rest is up to Him.

Chapter 9

A Heart of Self-Control

The second major character trait you want to see developed in your child by the end of this foundational stage is a heart of self-control.

What is self-control?

Obedience has to do with actions, but self-control has to do with emotions and how we deal with them.

Do our emotions control us, or do we control our emotions?

Self-control is one of the fruits of the Spirit listed in Galatians 5:22–23. It is a requirement for those in spiritual leadership. "Since an overseer manages God's household, he must be blameless—not overbearing, not quick-tempered, not given to drunkenness, not violent, not pursuing dishonest gain. Rather, he must be hospitable, one who loves what is good, who is *self-controlled*, upright, holy, and disciplined" (Titus 1:7–8, emphasis ours).

This means that if we are going to raise passionate Jesus followers, self-control is an area in which we dare not fail to train our children. By incorporating training in self-control early in your child's life, you are actually giving him or her an opportunity to qualify as a leader in Jesus' church.

The Greek word for self-control is *egkráteia*. It means self-restraint, or mastery. Self-control involves the ability, through the power of the Spirit within you, to master your own impulses and emotions, your willfulness, your tongue, your behavior, and your moods.

And get this: the word translated as self-control can also be translated *continence*. As in the opposite of *incontinence*. Think "Depends" commercials! Incontinence is messy, smelly, disgusting. To lack self-control is to be an incontinent mother or father, or an incontinent child who becomes an incontinent teenager. Your aim in teaching your child self-control is to enable him to grow into an adult who is in control of his emotions—emotions that lead to actions and reactions.

By teaching your child to control himself at an early age, you enable him to *choose* his responses to people and to life, to have control over mood swings, over the sullenness and sulking that all too often define children and adolescents, over the powerful pull of anger and all the feelings that threaten to take control of our lives no matter our age.

Until your child can learn to control himself, *you will need to be his self-control.* From the beginning of their lives, you are in control of them with the goal that they will, over time, learn to control themselves.

Keep in mind that because we believe that the Bible is inerrant and foundational to all of life, we know that children are not born innocent. Theologians call this "original sin".

Some people say they don't believe in original sin—clearly, they haven't had children yet!

James Dobson, the child psychologist who has influenced and enlightened Christian parents for several decades, says, "Perhaps this tendency towards self-will is the essence of 'original sin' which has infiltrated the human family."[1] No parent has ever had to teach their child to say, "That's mine!" Selfishness comes naturally to every one of us.

The Bible teaches that we are all born with the infection of sin pulsing through our veins. David understood this when he wrote, "Surely I was sinful at birth, sinful from the time my mother conceived me" (Psalm 51:5).

As parents, we need to be aware of this and alert to the misunderstanding often promoted by modern-day parenting publications, which basically asserts that all children are born as a blank slate and they get messed up by their environment—*us!*

That tiny infant you hold in your arms is not innocent. He is born with the desire to control. He is beautiful—a reflection of God Himself, made in His image—but don't make the mistake of thinking he's all purity and goodness in those first months and then suddenly, out of nowhere puts on his sinful nature on his second birthday! Well before he turns two, your innocent little bundle of perfection will begin to protest—loudly—when he doesn't get what he wants when he wants it.

The key we have found is to catch things early so that you will be able to discipline less.

Rather than waiting until your child's temper tantrums reach ear-splitting levels of intensity, watch for the occasional outburst and firmly discipline. Your child will learn early on that outbursts of anger are ineffective. Still, some children, perhaps even *most* children, will need continuous training to keep their immature emotions from overpowering them.

DIANE:

I well remember our firstborn's first temper tantrum. I was carrying groceries in from the car, and he wanted something NOW. When I told him he'd have to wait, he threw himself on the ground in a fit of drama.

I'd been told that if you just ignore temper tantrums by not paying them any attention, children will simply stop on their own.

Unfortunately, my strong-willed son hadn't heard that!

So he threw himself on the floor a couple more times, with no response from mom. With all the determination that makes him a fantastic leader today, John Mark stalked into his room, climbed up onto his tall bed, and threw himself onto the floor below. Then he really started to cry!

That was when I realized I had better deal decisively with his temper tantrums, or he was liable to really hurt himself. For a little over a week, I disciplined him every day for some sort of dramatic display or a willful temper tantrum.[2]

I was all prepared to deal with Rebekah a few years later, but her temper tantrums were a sort of female implosion. She'd just collapse on the floor in a heap of ruffles and tears. When it finally dawned on us that this was our daughter's expression of a temper tantrum, we decided to deal with those in the same way: firm, loving discipline to teach her that she could and must control her meltdowns.

Our third child, Elizabeth, watched all that drama with her older siblings and the ensuing consequences, and decided right then and there that she wasn't going to have any temper tantrums.

Smart girl!

I felt pretty good about that. I was ready to write the book on How to Handle Temper Tantrums.

Until Matt came along.

Matt-man, as we called him back then, wrote the book on temper tantrums! He was eighteen months old when he started in—every day, sometimes every hour, that horrific knockdown-on-the-floor-out-of-control variety. You know that embarrassed mother standing in the check-out line at the store? Oh yes, please don't judge—that was me!

Matt wanted his way, and he wanted it now!

I was tempted to give up. To settle for less. To shrug my shoulders and say, "Well, that's just the way Matthew is . . . I'll do the best I can and let him learn the rest on his own."

But Phil wouldn't let me. This is where the lamp and the light idea of Proverbs 6 is so valuable!

Looking back now at how hard that eighteen-month period of my life was, I am so thankful we stuck with the training. I am so glad I limited my life for those months in order to build into Matt's character the strength of self-control. But at the time, all I could see was that training wasn't working!

I wanted him to be over his tantrum phase in a week, or a month. But for eighteen solid months, every single day we dealt with Matt's temper tantrums.

PHIL:

I remember the day Diane said to me, "If I have to go to the grocery store again with all these kids, we'll starve!"

I love my wife's cooking, so on Monday nights I volunteered to feed the kids dinner (of course Diane had already cooked it!), bathe them, do Bible time, and put them to bed while Diane took her sweet time at the grocery store. She meandered up and down those aisles, relishing her time alone! I thought she'd never come back!

You will hear people recommend that you ignore your child's temper tantrums or try to reason with them while you wait it out. We do not agree. Temper tantrums are not only dangerous, they are the beginning of a rebellious spirit and can lead to serious issues with sinful anger.

When parents ignore or cater to their child's temper tantrums, they may go underground for a season, but will invariably pop back up in later years as out-of-control, manipulative behavior.

If a child's temper is not dealt with in early childhood, James Dobson warns that, "the thorny weed which it produces may grow into a tangled briar patch during the troubled days of adolescence."[3]

Be very alert here! If a parent caves to a child's tantrum, catering to him by pleading or trying to bribe him out of it, the child learns that anger is an effective means of controlling the people around him. Proverbs 29:11 warns, "A fool gives full vent to his anger, but a wise man keeps himself under control" (NIV 1984).

Teach your child to control his anger, lest he grow into an adult whose anger dictates his out-of-control responses to people and to life.

Remember, children do not grow out of anything but their clothes!

We all know adults who have temper tantrums. Many parents are still trying to gain mastery over their own tempers because their parents failed to train them in self-control. The shame can feel unbearable and may even cause a father or mother to feel unqualified to train their child in self-control.

Don't make this mistake! Instead, take it on as a quest *together*, asking your child's forgiveness when you lose your temper, explaining why it is hurtful and wrong. Tell your children you're asking God for the strength to live a life of self-control as you help them to do the same. Remember, God is a God of self-control, and His Spirit lives in you. As we draw near to Him, filling our souls full of His grace and beauty, He weaves self-control into our character, making us what we cannot become on our own.[4]

Be diligent as you discipline your child's tantrums. You love him enough to give him the tools he needs, so that he is not defeated by his own raging emotions.

Our son Matthew is a man now—and an amazingly peaceable person! He is not easily angered and shows no tendency towards a violent temper. When pushed to the very limit of his patience, Matt knows how to deal with it gracefully, but he is not the least bit passive. He is a strong and compelling leader with the self-control to deal with his emotions in a healthy, godly manner.

As we wrap up this chapter on discipline and the development of obedience and self-control in your child, mull over these words about training spiritually mature leaders by J. Oswald Sanders:

> "We need to be willing to pay a price higher than others are willing to pay . . . fatigue is the price of leadership . . . the world is run by tired men."[5]

These first five years are backbreaking work as you lay a solid foundation for the years ahead. Yet nothing is more important! Every moment is worth your focused attention. It took King Solomon seven and a half years to build the first temple in Jerusalem. For the better part of four years before that, he was making preparations: digging into the hillside, building huge stone retaining walls, getting water to the site—underground work that wouldn't have been visible once the entire temple was built.

It was all foundation work!

Like Solomon's building project, parents who do the heavy lifting during these foundational years are creating a solid base upon which the rest of their child's life can be reliably built. It's exhausting work! But so worthwhile.

Although your child will remember very little of it, the training you do in these early years will make all the difference as to the kind of person your child will become. Think about it—for most of us, our earliest memory is probably from around three to five years of age. *By then your parents were undoubtedly exhausted, and yet you remember none of it!* To those of you who are currently in this stage, keep up the hard work! You will be so glad you did. One day you will stand back and see the godly man or woman your child has become and you'll say, "It was worth it all."

Raising Passionate Jesus Followers

Laying the Foundation
(birth to 5 yrs.)

The aim is to help your children develop a heart of obedience and *self-control*. This early time in the home is like boot camp with lots of training.

Nearing the end of this stage, your child...

☐ Obeys commands when given. Exhibits self-control.

☐ Infrequent willful temper tantrums.

☐ Accepts "No" as a final answer.

☐ Grasps that he can control his attitude.

☐ Responds enthusiastically to stories about Jesus & Bible heroes.

☐ Has started memorizing Scripture.

☐ Prays authentically.

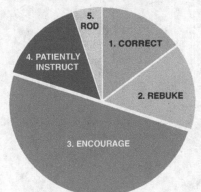

1. Gently show your child his fault. Don't ignore it, excuse it, raise your voice, or think they'll grow out of it. Use the **Ten Year Rule**—ask yourself, "What will this behavior look like in 10 years?"

2. Warn sternly, admonish strongly. This should be done in private, not in a way that publicly shames them. A warning ignored should always be followed by action, not more empty warnings.

3. Come alongside to help, comfort, and bring courage. This is the most important tool—use it **frequently & generously**. *Your child will become* who you tell them you see them becoming.

4. Train your children through **practicing**. Actively teach: "Not that way ... this way."

5. Spanking is a biblical concept and should be handled **prayerfully, and carefully** ... Never in public or in anger, & never to harm.

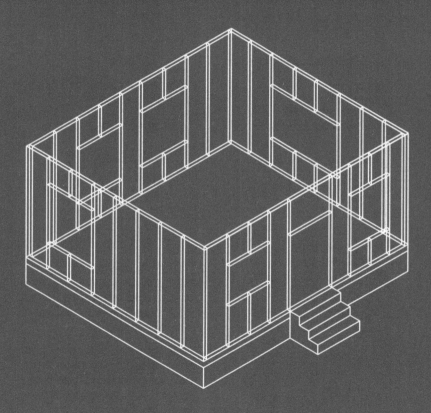

Part 3

Doing the Framing

Ages 6–12

"By wisdom a house is built,
and through understanding it is established;
through knowledge its rooms are filled
with rare and beautiful treasures."
PROVERBS 24:3–4

Chapter 10

Bring Them Up

I n this section we are going to focus primarily on the elementary school years, ages six through twelve. But remember: *these are stages, not ages!* Every child develops at their own pace, growing in the ability to grasp what you are teaching them while growing in the maturity to follow through. All along the way, we need to be asking God for insight into the hearts of our children. If we don't, we may miss specific instructions He wants to give us about the way He wired this child.

And He does want to speak to you! Over and over again we hear Jesus' phrase, "He who has ears to hear, let him hear" (Matthew 11:15 NASB). As you tune in to listen, you'll hear Him speaking, teaching, convicting, showing you how to work with Him as He shapes your children into these "rare and beautiful treasures" (Proverbs 24:4).

This home you are building *with God* is becoming something beautiful and rare.

The framing stage in the building of a home is a lot of fun to watch. Up until this point, you've been staring for weeks at a bare concrete slab, trying to imagine what it's going to look like. Then the framing crew shows up, and in just a few days you actually begin to see your new home take shape.

Just as in building a house, this stage of raising godly children is a lot of fun. All the hard work you did during the foundational years now begins to bear fruit. You're seeing a heart of obedience take shape in your child's responses. Not perfect obedience, but at least a leaning towards wanting to obey you and an understanding of the consequences of disobedience.

Although you will continue to work on training your child in the skills of self-control, by now you are beginning to see the fruit of your teaching. Temper tantrums are nearly gone. Your child is able to snap out of a bad attitude more quickly, resisting the temptation to lash out in anger.

During this stage you want to focus on developing in your child a heart of wisdom.

Proverbs 23:15–16 expresses the goal of this stage:

"My child, how I will rejoice if you become wise! Yes, my heart will thrill when you speak what is right and just." (NLT 1996)

And down in verse 24,

"What a pleasure it is to have wise children." (NLT 1996)

It is the parent's job to direct and supervise this framing stage as it develops in your child. And God tells you how to do it in Ephesians, chapter six.

In the previous chapter we studied Ephesians 6:1–3, focusing on God's instruction to *children*. Now, in verse 4 we see His command to *parents*, specifically to fathers. There are two parts to God's charge: one is negative (what you *are not* to do), and the other is positive (what you *are* to do).

First, the negative. Let's look at Ephesians 6:4:

"Fathers, do not exasperate your children."

This raises a pertinent question: What does God mean when He instructs parents to avoid exasperating their children?

The Greek word *parorgízō*, translated *exasperate* or *provoke*, means to *make angry* or *bring to the point of anger*. A working definition would be, "an ongoing pattern or treatment that gradually builds up a deep-seated resentment that finally boils over."

In Colossians 3:21 we see this same command repeated:

"Fathers, do not embitter your children, or they will become discouraged."

In the New American Standard Bible, it is translated slightly differently:

"Fathers, do not exasperate your children, so that they will not lose heart."

The Amplified Bible expands it this way:

"Fathers, do not provoke or irritate or fret your children—do not be hard on them or harass them; lest they become discouraged and sullen and morose and feel inferior and frustrated; do not break their spirit." (AMP 1987)

Do you get the picture?

Although the Greek word translated fathers here (*patér*) means just that, a male parent, this idea can apply to either parent. A mother is equally capable of doing the very same thing: being too hard on her children, causing them to feel inferior and frustrated. For some of you, it was your mom and not your dad who consistently hurt you in this way.

Both of us had to face our innate tendency to exasperate our kids—as does every parent we know. Diane by *fretting* them endlessly, being too picky and perfectionistic about minor things, and Phil by *expecting too much of them* at times rather than asking questions.

Being willing to identify your own "exasperating" patterns gives you the ability to bring those negative character deficiencies to

God—to humble yourself before Him and before your kids—and then to tap into the power of the Spirit to overcome them.

Because this is such a pervasive problem among parents—including good, intentional parents—we have listed a few ways parents aggravate their children, bringing them to a boiling point of deep resentment. These are by no means the only ways parents can aggravate their children, but they are five of the most common.

FIVE WAYS PARENTS PROVOKE THEIR CHILDREN

By speaking unkindly or harshly to them

We are talking about words like: "You did that again?!" "What is wrong with you?" "You make me so mad!" and "I've had it with you!" Be ever so careful about using shaming, discouraging words that sum up your child as inadequate or unlovable. Proverbs 18:21 warns: "Death and life are in the power of the tongue" (NASB). Those words, spoken rashly, linger in your child's head for a long time.

PHIL:

One day I was in my office upstairs working on this very section of our Intentional Parenting material when I heard our son Matt yell, "Bye, Mom and Dad, I'm heading out!"

At the time Matthew was a twenty-one-year-old college student living at home. He was a godly man, fighting for purity, enrolled in Bible College, training to be a pastor. We were letting him live rent-free in our recently remodeled daylight basement apartment.

But—well, let's just say he hadn't inherited his mom's love of neatness and order!

Diane had been trying to get him to clean things up in the basement for a week; out-of-town family were coming, and that's where they would need to sleep. But Matt had packed his schedule so tight, he hadn't gotten around to it.

Finally, in frustration Diane came to me and said, "I've tried being nice about it, but Matt just won't do it. Will you talk to him? You need to tell him he can't go hang out with friends until he gets that basement cleaned up!"

Which is why, on that morning, I yelled down to him, "Matt, did you do what Mom asked you to do?"

"No Dad," came his answer, "I'll do it later."

I lost it! Raising my voice, I bellowed, "How many times do we have to tell you to do something?!"

Silence.

Then I heard Matt's soft response.

"Dad, I feel like I can never please you."

Right while I was typing these very words!

I pushed back from my desk, walked to the top of the stairs, and by God's grace, apologized as I looked down at Matt's strong shoulders slumped in defeat. It was as if I had taken a knife and burst a balloon.

The proverb I had read that very morning popped into my head: "There is one who speaks rashly like the thrusts of a sword, but the tongue of the wise brings healing" (Proverbs 12:18 NASB).

By the way, a humble and sincere apology is the *best way* and the *right way* to bring healing when you've blown it with your kids. Ask their forgiveness. Name what you did wrong. Identify how your words hurt your child and how badly you handled the situation. Not only will you restore your relationship with that child, you are also demonstrating to them that you, too, live under the authority of Jesus. They will see the way He is changing and growing you, and they will be encouraged as you change and grow together— *in grace.*

Are you building your children up with your words or tearing them down?

By comparing them

Our children are supposed to be different! God made each of them unique, and He relishes the nuances of their personalities. He likes the way He wired them! When parents have a narrow ideal of what they want their child to be like, they are in danger of discouraging and exasperating their child.

Just like adults, children go at different paces. They are drawn towards different activities; they develop different interests and passions. They have different abilities and capabilities. Be very careful that you are not comparing your children to each other—or to yourself!

Remember the story of Jacob and Esau? They were the twin sons of Isaac and Rebekah, the great-grandchildren of Abraham and Sarah. Their animosity for each other was legendary, spanning multiple decades! This phrase takes us to the root of the trouble:

"Isaac . . . loved Esau, but Rebekah loved Jacob" (Genesis 25:28).

Contrast their tragic family story with the studies done by George Barna and his team. They found that "Ninety-six percent of the Revolutionary Parents we interviewed took the time and effort to learn the unique nature of each of their children and to build a parenting framework around each child's distinctives."[1]

For help in learning how to know your child's unique wiring, see Appendix C. We have listed books and resources that we have found helpful in our own quest to know our children's hearts.

By over-protecting them

This is the parent who smothers their child, overly restricting them, never trusting them, constantly questioning their judgment as if expecting them to fail. A parent who falls into this pattern may erode their child's confidence as the child intuitively senses their parent's lack of confidence in them.

This kind of nit-picky oversight eventually builds a barrier between the parent and the child, a barrier that must be breached if you are going to have a significant influence on your child as he gets older.

"It's not easy to sit idly, keeping hands and opinions to ourselves as we watch our children struggle to solve problems in their time and in their way. But this is the necessary discomfort of learning. Creativity involves painstaking trial and error. We don't want to deny our kids this privilege."[2]

The only way we know to be able to do this is by entrusting your child to the Father every single day, recognizing that He is leading, bringing wisdom and insight to you as you ask for it, then doing what He tells you to do for that particular child.

By pushing them beyond what they are capable of achieving

There is a fine line between believing in your child's capabilities and expecting more from them than they are able to consistently deliver. While each of our children had all the intelligence needed to get A's in school, two of them had personalities that would have caved under the pressure to perform at that level all the time.

Our middle daughter needs time and freedom to think and gather information. From that steady pace, her mind connects the dots, drawing conclusions that come out of her mouth with incredibly insightful wisdom. We noticed that when we pushed her too hard too fast, she lost the best parts of herself in the hurry. In high school, that translated to a lot of B's when she couldn't get it all done by pushing herself to an A level. It meant we needed to cheer as loudly for her B's as we did for A's.

Many children eventually give up entirely if they feel that no matter how hard they work, they cannot please their parents. Or the opposite happens: they grow into emotionally unhealthy adults whose incessant striving to over-achieve warps their personalities and prevents them from ever being at rest.

Know this: *you won't do it perfectly*. Just last week Diane ached with her daughter as they talked about the ways she had passed on her perfectionistic tendencies. While trying to teach her to work well, to *do it right*, Diane had inadvertently created a silent mental committee that sits on Rebekah's shoulders. Together they wept at the burden that kind of thinking creates. There were no accusations or anger, just a shared time of mourning for the loss of rest and peace that perfectionism brings.

Be wise and discerning—know your children! Then guard their hearts as you help them to know themselves. And recognize your own emotionally unhealthy tendencies, lest you burden your kids with your own unresolved issues.

By neglecting them

In this era when both parents are often working long hours or are distracted by texts, emails, and endless responsibilities, we are in danger of neglecting our children's relational needs. But as author and blogger Rachel Stafford teaches in *Hands Free Mama,* "To grasp what matters, you must let go of what doesn't."[3]

There is a death to the self-life when we have kids! There is a time when we need to put our children's needs ahead of our own wants. But this is what Oswald Chambers called "the good death," when we let go of our own ambitions and interests to put our children's vulnerabilities first, and we surrender our lives to God in absolute trust. This is not the same as child-centered parenting; it is simply a mature way of fulfilling the privilege of raising this child God has gifted you with.

Obviously, the extreme version of neglect happens when dad or mom leaves the family. Abandonment by a parent marks a child for the rest of his life. Yet this sense of neglect also happens when you are too busy or too distracted to listen to your children—to know their dreams and dream with them. They may think you do not actually love them enough to spend more time with them than is absolutely necessary.

Think about this! You can be loving your child by working extra hard so he can have all that he needs while your son or daughter is interpreting your busy-ness as disinterest. *Dad and mom are too into their own lives to care about mine.*

Just the other day, our thirty-seven-year-old son thanked Phil for taking him on an overnight camping trip when he was just eight years old. He still remembers it! Phil remembers fitting it into his too-busy schedule—a twenty-four-hour camp-out a couple miles from our house. Something so simple is still bringing good memories nearly three decades later.

DIANE:

My father grew up in poverty. Both of his parents worked just to put food on the table, and that's about all they could manage. Dad watched that hardship and determined to go to college, to find a career that would enable him to move out of the poverty he had known and earn a good salary. Providing well was a driving value of my dad's, thus he worked hard and put in long hours to succeed.

When I was in high school, struggling with defeated feelings that led to a drop in my grades, my dad set out to build me up. It was the summer between my junior and senior years of high school, and I managed to get my first job at a nearby amusement park. My uniform was a frumpy, red-and-white striped skirt and white blouse, and I was required to wear a gigantic bow in my hair. Red Converse sneakers—ridiculously unstylish in the late '70s—left me feeling like a clown.

My dad called me beautiful.

For that entire summer, at least once a week he left his office at lunchtime, donned his cowboy boots, and paid the entrance fee to the Western-themed park to have a burger—made by me—for lunch. My cheeks flamed as he announced to all who would listen that his daughter was the best burger flipper ever. He made a big deal of everything I did at that job, praising me, telling me what a great employee I was, making me feel like I had the most important job in the world and that whatever I did with my life, I was sure to be wildly successful!

Everything changed for me that summer. I stood taller, gaining confidence and the drive I needed to go back to school as the success

> my dad said I was. And all that time, Dad had me convinced that he
> loved every minute he could sneak away to be with me at Frontier
> Village.
>
> Instead of ignoring me as he drove himself to success in his career,
> my dad *saw* me. He heard me when I didn't even know what I needed.
> And he rescued me, showing me more than any sermon could have, the
> way of the Father.

When children perceive a parent's indifference to what matters to them, anger often takes hold in their hearts. Taking the time to ask questions, to attend games, or hear their stories affirms your child in a way he or she can grasp. Be present to your child, showing him the interest he needs to thrive.

Let's keep going! After telling fathers what *not* to do, "Fathers, do not exasperate your children," the second command in Ephesians 6:4 is a positive one about what we *are* to do:

"Instead, bring them up in the training and instruction of the Lord."[4]

The phrase "bring them up" contains a fascinating and easily overlooked concept. The word in Greek is *ektréphō*. It means "to nurture to maturity."

Nurturing isn't only confined to providing food and clothing—it includes training our children in all aspects of life: bringing them into health and maturity emotionally and spiritually. This is the same word translated as "nourish" (NASB 1973) or "feed" (NIV 1984) in Ephesians 5:29, wherein husbands are commanded to love their wives as Christ loved the Church.

A WORD ABOUT MARRIAGE

After leading your son or daughter to Jesus Christ, the greatest gift you could ever give your kids is the gift of a good marriage!

PHIL:

After I quit the band I played in for nine years, I got a job with a cement company while I was finishing my business degree. Cement trucks rolled up one after the other while we were pouring the foundations for huge industrial buildings.

Before the cement trucks arrived, thick steel rods called rebar were laid on the ground and tied together with wire. While the cement was being poured, it was my job to lift up that rebar, using a crowbar, so it would sit in the middle of the cement floor. This created a strong, four-inch-thick, unbreakable floor with a steel rod in the middle that could withstand just about anything.

Having (and maintaining) a good marriage is like putting rebar in the foundation of your home!

Like us, you'll make a lot of mistakes while raising your kids, but if you have a good marriage with Jesus at the center—if your children see you loving each other and apologizing to each other when needed—you'll give your kids a great gift. They will know deep down in their souls that their mom and dad love each other and are never going to leave each other. The foundation of your home will stand strong, and your children will thrive.

How about that last phrase, "bring them up *in the training and instruction of the* LORD"? There are three key points to understand there:

Training (*paideía*): Translated *discipline* in the NASB, this refers to the systematic training of children. It includes education.

Instruction (*nouthesía*): This Greek word means "putting in the mind." It is the kind of instruction found in the book of Proverbs, training that has to do not so much with fill-in-the-blank facts, as with right attitudes and principles for living skillfully. The word encompasses both instruction and correction.

Of the Lord: Don't forget this last phrase! Parents, you are to bring your children up in the discipline and instruction *of the Lord!* This is an education that is theocentric, or centered on God.

Parents are to model a God-centered way of living life.[5] **They are to guide their children in learning the *way of Jesus* and living out the *mission of Jesus.***

Together, your family is "trying to learn what is pleasing to the LORD" (Ephesians 5:10 NASB). In our home this included which movies we watched and which ones we avoided, what kind of music we listened to and which magazines we subscribed to. Even more, this "pleasing the LORD" way of living inspired in us a desire to make room for the fragrance of Jesus (2 Corinthians 2:15) to permeate the walls of every room, which in turn led to convictions about how we spoke to each other, how we handled disagreements, how we loved.

ALL WISDOM COMES FROM GOD

All wisdom comes from God. "The fear of the LORD is the beginning of wisdom, and knowledge of the Holy One is understanding" (Proverbs 9:10). Therefore, the more I know the way of Jesus, the wiser I will be. And the more my kids know the way of Jesus, the wiser they will be.

Authors and researchers Steven Southsick and Dennis Charney, in their book *Resilience,* identified ten key factors that enable people to bounce back from tragedy and trauma. Every one of the character qualities they identified can be found in Scripture. The belief in a brighter future (optimism), courage, altruism, faith, being in community, having mentors, flexibility, self-control over one's thoughts, feelings, and body.[6] As we have so often noticed, social research confirms the wisdom God has generously given us in His Word.

What you are trying to do in these framing years is to build a godly young man or woman—not by outward behavior management, but by bringing your child close to the heart of God so He can begin the beautiful, life-long process of transformation. That's wisdom.

Being a Jesus follower is not just about obeying the rules, nor is it primarily about following a Christian code of conduct. You want your child to know and love the God who made the rules!

Your goal is to cultivate in your child a heart of wisdom, because children do not just automatically grow up to become who God wants them to be. They must be *taught* how to live life the way God has designed it to be lived!

Before we lay out specific instruction for what to teach in this stage, we want to introduce you to a way of putting together all the aspects of wise training into a workable format, something we simply call The Box.

Chapter 11

The Box

As you seek to develop a heart of wisdom in your child, we want to introduce you to The Box. What's *The Box?* Glad you asked!

The Box is the frame we build around our children's lives in order to offer a place of joy-filled security in which they can thrive and grow into who God wants them to be. It is a mechanism parents can use to bring all the elements of God-oriented child-rearing into a cohesive, cooperative, and calming way of doing life—even when your children are anything but cooperative and calm!

The Box is a way of putting it all together, a format to follow when discipline and training are needed. It is a guide to make sure all that training is creating in your child a whole and healthy heart towards God and towards his parents.

The Box starts off small and tight. Mom and Dad control everything in those early days of infancy and utter dependence. Knowing what is best for your child, you create a warm and responsive atmosphere while nourishing and cherishing him as God's gift to you.

Slowly, The Box begins to expand as your child matures. He is given more freedom, more autonomy, while you get the joy of discovering and unfolding this beautiful gift from God that is your child. With that expansion comes a less directive approach as your child learns how to do life in your home.

Sometimes The Box has to be tightened back up when your child goes through those inevitable times of testing you and losing control. During those times, The Box brings her back into sync with who she is and how she thrives.

The Box grows and expands until one day you reach the goal: *no more Box*.

What joy that day brings to parents! Your relationship with your children changes dramatically as they begin to create their own Box, managed and imposed entirely by themselves as they grow into a vibrant relationship with Christ.

THE BOTTOM OF THE BOX IS JESUS

The bottom of The Box must be strong and solid, a foundation upon which to build the rest of life. That foundation is *Jesus*. Not church, not the Christian way of living, not AWANA or any sort of program—just *Jesus*.

Paul said it this way: "That I may *know* Him" (Philippians 3:10 NASB, emphasis ours). The Greek word *ginosko*, translated *know*, is a picture of intimacy, of deep trust and freedom in Him. For his friends in Ephesus, Paul prayed that they would *experience* the love of Christ.[1]

From the moment they are born, we talk about Him. We rock them to sleep with songs about Him, we pray in His Name. We give our children comfort in a way that opens their hearts to crave the comfort the Holy Spirit gives to those who remain in Him.

As they grow a little older, we tell stories of His strength and fill in their imaginations with stories of His power.

To our grandboys, Jesus is the ultimate superhero! So much so that one Easter, when five-year-old Duke was asked to color a picture of the resurrected Jesus, he looked at it and wasn't satisfied with the results. After pondering it for a while, he knew what it was missing: a light saber! So Duke added one, and there He was—*Star Wars* Jesus!

Although we laughed as a photo of his drawing was texted to all the Star Wars-crazy aunts and uncles, we also cheered his understanding of Jesus' strength and power.

Later, when they are a little older, we delve deeper into God's Word with the idea of unveiling Him to our children: who He is, how He thinks, what He loves. Not academics but just Him—*Jesus*. We want them to want Him, so we paint a compelling picture of who He is.

ONE SIDE OF THE BOX IS DISCIPLINE

There are times in a child's life when the discipline side needs to get a little firmer. You know it, you see it, and so you step in and tighten up this side of The Box. Instead of just reacting, you look for opportunities to address the problem.

DIANE:

I've told you about Matthew's infamous temper tantrums and how I was tempted to give up. Although he was a delightful, fun child, his will was so much stronger than mine, and I often shrank from the confrontation that entailed.

On one of those days, instead of dealing decisively with his behavior, I sent him to his room. I just couldn't go through with the ordeal of spanking him again.[2]

Matt-man (as we called him back then) stomped up the stairs, down the hall to his room, and slammed the door behind him. I just sat on the sofa, fearing for my son. Why couldn't we seem to get through to him? Why wasn't this working?

Then I heard a loud *bang!* I actually felt the walls tremble, like in those California earthquakes I'd felt when I was growing up along a fault line. I had to go up there and see what was going on, but gosh, I was dreading another confrontation.

When I got there, Matt was sitting completely calmly and oh-so-innocently on the side of his bed. But the shelf above his bed, which usually housed a display of vintage toys and books, was empty. Matt had climbed up on his bed and in one angry outburst, swept all those toys off, leaving one of the antique metal toy trucks embedded in the far wall!

> Now, with our smart phones and social media, we'd probably have Instagrammed a photo of that truck sticking out of the sheetrock—but at the time it felt anything but funny!
>
> Obviously, it was time for us to tighten The Box!

THE OTHER SIDE OF THE BOX IS ORDER

The discipline of a well-ordered life will follow your child from infancy through adulthood. It is simply the concept, taught throughout Scripture and lived out by everyday people, that *there is an appropriate time for everything.*

In the book of Ecclesiastes, King Solomon wrote what he had learned by listening and observing the wisdom of God. His words are a treasure for parents:

"... the wise heart will know the proper time and procedure ... for every matter." (Ecclesiastes 8:5–6)

"There is a time for everything, and a season for every activity." (Ecclesiastes 3:1)

"He has made everything beautiful in its time." (Ecclesiastes 3:11)

If we fail to put up this side of The Box, our children will live in a continual state of chaos and disorder. They will be stressed out and ill-equipped to function well.

With the current emphasis on simplicity and minimalism, the maxim from our parents' era rings truer than ever: "A place for everything and everything in its place."

We are convinced that our firstborn would have been labeled ADHD if we hadn't recognized his need for order at an early age.

In order for him to settle down for a nap, or when he was older, to study, we had to make sure his visual space was tidy. Disorder and chaos made him hyper and hard to soothe.

Some children need this kind of order more than others. These are the children who thrive on routine, yet who may be naturally scattered and unfocused. Kids who are especially creative and extremely sensitive to their environment often need a sense of wide-open, uncluttered space in order to flourish.

When they are guided by clear parameters, all children respond to order with a sense of contentment. Healthy food keeps the body functioning smoothly, preventing the documented effects of too much sugar and processed food. A bedtime routine allows the brain to ease into rest without the discomfort and unrest brought on by exhaustion.

We found that our children resisted settling down for sleep unless we kept them in a restful routine. Thus, our evenings were times of lowered voices, softer music, good stories. Order can overcome the fear that sometimes rises to the surface of a child's heart as he lets go of control. Routines involving warm baths and soft blankets generate feelings of safety, inviting the fearful child to rest. Such a simple routine enables our children to trust us, to sense our dependability—and to trust the Father who keeps us safe in His care.

Children thrive with a flexible structure to outline their days. Our youngest son woke up with the same two questions every morning:

1. Where is everybody? (He's definitely our extrovert!)
2. What are we doing today?

Knowing where everybody was and having a schedule laid out for him first thing in the morning enabled him to get up cheerfully and do what he needed to do.

Your children need to know what to expect so they're not constantly testing you. By remaining flexible and consistent while creating a safe, orderly world, you set your children up for success.

But don't forget about the top of The Box because it is really, really important.

THE TOP OF THE BOX IS AFFECTION, AFFIRMATION, AND FUN!

Our kids need to know—right down to the marrow in their bones— that we love them, that we think the world of them, and that we're so glad they're ours—whether they are three or thirteen or thirty-three.

Pastor and author Dave Stone, who devotes an entire book to the often-overlooked need for fun and joy in our families, advises, "Laughter and joy shouldn't be guests in your house; they should be permanent residents in our everyday life."[3]

Yes!

With all the hope and freedom Jesus brings into our lives, our homes should be bursting with joy! Words of affirmation and demonstrations of fond affection combine with fun to bring laughter and joy right into the heart of our homes.

That's The Box.

Here's the key: When you need to tighten The Box around your child because he's acting up, getting in trouble, or creating conflict and confusion, you don't just stomp on him with discipline. You must utilize all four sides of The Box—Jesus, discipline, order, then affirmation, affection, and fun—together to restore your child to a place of calm, a place of happiness and assurance. When you tighten all four sides of The Box at the same time, your child thrives. Instead of becoming sullen and angry, he lights up with the happiness of a child well-loved. Badly behaved children are miserable! Just remember, though: Tighten every side of The Box *simultaneously*. This is the difference between heavy-handed discipline and loving, biblical training.

PHIL:

We got to test this concept of The Box one day when we were watching our school-age grandchildren. We had them with us for a week while our son and his wife were in England. At the time, we were living in a friend's guesthouse while we were remodeling a fixer-upper. The commute to and from school every day was long, wearing everyone out by the weekend. By the time we were on our way home from church Sunday evening, we were all pretty much exhausted—and showing it! When the kids started bickering in the back seat, teasing each other with that particular sarcasm so prevalent in the schoolyard, Diane and I looked at each other and realized, *Uh-oh, we're in charge!*

I turned to the kids and said, "Hey guys, this needs to stop. We aren't going to speak like that to each other." Just a gentle correction to let them know what we expected. That was the discipline side of The Box.

Their dad had texted to check in that morning and told me about a cool, young worship leader who had led a song he remembered me leading when he was young: "Glorify Your Name." This made me feel that maybe I was still at least a little cool! Or at least not totally uncool!

So I told the kids about the call and then said, "Do you wanna hear the song?"

No response.

I sang it anyway!

Still no response.

"Hey, do you want to hear the first song your dad wrote when he was ten?"

They looked slightly interested, but by no means enthusiastic—it had been a really long week, and the traffic was barely inching down the freeway.

So I sang it.

Gradually the atmosphere in the car started to change—a lot less animosity and a shared story. I asked them to sing with me, and they did!

A song about Jesus, bringing Him in—there was the bottom of The Box.

After singing the song together a few times, they started smiling and joining in enthusiastically—that was the affection, affirmation, and fun to top The Box!

By the time we got home, Diane directed everyone to get their pajamas on while she made quesadillas. They marched off obediently and did what was asked of them cheerfully. By the end of dinner, they were filled with good food, having fun and being nice to each other—all the bickering forgotten. These are terrific kids who want to get along, after all.

Diane and I turned to each other, smiling, and said, "We just did The Box! It works!"

Using The Box enabled us to transform the atmosphere of tension and complaining into fun and camaraderie—and we did it with a minimum amount of discipline, which made all of us happy.

Tighten The Box when your child needs help, and you will see that the way the Father disciplines us is the way to freedom and joy.

We will be talking more about The Box throughout the book in order to help you apply it during every stage of your child's growth and development. We have seen this strategy work especially well during the teenage years, when most parents are at a loss to know what to do. Many parents are finding the concept of The Box to be a wonderful alternative to the tension created when we rely on negative discipline alone.

Chapter 12

Character Development

During these framing years, as you work toward the goal of creating a heart of wisdom in each of your children, there are three primary areas—found right in Scripture—on which to direct your focus. In the Gospel of Luke, God says this about Jesus when He was twelve years old:

> "And Jesus kept increasing in wisdom and stature, and in favor with God and men." (Luke 2:52 NASB)

As your child continues to develop physically (stature)[1], you'll want to intentionally focus on the other three areas Jesus Himself continued to grow in:

1. Character development (growing in wisdom)
2. Relationship building (favor with men)
3. Spiritual training (favor with God)

First, let's look at character development.

When the biblical narrative tells us that Jesus "continued to grow in wisdom", why do we call that "character development"?

The word translated *wisdom* in the original Greek is *sophía*. It means, "skill in the everyday affairs of life, including good sense and sound judgment."

How Jesus, who was fully human and fully God, was capable of growth in these areas of his life is an unfathomable theological mystery, yet the Bible says He was! If Jesus Himself grew in wisdom, in skill in the everyday affairs of life, how much more must we need to as well, right alongside our kids!

As you seek to cultivate Christlike character in your child, helping him grow in wisdom as Jesus did, there are four areas—four "biggies" to focus on.

TEACH THEM TO RULE THEIR SPIRIT CONSISTENTLY

Proverbs 16:32 declares that "He who is slow to anger is better than the mighty, and he who *rules his spirit*, than he who captures a city" (NASB, emphasis ours).

The opposite of being "slow to anger" is to be quick-tempered and impatient. A man or woman who is quick-tempered lacks the self-control to respond wisely under stress or to answer calmly in tense conversations. Instead of knowing how to "rule their spirit," they just "let it all hang out," spewing whatever it is they are feeling in the moment.

Quick-tempered people lack self-control.

By continuing to teach and train your child how to control himself when he is angry, you are setting him up for success. If, on the other hand, you watch helplessly while he lashes out, it will cause him no end of trouble. He may get fired from a job, and it may one day cause problems in his marriage as well as in his own parenting.

People will want to avoid your son or daughter if his impatient, quick temper affects their relationships. Proverbs 22:24 says, "Do not make friends with a hot-tempered person, do not associate with one easily angered."

Parents take heed: you do not want your son or daughter to be that person other parents don't want their kids to be around! The Bible teaches that this character deficiency is one that can be brought under control with diligent training. Before you begin that training, however, you'll need to ask yourself some questions:

Are you a dad or mom who vents in anger?

Are you learning to control your own outbursts?

There are two primary kinds of sinful anger: explosive anger and simmering anger. Both are equally harmful. Is anger an area of your life that needs to be repented of and brought daily to Jesus for redemption? If so, learning to rule your spirit is going to be a family affair!

We found that memorizing Ephesians 4:25–32 together and focusing on verse 29 worked wonders to diffuse angry outbursts in our home—from either us or the kids!

It says, "Let no unwholesome word proceed from your mouth, but only such a word as is good for edification according to the need of the moment, so that it will give grace to those who hear" (NASB).

We quoted this wisdom-packed verse constantly in our house!

And then we often added verses 31 and 32 to work with our kids in those heated moments between siblings:

> "Get rid of all bitterness, rage and anger, brawling and slander, along with every form of malice. Be kind and compassionate to one another, forgiving each other, just as in Christ God forgave you."

The next two verses explain why more fully:

> "Follow God's example, therefore, as dearly loved children and walk in the way of love, just as Christ loved us and gave himself up for us as a fragrant offering and sacrifice to God." (Ephesians 5:1–2)

It is your job, mom and dad, to help your children learn how to resolve conflict in a God-honoring way. If left to themselves, the meanest child will win every time!

Teach your kids that:

- No one has the power to make you angry.
- Lashing out in anger is a choice—one we can choose not to make.

Yes, things can happen to upset you, people will be rude and mean, teachers will sometimes seem unfair, and things won't always work out as fast or as well as you think they should. But that does not give anyone the right or justification before God to react with verbal or physical displays of uncontrolled temper. Sinful anger is never God's way.

We wanted our children to understand the truth that their response is their responsibility.[2]

We cannot understate the importance of teaching this truth to your children *now* before they swallow the two-sided lie:

- It is your fault that I am angry.
  - This is, in the extreme application of this lie, what abusers believe!
- It is my fault when someone is angry with me.
  - This is what victims of abuse come to believe, often binding them to their abusers!

While there is such a thing as righteous anger, that is not usually what gets us into trouble. True righteous anger accomplishes good things, making a strong statement for God's ways, as when Jesus overturned the money tables in the temple courtyard.[3] We experience this when we see injustices like little children being trafficked or abused. In Psalm 97:10 we are urged to "hate evil, you who love the LORD" (NASB) and Ephesians 4:26 says, "In your anger do not sin."

God gets angry at sin! With Him, our souls cry out for justice with fierce, compelling anger—the kind of anger that leads us to do something about injustice. Sinful anger, on the other hand, is when we want to hurt others, when our impatience or selfishness grapples for control.

So what do you do with your son or daughter who is displaying angry outbursts or bitter speech? Is there a sure way of obliterating anger from your child's go-to response? A simple, universally effective plan to eliminating anger?

Unfortunately, strong emotions are not easily cured with a simple three-step plan guaranteed to give you success. This is why we take James 1:5 seriously:

"If any of you lacks wisdom, you should ask God, who gives generously to all without finding fault, and it will be given to you."

Ask God for His wisdom concerning your angry child. What is at the root of it? Why is he hitting his little brother? What's up with your daughter's angry outbursts?

"The Bible's emphasis on the inward origin of anger suggests that helping angry children involves more than mere anger management techniques. To solve your child's anger problem, you must target the source of his anger: his heart."[4]

Three Root Causes of Anger

Anger, we have seen, can usually be traced to three root causes.

Control

It seems that some people are just born with a tremendous need to control everyone and everything around them. Sometimes these kids are loud and obnoxious—usually boys, but not always. Sometimes little girls (and not-so-little girls!) can turn manipulative and become viciously angry when someone will not submit to their control—including you!

Here's the good news: If you catch this early on in their development, and you don't overlook it or cater to it, there is a pretty simple (although not easy by any means) fix.

Instead of reacting in anger or giving in to your child's anger, rummage around in that box of disciplinary tools from Part 2 to discern which one is the appropriate tool for the situation. Remember those biblical tools? *Correct, rebuke, encourage, patient instruction, the rod of correction.* By understanding your child and the reason for his anger, you can choose whichever tool will most effectively target his heart. Talk together with your spouse about specific ways you will consistently deal with this child's anger.

Be sure, Mom and Dad, that *you* are filled with and under the control of the Spirit when you step in to correct your child's anger issues. Remember James 1:20: "Human anger does not produce the righteousness that God desires." If you respond to their anger with your own sinful anger, it will not bring about the desired result that pleases the Lord. Instead, your own anger may reinforce to your child that sinful anger works! And yes, anger *is* a means of controlling people, but it's not God's way!

Andrew Murray concluded that the great secret to a peaceful home is for parents to "first [be] ourselves what we want our children to be." Ultimately, it's about modeling, isn't it? So don't get mad at your child; instead, teach and train him or her to be wise and self-controlled—to be mighty in spirit.

Frustration

Some kids (and many adults!) seem to have a lightning-quick fuse when it comes to obstacles in their path. This is the child who throws things when they don't work out the way he wants or erupts in angry tears when his own limitations keep him from doing what he wants to do.

Your child does not have issues. He has anger.

Yes, there are issues (dyslexia, sensory reactions to uncomfortable clothes, etc.) but those are just the triggers of inappropriate anger, not the cause. Your child can, with your help, learn to control his responses and be patient with himself and others.

So, what can you do to help your frustrated child?

The solution is so simple and so clearly laid out in the Scriptures: slow down your life!

Your child may have too many toys, too many people clamoring for his attention, too much stimulation, and not enough time to go at his own pace.

PHIL:

When our daughter Rebekah was in this framing stage of her life, we noticed, seemingly out of the blue, that she was starting to stutter. She'd try to get her words out, but would often be so frustrated that she couldn't seem to string a sentence together without tearful stuttering. It scared us!

I had grown up with a friend whose stuttering had become habitual and severely limiting by the time he was in college. He had a heart of gold and could sing beautifully, without any hesitancy, but a conversation was nearly impossible. Everyone who knew Fred loved him, and our hearts ached for him when he struggled to get his words out. So when Rebekah started to stutter, I was filled with fear for her future.

After worrying about it, we decided to pray about it! Isn't that the way we often are? When we did, God spoke to both of us, revealing that our young daughter's stuttering was our fault.

Our life and church ministry had become frantic. I was a worship pastor in a growing church with six gatherings every Sunday, and I was often out five nights a week. Diane and I were doing life at a hectic pace, and Rebekah was sensing that she had to rush to get her words out or she'd miss being heard.

The Lord showed me we needed to slow down through Scripture during my regular Bible reading time! I was reading in Genesis and came across the story of the reunion of Jacob and Esau. After years of estrangement, Jacob was terrified that his brother was going to make good on his threat to kill him. Instead, Esau forgave him, they reconciled, and then,

> "Esau said, 'Let us be on our way, I'll accompany you.' But Jacob
> said to him, 'My lord knows that the children are tender . . . so
> let my lord go on ahead of his servant, while I move more slowly
> at the pace . . . of the children until I come to my lord in Seir.'"
> (Genesis 33:12–14)
>
> *I will move more slowly at the pace of the children.* The Lord showed
> me what we needed to do right then and there.
> We needed to slow down.
> So we did. We sat on the ground when Rebekah talked to us, giving
> her room to get her tangled thoughts out. We tried to make her feel like
> we had all the time in the world to listen and hear. Within a week, her
> stuttering stopped.

The first time we shared this story at our parenting conference, a woman came up to us afterwards and introduced herself. After giving her name, she said, "I'm a pediatric speech pathologist, and I just wanted you to know that when parents come in alarmed that their child has started to stutter, that's the first thing we tell them to do: *Slow down!*"

We realized then that sometimes our children's anger, frustration, or stuttering was our fault. We were still trying to go at the pace we went at before we had kids, dragging them along, speeding up when we should have been slowing down. Slowing down wasn't easy by any means. (It still isn't!) But over time we adopted a slower pace of doing life and as we did, we saw Rebekah flourish.

Be careful, moms and dads, that you remember to live at a pace that works for your children. Simplify every area of your life in order to create a home environment that is uncluttered and calming. Your children will respond immediately, increasing their ability to live life peacefully.

And take note of a powerful truth here: The passage of Scripture God used to speak to us about this serious situation had nothing whatsoever to do with stuttering or angry outbursts. Yet God used it to speak to Phil, to lead us to a workable solution for our problem. We have seen this over and over—God has spoken wisdom to us straight from the Scriptures *when we asked for it.* Such is the power available to any and all who follow Jesus.

Willfulness

By far the most common cause for angry outbursts from a child is willfulness: *I want my way and I want it now!*

That is what most temper tantrums are about. That is what *all* of Matthew's temper tantrums were about!

We chose to consistently use the rod of correction—a carefully controlled, God-honoring spanking—to train our children to control their willfulness. Taking away privileges or sending them away by themselves rarely did what was necessary to soften our children's hearts or enable them to yield their strong wills. Although some children certainly will respond to a less authoritative means of discipline, ours did not. We decided that a willful temper tantrum was unacceptable in our home.

You will need to talk together about which tool you will use to teach your child that temper tantrums will not be tolerated. It will take patience and time on your part, but the resulting self-control will be well worth it.

Dealing with Fear

There is, however, one emotion that often masquerades as anger—*fear.* The most delightful child in the world can seem stubborn and angry when she is in the grip of hidden fear. Fear is such a powerful and unreasonable emotion that no amount of correcting or rebuking or training or spanking will make a dent. You will just escalate your child's fear by attempting to reason it away, or worse, to spank your child into compliance.

Our granddaughter Scarlet is one of those children who grapples with fear. She is cheerfully obedient, extraordinarily helpful, and eager to please—until bedtime. The process of letting go of control enough to fall asleep sends her into a spiral of fearfulness.

When she spends the night with us, she outlines every step of the process:

"First, I'll lie down in the hallway so I can see you. Then when you're taking your bath, Amma, I'll go to your bed. I'll get the bed warm for you. Put your soft blankie on me! When you're all done with your bath, we can cuddle. Then I'll fall asleep, and then you can move me to my bed. Okay?"

Scarlet's need to control the process of falling asleep is not disobedience or obstinateness. In fact, she is learning to overcome her fears by arranging her environment, pushing through to courage. The soft vulnerability on her face right before she falls asleep lets us know that she has found rest, that she feels safe.

A fearful child requires great patience on the part of the parent. It will take a level of wisdom you don't have on your own—but real wisdom comes from the God who promises to provide it if you will sincerely ask. If you're unsure, someone else may be able to detect fear in your child. Ask a grandparent, an older woman, a pastor, or a counselor for help. You want to be the one to bring the Spirit's truth to your child's fear, and often it is the community around you who can help you see how.

It is important to note here that emotions in and of themselves are not bad. In fact, it is the wise parent who draws a child out and helps him to identify what he is feeling rather than just pushing those pesky feelings away. Sometimes an angry outburst from your child is a red alert that there is something going on inside him or her. Invite God into the situation, allowing Him to guide you to the hurt or wrong thinking that has led your child to this point.

Raising Leaders

Some kids are just harder than others from the get-go! They're just as valuable, just as loved, but ten times more challenging. Don't give up! You are going to earn every grey hair on your head, but hang in there—it's worth it.

You have been entrusted with the privilege of training a leader.

Think for just a moment of the leaders you know: politicians, leaders of businesses, leaders of movements and of churches. Can you imagine them as young children? It is doubtful that these strong and compelling leaders were compliant toddlers! Take heart, be persistent, and insist on obedience. Teach your strong-willed child to rule his spirit.

DIANE:

Our son Matthew preached his first sermon on Mother's Day a few years ago. As a middle-school pastor, he'd been given the opportunity to speak to the entire church that Sunday, and I was in the audience. He presented me with a beautiful bouquet of flowers, a delightful grin on his face. All I could think of in that moment was that this was the guy whose anger had sent that vintage toy truck flying across the room to be embedded in his bedroom wall!

Can we just give you hope to hang in there and do the hard work faithfully? Enable your strong-willed sons and daughters to gain mastery over their own wills, freeing them to be the leaders they were made to be. Someday you may get flowers!

TEACH THEM TO CONDUCT THEMSELVES WISELY

Proverbs 20:11 says, "It is by his deeds that a lad distinguishes himself, if his conduct is pure and right" (NASB).

The phrase, "distinguishes himself" means "to make himself

known." We all have a reputation, even our young children. A good reputation is a precious possession.

Proverbs 22:1 says, "A good name is more desirable than great riches; to be esteemed is better than silver or gold."

Sometimes we think something our son or daughter is doing is kind of cute and harmless when in reality, it is irritating to others.

DIANE:

When Matthew was eight years old, we were going to a church with lots of strong young men leading the children's ministry. Since Matt's older brother, John Mark, was one of those leaders, Matt tried hard to fit in and get their attention.

As boys do, he started to hit the guys whenever he saw them. *Bam!*

At first I thought nothing of it—no big deal, just kinda cute, with his buzzed hair and his little skate shoes. But then one day I observed the reaction of a group of three of these leaders as they noticed Matthew approaching. They instinctively stepped back and assumed defensive positions.

Now, I knew Matt as a sweet little boy, but his reputation as an annoying menace was preceding him!

Part of the problem, clearly, was their height and Matt's height and the area of the body where his punches were landing!

What I thought was cute, these guys saw as annoying.

Mom and Dad, it's our role as parents to protect our child's reputation by intentionally seeing past the cute factor and making sure his conduct is both pure and right.

We take on that role in these early years, not because we are afraid of what people might think, but because our sons and daughters are building their reputations. Without your intervention, he may start to develop a negative self-image because of people's reactions to his behavior rather than growing in the self-confidence you are working to instill in him.

Your job is to help your children learn to conduct themselves wisely because "foolishness is bound up in the heart of a child."[5] Children aren't born with good judgment; they must be wisely and intentionally trained.

TEACH THEM TO WALK IN INTEGRITY

PHIL:

When John Mark was eight, he became interested in model trains. He loved going to the train store near where we lived, planning his layout and which cars he needed to complete his set. But collecting trains is an expensive hobby, and his weekly allowance didn't come close to covering it, so, along with a paper route,[6] he started collecting soda cans to earn more money. There was a recycling machine just outside a nearby Toys 'R' Us where he'd bring his bag of cans and exchange them for cash. This particular machine actually dispensed money after you inserted your empty cans and bottles.

On this day, instead of spitting out two dollars, what his bagful of cans was worth, the machine gave him *twenty-two* dollars—a crisp, fresh twenty had stuck to one of the dollar bills! John Mark's eyes lit up! But then, realizing what had happened, he turned to me and asked,

"Dad, what do we do with this extra money?"

I answered his question with a question of my own: "What do you think we should do, son?"

He thought about that for a few seconds, then said, "I guess we should go inside the store and turn it in." The look on his face was a mixture of conviction and disappointment. All I could think to say was,

"God is going to bless you for your honesty, John Mark."

Still, he trudged into the store with the slumped shoulders of an eight-year-old who had to give up a small fortune.

The manager of the store had no way of getting ahold of the company that leased space for their machine, so they told him to keep it!

My little boy looked at me, eyes wide with wonder.

Me? I'd become a prophet! I knew God would bless him whether or not he got to keep the money.

The great thing is, John Mark was able to keep that money with a clear conscience because he refused to take what didn't belong to him. He'd been a person of integrity. While I had meant that God would bless him spiritually, God had decided to teach him a lesson and bless him financially as well.

How did I know how to help my son do that? Because I remember watching my dad find a twenty-dollar bill on the floor of a Safeway store when I was a little boy. And I remember walking with him to the manager's office while he turned it in.

I don't remember him saying, "Son, I am going to teach you about integrity!" He taught me integrity by example—the most powerful means of instruction.

Proverbs 20:7 says, "A righteous man who walks in his integrity— how blessed are his sons after him" (NASB). My dad was a man of integrity, and I was blessed because of it. Now I was able to pass that blessing on to my son.

The Hebrew word translated here as *integrity* is *tom* (/tome/). It has to do with who we are as a person as well as what we will and won't do.[7]

Integrity says, "I will do the right thing, whatever it costs me." It is one more character quality that must be modeled in your life, then intentionally taught to your children.

In Psalm 101:2–3, David said, "I will walk within my house in the integrity of my heart. I will set no worthless thing before my eyes" (NASB).

Mom, Dad, are you a person of integrity? If you are walking closely with God, your kids will see your integrity and copy it. Don't ever allow yourself to slip in honesty. Job said, "Till I die I will not put away my integrity from me" (Job 27:5 NASB).

TEACH THEM TO WORK HEARTILY

In the Gospel of John, Jesus said to His Father, "I have brought you glory on earth by finishing the work you gave me to do" (John 17:4).

One of the privileges you have as a parent is to teach your children the amazing truth that God actually has prepared "good works" for them to accomplish (Ephesians 2:10). Just as Jesus had specific tasks to accomplish while he lived on earth, so your son or daughter has significant work to do as well.

To highlight this truth to your kids, teach them verses like Colossians 3:23–24:

> "Whatever you do, work at it with all your heart, as working for the Lord, not for human masters, since you know that you will receive an inheritance from the Lord as a reward. It is the Lord Christ you are serving."[8]

The phrase "work at it with all your heart" can also be translated "work heartily" (NASB). It means to put your back into it, to give it your best effort. As with all of life, you will need to model this kind of work ethic and then turn around and patiently teach your kids what a well-done job looks like.

PHIL:

My dad used to say to me and my two brothers, "Hard work never killed anybody." We hated it when he said that! But we learned the importance of hard work by watching and listening to Dad's value of consistently doing his best work, no matter what the task.

Consequently, all three of us have passed on this same emphasis on the value of working heartily to our kids. For years, my brothers and I delivered the San Jose Mercury newspaper early in the mornings. We had 60–70 customers, and the papers had to be delivered by 6:30 a.m. 365 days of the year. We folded the papers, put a rubber band around each one, then delivered them on our bikes. First my older brother had the route, and then he passed it onto me. I passed it on to my younger brother. We had that same paper route for eight or nine years!

Every month we had to go door to door and say, "Collecting for the San Jose Mercury." Then we paid our bill for the papers and got to keep whatever was leftover.

Here's the deal: our dad made us put the paper right on the front porch so our customers could open their door and find their paper right there waiting for them. There was one man who called our house if his paper wasn't outside his door by 6:30 sharp!

Those years of working for the newspaper taught all three of us to work heartily. There are very few of those neighborhood routes available to grade school children now, but if you get creative, you will be able to find ways to teach your kids to work well.

Diane read once that one of the best ways to enhance the self-esteem of your kids is to get them to do chores, so she set out to make our kids the most self-esteemed kids on the block! Our kids really didn't like it when she acted like the commander-in-chief and started barking orders at them, though, so one day, Phil brought his fun into our day by making a game of it.

Phil could see that the tension was rising as Diane hurried everyone to get their chores done. Since he's usually the one to bring fun into our family circle, he came up with a plan. He took the kids aside and instructed them to line up in front of their mom and salute while saying, "Reporting for duty, Mother!"

This became a fun way of relieving the tension between our kids, who didn't want to do chores, and their mom, who was trying to teach them to be good workers.

DIANE:

The chore salute became so ingrained in our family lore that a couple of years ago, we added to it when all sixteen of us were spending a week together in my parents' cabin in the Sierras for what we call "Camp Comer." One evening after a fun day of playing at the nearby Stanislaus River, we all sprawled in a sunburned heap in front of a movie. I looked around at the mess we had created—thirty-two shoes in the front hallway, the kitchen counter stacked with dirty dishes from dinner—and I couldn't help but think about how my parents would react if they suddenly decided to come home from their vacation early.

Quietly, I slipped out and made my way to the kitchen. I knew it would take at least two cycles of the dishwasher just to get all these plates and glasses clean. While I was working, I sensed some shuffling behind me and turned around to find all our kids, their spouses, and the grandkids lined up from tallest to smallest with their hands in a salute.

As soon as they saw they had my attention, they shouted together, "Reporting for duty, Mama!"

Phil led our family with the idea that working together can be fun—actually, he managed to make just about everything fun!

Going the Extra Mile

In Luke 17, Jesus told his followers a story about a boss and his servant. In the story, He reminded them that an employee should not expect to be thanked for simply doing the things he was explicitly told to do. Instead, Jesus urged his followers to say, "We are unworthy [servants]; we have done *only* that which we ought to have done" (Luke 17:10 NASB). In other words, a "worthy servant" goes beyond duty to do even *more* than he is asked to do. We call this going the extra mile.

We thought we'd done a decent job of training our kids to work heartily and making it fun. But then our friends, the Waggoners, one-upped us! They taught their kids to report back to their mom or dad after completing a chore and say, "Mom, I did what you asked me to do, is there anything else you would like me to do for you?"

Wow! We wish we'd thought of that! We pass that on as one of the wisest ways we have heard to teach your children the value of going the extra mile. No doubt about it, those kids will grow up to be a shocking surprise to their first employers!

Chapter 13

Relationship Building

I n addition to character development (growing in wisdom), Luke 2:52 says Jesus increased in favor with men. We're going to call this *relationship building*.

Jesus loved being around people, and people loved being around Jesus. Luke 4:22 says that those who heard Him speak "marveled at the gracious words which proceeded out of His mouth" (NKJV). Parents, being unselfish and caring for others doesn't come naturally to most children. It's up to you to teach them how to be gracious.

Remember the great Shema? Our mandate is to love God with all our heart, mind, soul, and strength. Jesus linked it with another command: love your neighbor as yourself (Matthew 22:39).

Love God with passion and love people on purpose: these are the two great callings that weave through and undergird everything we are training and teaching and disciplining and developing, everything we are pouring into our children's formation.

It is first and foremost pressed on you, Mom and Dad, to teach your children how to love people on purpose, how to love your neighbor as yourself.

When we love the way God wants us to, we love unconditionally. His is a no-matter-what kind of love. It is generous, *lavish*,[1] considerate.

To love God's way is sacrificial; a giving up of our lives for others, expecting nothing in return. Not enmeshing our identity in another's, but a way of living that brings *life* to those around us.

When we love the way God wants us to, we love consistently—all the time. On good days when our children are adorable, and through the inevitable seasons in our children's lives when they are anything but loveable.

And yet, let's be honest. Neither Phil nor Diane is up to the task of loving unconditionally, sacrificially, and consistently. No one is! However, "His divine power has granted to us everything pertaining to life and godliness" (2 Peter 1:3 NASB). Or, as Jon Courson says,

> "Without Him I can't,
> Without me, He won't."[2]

Your part, Mom and Dad, is to know and experience God's love so that you can then pour out His love onto your kids. The people who have the hardest time accepting God's unearned love—His *grace*—are the ones whose parents were unable to show them this kind of love.

Why? Because parents who are not yet experiencing the love of God for themselves have a hard time expressing God-like love towards their children. James Dobson puts it this way:

> "The vast majority of our children are not dazzling, brilliant, extremely witty, highly coordinated, tremendously talented, or universally popular! They are just plain kids with oversized needs to be loved and accepted as they are."[3]

THE MANNERS OF GRACE

Being unselfish, caring for others, watching out for each other—love like this doesn't come naturally to a child. You as the parent need to take on the primary responsibility of teaching your child ways of welcoming and loving people well.

Training your children to love people on purpose includes teaching them good people skills. We saw this at work in our grandson, Jude.

PHIL:

Not long ago our grandchildren Jude, Moses, and Sunday were staying at our house while John Mark and Tammy were away. A friend from out of town came to our home for dinner, and when he came in, I introduced him to Jude.

"Jude, this is Mr. Kimball. He's a friend of ours, and he knows your dad too."

Immediately, seemingly instinctively, Jude grabbed Dan's hand to shake it and said, "Nice to meet you, Mr. Kimball!"

My friend Dan (aka Mr. Kimball) was taken aback by Jude's greeting. That a six-year-old would step so boldly and confidently into that brief introduction astonished him!

It took me back to the day, thirty years ago, when I introduced six-year-old John Mark to Dan, who was then a college student. I remember being so proud of my son when he stuck out his hand and said, "Nice to meet you, Mr. Kimball!"

John Mark and Tammy are training their kids to love people on purpose, giving them the skills they need to be gracious and loving people! Such a seemingly simple gesture, saying "Nice to meet you!" is a way of letting people know they are important and you care about them.

The hardest people to teach your children to be gracious towards is—surprise, surprise—their siblings! It shouldn't surprise any parent that the first murder in the history of mankind was committed by a brother who was jealous of his little brother![4]

DIANE:

Our third child, Elizabeth, had a dominant older brother and a strong-willed older sister. She was neither dominating nor especially strong-willed, so in order to cope with the hierarchy into which she was born, she developed what we came to call The Look. She could wither her bossy older brother with The Look!

That's when her brother gave her the nickname Queen Elizabeth: regal, cold, royal. The Look was Elizabeth's method of passive resistance. When she felt overpowered or intimidated by her siblings, she'd just freeze them out.

One afternoon I drove with my kids to a good friend's house across town. Peggy is one of the most vivacious women I know. Her unrestrained love enveloped our family as if we belonged to her. Her three boys and her husband, Jeff, embraced each of us, bringing us along on vacations, watching over us while Phil went on a three-week mission trip to the Philippines. We were more than friends; we were family.

That afternoon, when we drove up to their house, Peggy eagerly rolled open the mini-van door and said enthusiastically, "Hi Elizabeth!"

I was taken aback as Elizabeth scowled back at my friend, releasing The Look at its most ferocious. Then I watched Peggy's face fall as she instinctively took a big step backwards, as if Elizabeth had slapped her.

The Look had to go!

Obviously, we had to work on this! It would no longer work to say, "She's just shy." The Look was no longer cute and entertaining, but an unwelcome, unloving expression of resistance. We had to teach our daughter how to be gracious.

Graciousness Training

1. Train your child to look people in the eye when they are talking to them. Let them know that doing so conveys value and interest.
2. Train your child to always respond when someone asks them a question. Explain that small talk is a way of warming up to real relationship.
3. Go further and encourage your kids to ask a question in return, in order to keep the conversation going. Learning to stay present in a conversation is as easy as tossing

a ball back and forth. If one person drops out of the conversation, it is like dropping the ball in the middle of a game.

4. Train your child to thank a friend's mom or dad for having them over to play, for lunch, for their kindness. When your child comes home, ask him if he did. That way your son or daughter will know that expressing thanks is important.

5. Teach your child to first greet a sales person at the store, before getting straight down to the business of what you want them to do for you. "Hi! How's your day going?" is such a simple phrase that communicates the importance we place on people.

6. Train your child to care about others, to do what Philippians 2 urges all of us to do: "In humility value others above yourselves, not looking to your own interests but . . . to the interests of the others" (Philippians 2:3–4).[5]

That's what manners are really about. This wisdom is attributed to manners guru Emily Post: "Manners are a sensitive awareness of the feelings of others. If you have that awareness, you have good manners, no matter what fork you use." Good manners are people skills that show we recognize that other people matter. They matter to God, and therefore they ought to matter to us.

How our children treat the people in their lives—from sales people to siblings—reflects the depth of their understanding of God's love. As we begin to grasp how dearly God loves each person we encounter, we grow more gracious.

While there is no doubt that your kids are going to argue, that doesn't mean we just shrug our shoulders and do nothing. One may give The Look, another may lash out verbally. It's our job to intervene!

LOVING EACH OTHER

Have you heard the supposedly tried-and-true advice given to parents of bickering brothers and sisters? It goes something like this: "Don't intervene! They have to learn how to work things out for themselves. Just let them."

But what is the actual result of that pithy appeal? Think about it. *The meanest one wins—every time!*

If, on the other hand, you patiently teach your children how to work through conflict in a godly and gracious way, you will be setting them up for a future of relational maturity. They will be able to empathize with others, knowing how to "rejoice with those who rejoice, and weep with those who weep" (Romans 12:15 NASB).

In the eighties, when we were raising our children, a popular children's song helped to lighten the mood when intervention was necessary. The words of the chorus still ring in my head when relational tensions arise:

> *Get-a-long-ability, get-a-long-ability, get-a-long-ability,*
> *it comes from inside!*
> *Get-a-long-ability, get-a-long-ability, comes from God*
> *when you really try!*

As corny as that may sound now, it's the kind of truth that sticks.

Jesus talked about intentionally loving people in the Sermon on the Mount, saying, "Blessed are the peacemakers, for they will be called children of God" (Matthew 5:9). He upended cultural norms by telling His followers to "love your enemies and pray for those who persecute you, that you may be children of your Father in heaven" (Matthew 5:44–45).

Peter, having watched Jesus, exhorted us to respond to insults as Jesus did, saying, "When they hurled insults at him, he did not retaliate; when he suffered, he made no threats. Instead, he entrusted himself to him who judges justly" (1 Peter 2:23).

Making disciples of your own children by training them in this counter-cultural concept of loving people—especially their own siblings—is the high calling of Jesus-following parents.

There are a million ways to love well; some people love by giving thoughtful gifts, while others offer words of hope, mercy, or empathy. Maybe your way of loving people is serving them with beauty. Diane's dad fixed things, Phil's mom cooked soul-satisfying suppers. Dive into this with your kids, together discovering the thrill that comes when we love people on purpose!

The Proper Way to Apologize

One key practice to teach each of your children in wise loving is the proper way to apologize. This skill alone can set your children up for quick conflict resolution! Here's how it works:

Apologize for the specific offense.

"I'm sorry if I hurt you" is a hollow apology. Instead, teach your kids to be humble by being upfront and honest about what they did wrong. Something like, "I'm sorry for calling you stupid."

Accept responsibility.

Again, be specific and do not blame the other person. "I said such-and-such because you did such-and-such" puts the blame for your choices on the other person. Instead just say, "I should not have said that." Remember: my response is my responsibility!

Ask God's forgiveness.

All sin and selfishness hurts God first. When I wrong one of God's children, I am wronging God Himself.

Ask the person's forgiveness.

Saying, "Will you please forgive me for calling you stupid?" holds more weight than a sullen, grudging "Sorry." Asking forgiveness is a way of acknowledging that what you did hurt or inconvenienced or in some real way affected the person you offended.

Restore the relationship.

The burden for restoring the relationship falls squarely on the shoulders of the one who did the offending.[6] Don't miss this last step, or your son or daughter may expect a quick apology to fix everything they break.

When the prodigal son came home to his father after blowing his inheritance, he didn't expect to come back in an exalted position. He simply hoped to be taken in as a servant. His words give us a beautiful example of a genuine apology:

> "Father, I have sinned against heaven and against you. I am no longer worthy to be called your son; make me like one of your hired servants." (Luke 15:18–19)

The father exceeded his expectations, embracing him, and their relationship was restored.

The skills that will enable your child to grow up to be a good employee, a loving spouse, and a godly parent are to be learned right here in your home. The home is the primary training ground for relationships. It's a world in miniature.

With every moment you spend training your children how to love people on purpose, you are setting them up for a future filled with satisfying relationships.

Who wouldn't want that for their children?

Chapter 14

Spiritual Training

Luke 2:52 says that, in addition to growing in wisdom and in favor with man, Jesus also grew "in favor with God." The Greek word translated favor is *cháris*, in other places translated "grace."

Jesus grew in the grace of God.

Even as a young boy, Jesus had a growing relationship with His Father that was neither passive nor stagnant. His walk with God was alive and vibrant, intimate and growing.

These framing years are an ideal time for intensive spiritual training, helping your son or daughter to "grow in favor with God." Children at the beginning of this stage of life are generally able to grasp concrete facts and are beginning to understand metaphors that apply to their situations. Parents are in the perfect position to come alongside their children in the daily-ness of real life, to talk about the kingdom ways specifically taught by Jesus.

But where should you start? How do you teach your child what you may be just beginning to grasp yourself? Shouldn't this be left to the professionals? Preachers, seminary-trained leaders, or at least Sunday school teachers?

These are the questions that plagued us, serving up doubts and insecurity about our ability to teach our own kids. We were still relatively new believers when our kids entered this stage of life, and we feared getting it wrong. We were intimidated by the immensity of what we thought needed to be taught, yet at the same time growing in the conviction that teaching and leading and influencing our children's walk with God was first of all our responsibility. After all, who could possibly love these kids more than us?

After endless hours of talking and praying together, we decided that there were three main things we wanted our kids to grasp during these years—three things we wanted to see happen in their hearts. We believed that if they got these truths, they'd be well on their way to growing in the grace of God, just as Jesus did.

While there is a plethora of excellent material available,[1] it is not simply information that your children crave. In fact, too much information may actually mute your child's enthusiastic embrace of Jesus. What your children need at this stage of their development is to connect with God in a real and personal experience.

They need to fall in love with Him.

THE THREE LOVES

Love Jesus

We wanted to do everything in our power to make sure our children fell in love with Jesus. We wanted them to see Him as inviting and heroic, and worthy of their worship. At the same time, we wanted to watch for and dispel any boredom or disinterest before it could take root. As newcomers to the faith, we were in awe of Jesus and His grace-filled ways. We wanted our kids to share in that awe with us. *But how?*

Here's the beauty of this quest: you get the privilege of describing Jesus to your kids. You get to be the ones painting a compelling picture of who He is.

You point out to your child how He responded to people's hurts, how He soothed their fears, how He wanted children to come close when adults wanted to chase them away. You read the stories and you read between the lines, bringing those stories alive in a way your child can understand.

The Gospels will be your go-to place for uncovering the real Jesus, allowing your own preconceived notions to fall away as you set out to discover together who Jesus is and what He is really like.

- Read about His friendship with the siblings, Lazarus, Martha, and Mary in Luke 10:38–41 and John 11.
- Tell the story of His compassion towards the man born blind in John 9.
- Note how highly Jesus' cousin, John the Baptist, honored him in Matthew 3:11, John 1:25–37, and John 3:30.
- Enlighten your children's understanding of Jesus' respectful attitude towards women by reading the story of the Woman at the Well in John 4.
- Turn Easter into the greatest celebration of the year by telling the story of the cross and the resurrection. Tell it personally, repeating Jesus' forgiveness-filled words of love just before He died (Luke 23:34).

Do you get the idea? You are making Jesus out to be the hero that He is, paving the way for each of your children, in his or her own way, to fall deeply in love with Him.

Perhaps the most powerful tool you have is your own story of faith. Tell your kids how Jesus changed your life. How He is changing you still. Tell stories of His involvement in your everyday life—both the remarkable, off-the-charts miracle stories, and the seemingly coincidental stories that add up to a beautiful story of love and care over a lifetime. Make Him real in a way your kids, with their unique personalities, can relate to.

Love God's Word

Second, we wanted our children to love the Scriptures. As soon as your children can read, make sure each one has a Bible of their own, one that they are able to read and understand.[2]

Let them see you reading your Bible, studying and learning,

praying and taking notes. Let them see you ponder the truths you're learning.

Also, be sure you are involved in a Bible-teaching church where the leaders firmly believe in the authority of Scripture and are making it accessible and applicable to real life. Bring your Bibles with you every Sunday so your children understand the incalculable value of the Word of God. They will see your interest, and that sparks theirs.

Love the Church

Finally, we wanted our children to love God's church. Our years in pastoral ministry have shown us that no one lasts long as a lone ranger Christian. God made the church, this great big, varied, diverse community of believers with all her problems, to be the center of His plan to bring the world back to Himself. We wanted our kids to see the Church as the family it had become for us; imperfect but beautiful, embracing, a place where grace and forgiveness is lived out in real time. We wanted our kids to see that church is not just a place you go on Sundays, but a living, vibrant community that does life together.

THE THREE THINGS

To successfully pass on these three loves (loving Jesus, loving the Scriptures, loving the Church), we focused on three things. These are three easy-to-implement practices to bring the three loves into being: family Bible times, Scripture memory, and the Lord's day or Sabbath. These are just the beginning of bringing what many teachers call the "spiritual disciplines" into the regular fabric of your family life. They're a great way to leave your children hungering for more!

Family Bible Time

This practice of coming together regularly as a family to read the Bible out loud has become a rarity among Christian families. A recent Barna report noted the sad truth that in America, "fewer than one out of ten born-again families read the Bible together during a typical week."[3]

Most parents feel intimidated by the idea of a practice they may never have experienced as a child. But it's not that complicated, and certainly not too difficult to take on in a time when children's Bible resources are so abundant. Also, the earlier you begin, the better! By normalizing this practice while the kids are still eager to gather around you in their pajamas, you will have what few families experience: shared intimacy on a deeply spiritual level.

Neither of us had any experience with this concept of a time set aside to delve into the Scriptures together, so we simply set out to make it work for us in our own way. By trial and error we discovered five essential factors that enabled us to be consistent and genuinely enjoy what became a sweet time of fellowship in our family:

- Choose the proper tools.
- Keep it short.
- Make it fun.
- Include a prayer time.
- Schedule it for right before bed.

A NOTE TO MOMS FROM DIANE:

I have been listening to women open their hearts to me both privately and in small groups, in brokenness and in spilled-over frustration, for nearly four decades of church ministry. What I have heard over and over is a cry for husbands to take up the responsibility of spiritual leadership in our homes, and a sense that if they don't, our children will suffer and so will we. Over time, that frustration often turns into an underlying bitterness of spirit that our men rarely identify but always sense.

While there is much truth in our worries, I believe there is a great deal of falsehood as well. Somewhere along the line, many of us create in our minds our own definition of what spiritual leadership looks like.

We mix our deep desire for spiritual oneness with our husbands with idealistic renderings of what we are sure other men do. It's an unrealistic notion that we have idealized as the gold standard of spiritual leadership.

Moms, may I caution you? Oftentimes we expect far too much from our husbands when the Bible clearly indicates that the spiritual training of children is *both* the mother's and the father's responsibility. The lamp and the light, remember?

While I am convinced that Phil's commitment to reading and informally teaching the Bible to our kids resulted in adults who love the Word of God, there is absolutely no reason that a mother cannot do the same if her husband is not stepping into that role.

The Biblical example of this is tucked into a paragraph in an intensely personal letter Paul wrote to Timothy:

> "I am reminded of your sincere faith, which first lived in your grandmother Lois and in your mother Eunice and, I am persuaded, now lives in you also." (2 Timothy 1:5)

Scholars believe Timothy pastored the largest church in the world at that time—the church in Ephesus. No doubt this man was a spiritual giant in the early church, a young man any Jesus-following parent would be proud of.

Yet Paul does not mention Timothy's father. Many speculate that his father was not a follower of Jesus. We know from Luke's account that Timothy was a young disciple "whose mother was Jewish and a believer but whose father was a Greek" (Acts 16:1).

It can be presumed that Timothy grew up in a home with a father who was either absent or who took little or no interest in following Jesus. The influence of his godly mother and grandmother was remarkable enough to be noted by Paul.

Some husbands need to be encouraged—not manipulated or shamed or pushed—into their God-assigned role as the spiritual guide of their family. If your husband is a believer, he probably wants to lead his family, and he may even be secretly ashamed that he has rendered himself mute in spiritual matters, but he doesn't know how. He may not fully understand what is expected of him and lack confidence in his ability to fulfill that undefined role, so he remains passive. It is not uncommon for men to revert to a disinterested façade when they feel they have no chance at success.

We can make it much easier for our men if, instead of laying a guilt trip on them, we know their hearts and act accordingly. We should assume the best of our husbands, not making family Bible time a test of their spiritual leadership capabilities. Instead, we can step in to help make it happen.

We get out the Bible story book (that we researched and purchased) right after dinner. We gather the kids, maybe make a bowl of popcorn, and start a fire in the fireplace for atmosphere. We set it up! This is not taking over; it's being an encouragement and a helper to our husbands, recognizing their need for respect in every area of life—but especially in this intimidating role as spiritual leader.

Early on I learned that Phil would always rather do Bible time than clean up the kitchen after dinner, so that's what we did most nights. I cleaned up while Phil stretched out on the floor with the kids piled on top, and read the picture Bible to them. I took my sweet time, relishing some time alone to clean up (thereby feeding my manic perfectionism!) while our children relished time with their dad and learned to love the Scriptures.

Fathers, do not underestimate the impact you are having on your children when you gather them around you and delve into the Bible together! It isn't even so much what you teach and read to your kids as how they feel while you're doing it.

There is a sweet comfort there, a connection that cannot happen any other way. As you read the Bible together and ask questions, listening to each other's take on the stories, you grow close. You learn, and so do your kids. Over time what your children will learn more than anything else is to crave that connection they felt as they cuddled up to you and read the Bible.

Then, as they grow into young adulthood, they bring that craving for connection into their own walk with their heavenly Father, and they know how to go after it themselves.

The NBNB Rule

Remember how having fun is at the top of Phil's list of values? He found a way to make Bible reading fun for our kids too. When we sensed that our children were ready to begin developing a morning devotional time of their own, he presented what we came to call "The NBNB Rule":

No Bible, No Breakfast.

While Diane was filling our home with the scent of pancakes cooking on the stove, Phil urged our kids to take a few minutes to read their Bibles, quoting Jesus' words: "Man shall not live on bread alone, but on every word that proceeds out of the mouth of God" (Matthew 4:4 NASB).

We were teaching our children in a light-hearted, fun way that they needed spiritual food for their hungry souls as much as they needed the hearty breakfast their mom was preparing. We kept it simple and doable, just enough to establish a life-long habit without overwhelming their still-short attention spans. We asked them to read for a very short while at first, maybe five or ten minutes: one chapter of Proverbs, a Psalm, maybe a segment of one of the Gospels. Just enough to whet their appetites, but not enough to make it a grueling discipline.

We asked a mentor whose counsel we had often sought about raising godly kids, "Is it okay for us to require our children to read their Bibles? Wouldn't they resent it someday?"

His clear, logical answer made sense and made us laugh: "Every day you make your kids brush their teeth, right? And you're not in the least bit afraid that they will grow up and rebel against tooth brushing!"[4]

In case you're still worried, be aware that this habit you are working to instill in your children is for their flourishing. "Holy habits are that: the disciplines, the routines by which we stay alive and focused on Him. At first we choose them and carry them out; after a while they are part of who we are. And they carry us."[5]

We were simply "requiring" of our children what they had been watching Mom and Dad do morning by morning for as long as they could remember. In fact, they now reminisce fondly about those early mornings when they came downstairs to find their mom reading her Bible in the chair we called Big Green, or when they crawled under the covers of the "big bed" where their dad was reading his Bible. Snuggling in with blankies and Bibles of their own, they learned to taste and see the goodness of God.

Now that they are adults, this practice of reading their Bibles with hearts open to listening to the Spirit is firmly established in each of their lives. It brings us such joy and confidence to see them actively seeking God, listening, waiting, hearing what He needs them to know.

When we visit Rebekah in L.A., she invites us into their loft's tiny tearoom for a time of quiet reading by candlelight. Her travels to the Orient led her to create an intentionally peaceful space as a place for meeting God before her work begins.

Elizabeth gets up ridiculously early in order to sneak in that quiet time of feasting on the Word of God before her young children get up. They wake up every morning to find their mom and dad immersed in the Scriptures.

John Mark is already passing this delight-filled spiritual discipline on to his own kids. Even when they come to spend the night at our house, he gives them instructions to start their morning in the Scriptures. When his son Jude voluntarily read the entire book of Exodus, John Mark rewarded his effort by taking him out for a special father-son breakfast so they could talk about it.

When Matthew was in Bible college and feeling his soul beginning to shrivel in the dryness of too much theological debate, he reinstituted that morning quiet time as a means of listening for the fresh food the Spirit feeds us if we are willing.

And not one of them is doing it because of the NBNB rule!

Are we saying that establishing a morning routine that includes Bible reading while your children are young will guarantee that they'll be avid Bible students as adults? No. But if you will nurture and reward and encourage this morning meeting with God through His Word, you will be paving the way for them to decide on their own if this way of starting their day really makes a difference. In the years ahead, your children will likely move in and out of this practice until they experience for themselves the life-changing intimacy with God that is possible through studying His Word, and they won't want to miss out on it.

Scripture Memory

These framing years are the ideal time to memorize Scripture together. Their brains are amazingly quick to memorize verses, and if you'll do it together, most kids this age are ignited by a little healthy competition. This is also the age when God's Word can effectively take root in your child's heart and begin its deep work.

In 2 Timothy 3:16–17, Paul tells us, "All Scripture is God-breathed and is useful for teaching, rebuking, correcting and training in righteousness, so that the servant of God may be thoroughly equipped for every good work."

God's Spirit breathes life into our souls, and into the souls of our children through His inspired words.

The words we memorize together can be His means of teaching and training our children (and ourselves!) right in the moment when we need His guidance. The Spirit of God brings these verses to mind later, using His own words to speak truth to us when we need it.

Do you realize that if you and your children would memorize just one verse every week for fourteen years—from when your child is four until he's ready to go off to college at eighteen—that adds up to *728* verses tucked into your child's head and heart!

Ok, let's be honest here: most of us won't memorize 728 verses. But what if we memorized 400? Or even 100? Those verses will be used by the Spirit to speak to your son or daughter when you're not there. Could there be any better use of your time?

One of the families we looked up to had a simple system using notecards to write their verses on. Every night around the table (yes, they actually ate dinner together!), they talked about their day and passed the card around. Each family member said the verse out loud—seeing it, hearing it, touching it, until they had it memorized. Then they started a new verse.

Our son-in-law Steve told us about one of his favorite childhood memories. He was often invited to his best friend's house for dinner, and he always accepted because his friend's mom was an especially great cook! But what always stood out to him was what happened right after everyone finished eating dinner.

If Steve and his friend started to leave the table in order to rush off to wherever they wanted to go, his dad would stop them, saying, "Wait! We always read a chapter of the Bible out loud together after dinner. Listen in, and tell me one thing that stood out to you—then you can run off!"

Rather than causing resentment, this practice intrigued Steve so much that he determined to do the same when he had kids. Don't forget; it's your child's heart that you're after. You want your child to delight in God's Word like Jeremiah did:

> "Your words were found and I ate them. And Your words became for me a joy and the delight of my heart; for I have been called by Your Name, O Lord God of hosts." (Jeremiah 15:16 NASB)

When your child learns to delight in God and to connect with Him by listening to His Word, he will never be satisfied with lesser food! Instead he will be like the person described in Psalm 1:

> "Oh, the joys of those who do not
>> follow the advice of the wicked,
>> or stand around with sinners,
>> or join in with mockers.
> But they delight in the law of the LORD,
>> meditating on it day and night.
> They are like trees planted along the riverbank,
>> bearing fruit each season.
> Their leaves never wither,
>> and they prosper in all they do." (Psalm 1:1–3 NLT)

The Lord's Day

DIANE:

One day when our oldest son was about eight, he came to me and asked, "What day is it tomorrow?" When I said, "Sunday," his shoulders slumped and he declared emphatically, "Oh! That's the worst day of the week!"

To say the least, that comment made me think long and hard about how I was handling the stress of Sundays in a pastor's home.

Phil always left for church early to get things ready for the multiple services, and I had the task of getting the kids cleaned up and out the door—after putting a nice dinner to simmer in the oven or Crock-pot, of course—while also getting myself dressed in my best so I could look like the perfect pastor's wife.

Sheesh!

All the pressure I put on myself created such a tense atmosphere in our home that at only eight years old, John Mark already dreaded Sundays!

His straight-from-the-heart comment led me to make some changes, let go of some things, and start intentionally transforming our family's Sundays into the best day of the week.

One of my children's favorite changes was when I told them they no longer had to make their beds on Sundays, which, for a neat-freak like me, was a big deal! This is exactly what we mean when we write about being careful that your values do not get in the way of your goal to raise passionate Jesus followers! I could see that my value of a well-kept home had superseded our value that our children love church.

To motivate them to hustle without having to cajole and hassle them out the door, I promised to take them down to the beach for a few minutes on our way to church if they got ready in time. Since we lived less than a mile from the beach in Santa Cruz, that promise was pretty easy to fulfill. How they loved peeling off their shoes and socks for a quick dash from our minivan to the edge of the ocean before church! I can still see the delighted grins on their faces and remember the sweet smell of sand and sea that lingered as we drove to church.

As for Sunday dinner, it became a quick trip through the drive-thru to pick up fast food—a rare treat—on our way home from church.

Our kids loved going to church; it was their mom's frantic frenzy of getting us there that about did them in![6]

It's important that we understand the attitudes we are encouraging in our kids towards church. Do we show them that we find joy and delight in going to church? Or do we drag ourselves there reluctantly and then eat "roast pastor" for lunch? Our children hear it all, and we might be dismayed if we could take a peek inside their heads!

If your child resists going to church, utilize your most persuasive, fun-loving leadership skills. Take the time to be alert and aware of how your child responds to your church's Sunday school program. You can find ways to make it work for both your reluctant introvert and your all-in extrovert.

When our most introverted child balked at going to his class week after week, Diane asked the director of children's ministries for advice. This wise older woman suggested that she try to arrive fifteen minutes early and walk all the way in with him. That way he could get comfortable in his environment with his mom by his side, chatting with the teacher as she prepared for class.

Arriving early also prevented this highly sensitive child from feeling overwhelmed by a loud, active class full of moving, talking, shouting kids. As the other children arrived one-by-one, he waded cautiously into the social waters without feeling like he was drowning.

And now? That same son leads a church in the urban core of Portland, using his compelling leadership skills to compel people to walk with him in the way of Jesus.

Over the years we have heard from well-meaning parents who don't feel it is their right to "make" their kids go to church when they don't feel like it. They are afraid that their kids will grow up to hate church because they had to go every week. When those parents offer compelling yet firm leadership, invariably their kids respond. So go ahead and invite discussion, ask questions, stop for doughnuts on the way—just *go to church!*

Your only other option ties right into a new term sociologists have coined for children who insist on dictating their family's values and the parents who give in: *Kindergarchy!*

Kindergarchy is defined as "The state or phenomenon of children dominating, particularly in the context of children's needs, and preferences being accorded equal or greater status than those of adults."[7]

This is a huge mistake! Unless your child is sick, you simply set about to make sure the day is happy and fun, not giving in to your child's efforts to rule the roost.

By going to church regularly, we are modeling for our children and teaching them that passionate Jesus followers live in community and gather with the body of Christ. We are showing them that we do it whether we feel like it or not, and that we do all we can to get our feelings in line with what we know to be true: the church is our family. We go there to be part of that family, to give as well as to receive. We love the church, and we wanted to teach our kids to love the church!

Just as the Jewish people prepared for the Sabbath, we learned that Sunday mornings were much happier for all of us when we prepared for church the evening before. Saturday nights became a fun time of getting ready for the next day—together.

Diane did all she could to ease the morning rush by packing diaper bags and laying out clothes, while Phil paid out allowances and taught our children the value of tithing. Each week he'd count out their allowance in change and then help the kids to put ten percent aside for God. The kids loved to color on their envelopes, writing love notes to God and tucking their envelopes into pockets for the morning. It was such a simple thing, but it worked wonders to arouse in our children's hearts a sense of belonging, of purpose. They marched into church with their lovingly prepared envelopes, eager to be part of something bigger than themselves.

Teach your kids that everything we have comes from the hand of a good Father (James 1:17). Help them to understand that all we have really belongs to Him (Psalm 24:1) and that we have the privilege of partnering with God as trustworthy stewards (1 Corinthians 4:1–2).

Read Malachi 3:10 to your kids and teach them early to give God the first part of every dollar they earn. And don't forget to teach them to give joyfully, as God expresses His delight in a cheerful giver (2 Corinthians 9:7).

This practice—a vital spiritual discipline—will stick with them throughout their lives, as they learn to trust God to provide all they need, and as they learn to live with less so that others may have what they need.

As we wrap up this section, remember Luke 2:52 says "Jesus grew in wisdom and in stature, and in favor with God and man."

The key phrase here is *grew in*. This word is *prokóptō* in the original Greek. Pro means *toward*, while kopto means *to impel*. Jesus was *impelled toward* wisdom and stature and favor with God and man.

This framing stage is about six years long. Your children will stumble along the way, and sometimes they will race to catch up. It's okay! They are being impelled toward the goal of becoming passionate Jesus followers.

DIANE:

Our daughter Rebekah was one of those children who actually wanted to please. Like many people-pleasing children, she would sometimes lie in order to avoid getting into trouble. When she was about ten or so, I caught her in a long, ongoing lie. Unbeknownst to me, she'd been cheating on her math homework—not because she couldn't get it, but because she wanted to get it over with and head to the barn behind our house, where she boarded her horse. Just before we caught the lie, Phil and I had been praying for wisdom, trying to figure out why our happy little girl had suddenly become unhappy and cranky. That's what hidden sin does to us, doesn't it? It makes us miserable!

When I discovered Rebekah had been cheating, she was devastated, genuinely repentant, and even relieved to get it out in the open. It was one of those rare teachable moments—we get just a few of them when we're raising our kids. Rebekah's heart in that moment was wide open and vulnerable. Tears flowed down her cheeks.

We sat on the front porch and spent a good long time talking about failure. About Paul saying in Romans 7:18–19:

"For I know that good itself does not dwell in me, that is, in my sinful nature. For I have the desire to do what is good, but I cannot carry it out. For I do not do the good I want to do, but the evil I do not want to do—this I keep on doing."

I didn't punish her—that would have been a crushing mistake! Instead I just held my little girl as she cried. I told her all about God's astounding grace—that God covers her sin, that freedom is just one step of repentance away. That He welcomes her with open arms, failure and all. And that the way of grace is not about following the rules perfectly, but about coming back to Jesus over and over again and saying, "Without You I can do nothing. I can't even be honest."[8]

I watched Rebekah's faith become real that day on our front porch. I watched her fall in love with her Savior. I saw her sweet, Sunday-school faith progress to a real, vibrant, going-after-God kind of faith that would hold her close to Him in the years ahead.

Don't be afraid of your children's failures! Just like Paul and Peter and Jacob and David, mistakes can be the very realities that bring them into an authentic faith of their own.

It was Albert Einstein who observed that, "In the middle of every difficulty lies an opportunity."

Of course, we want to guide our children around the quicksand of habitual sin, but even more, we need to introduce them to a Redeemer who can take the worst about us and turn us into people who are all about Him. Be alert to those moments of vulnerable brokenness, and show your children the way of God's amazing grace. Teach them the beautiful truth of Romans 8:1:

"Therefore, there is now no condemnation for those who are in Christ Jesus."

John Lawrence said, "Greatness does not consist of not making mistakes, but in what we do with them."[9]

Moms, dads, remember this: You aren't trying to raise perfect children, you are trying to raise *godly* children—people who love God with all their hearts and who are following hard after Jesus.

◆ Raising Passionate Jesus Followers

Doing the Framing
(6 to 12 yrs.)

The aim is to help your children develop a heart of *wisdom: living life skillfully*. In this stage, do not provoke your children through an ongoing pattern of ill-treatment that breaks their spirit and builds up a deep-seated resentment.

Nearing the end of this stage, your child...

☐ Has received Jesus as Savior and King.

☐ Understands and has considered baptism.

☐ Reads the Bible on his/her own.

☐ Memorizes Scripture.

☐ Has an emerging work ethic.

☐ Exhibits honesty and integrity.

☐ Treats people graciously and respectfully.

Affection, Affirmation, and Fun

Discipline

THE BOX

Order

JESUS

1. Jesus - He's the foundation /base,

2. Discipline - correct, rebuke, encourage, patiently instruct, rod of correction

3. Order - routine, bedtime, healthy eating, outdoor play, etc.

4. Affection, Affirmation, and Fun

If your child is acting up, don't just stomp them with discipline. Tighten every side of the box *simultaneously* and you will see them thrive.

Three areas to focus on during this stage:

1. **CHARACTER DEVELOPMENT**—teach your children to rule their spirit consistently, conduct themselves wisely, walk in integrity, and work heartily.
2. **RELATIONSHIP BUILDING**—teach your children how to love people on purpose, treating others respectfully and apologizing sincerely when necessary.
3. **SPIRITUAL TRAINING**—You want them to fall in love with Jesus, love the Scriptures, and love God's church.

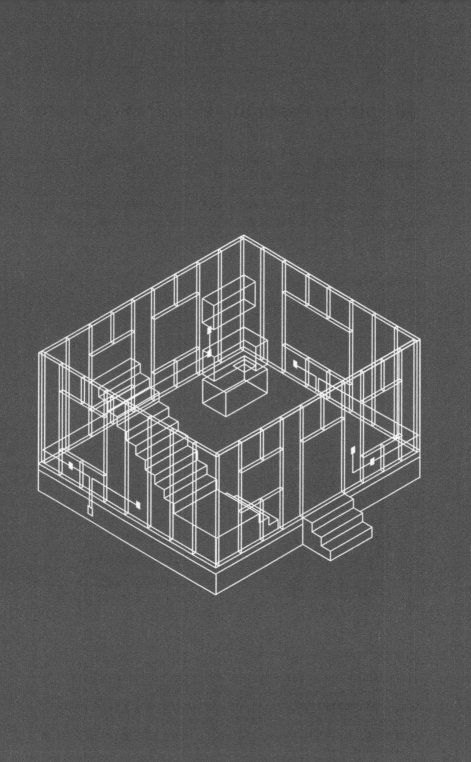

Part 4

Installing the Functional Systems

Ages 13–17

"Therefore as you have received Christ Jesus
the Lord, so walk in Him, having been firmly rooted
and now being built up in Him and established
in your faith, just as you were instructed,
and overflowing with gratitude."

COLOSSIANS 2:6–7 NASB

Chapter 15

Four Things You Will Need

Some years ago, the Houston police department published a leaflet entitled, "How to Ruin Your Children." Facetiously written, this booklet on raising children was guaranteed to be 99% effective. In part, this is what it said:

"Never give him any spiritual training. Wait until he's 21 and then let him decide for himself what he believes."

That's a far cry from the Beit Sefer, the Jewish equivalent of elementary school in Jesus' day, where by the time children were twelve years old, they had memorized large sections of the Torah—the first five books of the Bible!

In this section we are going to cover the teenage years, that developmental stage of your child's life between the ages of thirteen and seventeen. Remember, these are *stages*, not *ages*. Think of the difference between a thirteen-year-old boy and a seventeen-year-old girl—a wide gulf of mature judgment and sophisticated thinking separate them! Yet the principles for guiding your son or daughter through these notoriously turbulent years apply to every teenager.

In the foundational stage, your aim was to develop a heart of obedience. You moved into the framing stage focusing on a heart of wisdom—the ability to do life skillfully.

Now in these teenage years, your goal is to see your child develop *a heart of godliness*. You want to see their faith become their own.

As Colossians 2:7 tells us, you want your kids to become firmly rooted and established in their faith, just as you have been instructing them.

Unlike a sixteen-year-old who has been given no spiritual instruction, they have been receiving instruction from you for years! Now you get to see them begin to live out what they've been taught. Even better, you will get to see them enjoying their own walk with Jesus.

Someone once said, "You can teach a child to be thankful, but you cannot force them to be grateful." God must do this work in your child's heart.

To continue the house analogy, in installing the functional systems—heating, electricity, ventilation, plumbing, and so on—you don't want your house to just look good on the outside; you want it to function properly on the inside.

In the same way, by the end of this stage you want to see your son or daughter living life—functioning—as a fully devoted follower of Jesus, a young man or woman who is rooted and established in faith

This can be the most rewarding of all the stages of your child's life—honestly!

When you build a house, laying the foundation is just hard work. It's difficult to imagine what that house is going to look like. Then the framing gives you an idea, and it gets much more fun. Your imagination takes hold, and you start to get excited.

Then there seems to come a pause as all the systems are installed. It's not particularly exciting, but you know this is how your house will become a home, how it will stay warm, how the lights will come on when you need them.

That is what begins to happen in the early teenage years. You've done all that work and now you see it working. The lights start to come on. Your child begins to look like a young man or woman of God. She gets up early to read her Bible before going off to her summer job at Starbucks.

DIANE:

I well remember the first time I saw Rebekah get up crazy early in order to read her Bible before heading off to her job at a coffee shop. I woke up at four in the morning and noticed a light on down the hall. I thought maybe one of the kids was sick, so I hurried out of my own warm bed to investigate.

There sat Bekah, propped up in bed, reading her Bible.

When I asked her what in the world she was doing up when she didn't need to be at work for another hour, she said: "I just can't go in there without this time with the Lord. It's harder than you know, Mom. I need this."

She wasn't doing it because of the old NBNB rule! She was delving into God's Word because she personally felt the need. Amazing! She was being built up and established in a faith of her own, just as we had been instructing her for so many years. But still, it came as a bit of a shock to me—it had worked! My girl wanted Jesus.

It was all I could do not to dance my way back to my bedroom!

Remember: you are partnering with God as He is building a spiritual house in your child. God is drawing your son or daughter to Himself, and He longs for them to be close to Him—even more than you do!

You, Mom and Dad, are the primary tool in His hands to accomplish this. As you keep close to Him, He will generously work in and through you to bring your child into an authentic and intimate relationship with Himself.

With that picture in mind, even though we know these years can be challenging, we want to give you four things you will need in order to navigate through the teenage years.

COURAGE, TO STAND AGAINST THE TIDE

When the Israelites faced formidable obstacles on the way to entering the promised land, God spoke these words to their leader, Joshua:

"Keep this Book of the Law always on your lips; meditate on it day and night, so that you may be careful to do everything written in it. Then you will be prosperous and successful. Have I not commanded you? *Be strong and courageous.* Do not be afraid; do not be discouraged, for the LORD your God will be with you wherever you go." (Joshua 1:8–9, emphasis ours)

Remember, you are partnering with the God who gives courage! He longs for your son or daughter to love and serve Him. He is at work in your child's heart. As you draw close and pray, He will give you the courage you need to stand against the tide of wrong thinking that threatens to sweep your child away from Him.

Every parent knows they'll face some difficult challenges during the teenage years. At times you may even feel like throwing in the towel and running away or giving up and leaving your child to his own devices.

This is where courage comes in—and an unflagging sense of humor!

Somebody once jokingly asked, "Do you know why God asked Abraham to offer up Isaac as a sacrifice when he was twelve? . . . because by age thirteen it wouldn't have been a sacrifice!"

Mark Twain is credited with saying, "When a boy turns thirteen you should put him in a barrel and feed him through the hole . . . when he turns sixteen, you should plug up the hole!"[1]

Seriously, though, if you've done the hard work in the earlier stages, these years don't have to be a burden; they can actually be a blast!

There are, of course, some children who will chafe against their parent's authority at this stage. They resist instruction, and that tempts parents to give up, to settle into a safe place of simply staying quiet or worse, to settle into a sort of passive-aggressive disapproval that ekes out of their pores. Sarcastic jabs and social media rants are all too common, not just among teenagers, but also among parents of teenagers!

We have talked to many college-age people in our church who actually feel their parents abandoned them during their teenage years. We want to warn you, because we don't think those parents had any idea that their kids would interpret their backing off as abandonment. They just didn't know how to have that notoriously uncomfortable sex talk. They couldn't figure out how to give their teenager some reasonable freedom yet still stay involved in their dating life. They simply didn't know what to do, so they bowed out.

In this stage of your child's life, you have got to be willing to be the bad guy at times. Mary, a very wise woman who raised four passionate Jesus followers, gave us this advice: *Fight for your child!*

She painted a vivid picture as she described feeling as though she was hanging onto the back of her daughter's shirt while this girl she loved teetered on the edge of a cliff. Her daughter would have gone right over that cliff and been so broken if Mary had not determined to hold on tight. She refused to abandon her daughter to her own poor judgment.

Refuse to abandon your child!

Sometimes during these teenage years, you may even have to be willing to temporarily sacrifice your relationship with your teenager in order to save him from self-destruction. But take heart! And be patient.

Your teenager is aware of your desire to help him. He knows it is love that propels you to investigate an activity; she realizes you are protecting her from unknown threats to her well-being. But all those hormones and the pressures and fears involved in this almost-but-not-quite-grown-up stage often sabotage a teenager's ability to communicate graciously.

One study found that, "Finding the right blend of freedom and limitations proved to be a taxing proposition for the parents we interviewed."[2]

DIANE:

It's not always a compliment when your daughter says of you at this stage, "My mom is my best friend." While we were close, neither of my daughters would have said I was their best friend when they were fifteen! That comes later.

Our girls needed me to be willing to stand strong for them when they were wavering, to make them do the right thing when the right thing seemed impossible for them. Not for one second could they doubt my love for them; in fact, loving them even in those testing times was one small way I could point them to the faithful love of God.

PERSEVERANCE, TO KEEP THE TRAINING GOING

It's way too soon to let go. You're getting a little weary, your hair may be showing some grey, and now you're facing the daunting teenage years, gearing yourself up for the rebellion you've been told is inevitable.

You *can* raise children who don't rebel. Josh McDowell reminds parents that "rules without relationship lead to rebellion."[3] Yes, there is a natural (and sometimes messy) pulling away, but it's not your rules they're liable to rebel against. It is a fractured or hurtful relationship that often sets teens against their parents.

At this point in your child's life, your goal is that they are maturing spiritually. They aren't babies anymore; they're beginning to move from "milk" to "meat." That is what the writer of Hebrews means when he writes:

> "Solid food is for the mature, who because of practice have their senses trained to discern good and evil." (Hebrews 5:14 NASB)

Remember that one of the Greek words translated *training* is where we get our English word *gymnasium*. A gymnasium is a place of exercise where you go to get in shape and stay in shape. It is used metaphorically here as a way of expressing this idea of training for the purpose of godliness.

Paul wanted his "son in the faith," Timothy, to understand that "physical training is of some value, but godliness has value in all things, holding promise for both the present life and the life to come" (1 Timothy 4:8).

So don't quit the gym! Keep the training going; stay actively involved in your teenager's life.

DETERMINATION, TO KEEP YOUR FAMILY CLOSE

During this season, keeping your family close will be one of your greatest challenges. It will not happen without concerted effort and a great deal of planning. You will have to *make* it happen.

DIANE:

Moms, this is mostly up to us. You will need to be both creative and determined. Work schedules, athletic practices, heavy homework loads, and growing social needs will all seem to conspire against your efforts to keep your family tight and together. Don't give up!

By the way, this is a role we will need to play for the rest of our lives in order for our families to stay connected. Even now, with four married children and a growing cadre of grandkids, it is most often me who initiates the planning needed to keep our family close.

Four Ways to Keep Your Family Close
Family dinners

Everything will seem to work against against your family sitting down to share a meal together with any sort of regularity. But there is nothing that even comes close to the camaraderie that comes from sharing your lives around the table.

According to a 2009 study,[4] teenagers who participate in regular family meals (five to seven family meals per week) are far less likely to engage in at-risk behavior. On the other hand, kids who infrequently sit down to meals with their family (fewer than three times per week) are twice as likely to use tobacco or marijuana and one-and-a-half times more likely to have used alcohol. As if that isn't enough, teenagers who have fewer than three family dinners in an average week get considerably lower grades through high school. These are sobering statistics, yet so solvable!

Use mealtimes to talk over issues that come up during the course of your children's lives, to discuss the highlights and hard times of their days. Make sure there is friendly banter and laughter. Enjoy each other's company while being nourished by good food.

With sports, school activities, and part-time jobs, it may not be possible to celebrate the family dinner table every night, but you can set certain nights in concrete.

Our friend and literary agent Bill Jensen made Sunday Supper the highlight of his family's week when his girls were teenagers. His job often kept him away from home during the work week, but he always tried his best to be home by the weekend. And since he loves to cook, and everyone loves to eat whatever he cooks, he found this to be a compelling way to keep his family close.

Bill was really smart! He included an open invitation for his daughters to bring friends and boyfriends home for Sunday Supper, and made sure the afternoon was a treat for everyone.

In her best-selling book *Bread and Wine*, Shauna Niequist paints a picture of what the dinner table represents:

"We don't come to the table to fight or to defend. We don't come to prove or to conquer, to draw lines in the sand or to stir up trouble. We come to the table because our hunger brings us there. We come with a need, with fragility, with an admission of our humanity . . . The table is the place where the doing stops, the trying stops, the masks are removed, and we allow ourselves to be nourished, like children. We allow someone else to meet our need . . . the table is a place of safety and rest and humanity, where we are allowed to be as fragile as we feel."[5]

Let *your* table be this safely nourishing place for your whole family.

Vacation together

We never had the finances to take our kids on fancy vacations, but we found ways to go on vacation together every year, even when our kids were teenagers. We had to get creative, and maybe that's one of the reasons we had so much fun.

Most often we either went camping or to Diane's parents' cabin in the Sierra Mountains of California. We swam in snow-fed lakes and discovered slippery slides in boulder-strewn rivers. We fished and got sunburned, hiked and had our own family church high in the mountains. Once while Phil was playing his guitar at a lookout over the Sierras, a hidden rattlesnake kept time with our singing. We couldn't scoot out of that spot fast enough!

We resisted bringing our children's friends along, because we wanted our teenagers to enjoy each other's company. By the time they were teenagers, their lives were busy, making it hard to carve out time to know and enjoy and just hang out together. We were hoping to create a bond between our four that would outlast their time at home—real friendships that would endure long after we were no longer in an authority role in their lives.

When Matt was the only one still at home, we did let him bring a friend. But we made sure it was a friend he wanted to bring and one we liked! Someone who was able to enter into our family easily and who helped rather than hindered our son's ability to power down and have fun. Once we even bought a return airline ticket for a friend who needed to get back for baseball practice. It was a great investment!

Since your teenagers will likely have summer jobs, you'll need to plan ahead, giving them the dates well in advance so they can get the time off work.

DIANE:

Teenage boys equate leisure time with good food, so I cooked more on vacation than any other time! A wise mentor advised me to see our family vacations as a unique time to grow closer as a family rather than as a vacation for myself. By the time we had teenagers, I knew our times together were limited, so I took her advice and made sure my teenage boys got plenty of their favorite foods while we were camping or at the cabin. Somehow it seemed that they understood that, making my efforts worth it.

Now, with our oldest grandson on the brink of his teenage years, his family spends a portion of their vacation every summer with other families in their community group. Thus our grandkids have the advantage of doing life with different people who do life differently. At the same time, they are able to experience families with similar values and a shared love for Jesus.

Be there when your teenager comes home

If at all possible—and we know it is *not* always possible—arrange for one of you to be home and available when your teenager gets home from school every day. Some of you may need to get creative in order to make this happen. Perhaps it means trading after-school hours with a friend who shares your values. Maybe it means leaving an encouraging note or calling as soon as your son or daughter gets home.

Why? Because this is a dangerous age to be alone and unsupervised. The internet is a quick fill-in for loneliness. For your children to know you are waiting for them to come home, that they have your full attention, that their welcome is warm and accepting—these are rare gifts and a strong support for your teenage son or daughter who wants to walk with God but whose judgment is still developing and whose emotions can be fragile. If you can be there with a snack and time to listen, those will be some of your most intimate and revealing conversations.

DIANE:

I wish I had understood what a high-impact ministry was available to me at this stage of our children's lives. I was a stay-at-home mom with a toddler still keeping me busy while my oldest son started high school. I could easily have invited my kids' friends into our home after school!

I had a friend who was a single mom raising four kids, and I look back now with real regret that I was so unaware of her need. Although it wasn't easy, we managed to squeak by on a single salary, but there were friends of ours for whom that was simply not possible. This is the way the body of Christ functions at its finest: when we are alert to each other's needs and offer to step in with help when we can.

Make your home the place their friends want to hang out

When our children were teenagers, we were surprised to find how few parents were willing to open their homes to their kids' friends. Since teenagers love to congregate in groups, that becomes a problem.

As both of our parents had done for us, we threw open the doors of our house for these kids. Sure, they were hard on our house. Your pantry will empty, your carpet will get stained, your sofa will suffer. Teenage boys carry a certain scent with them, and teenage girls sometimes leave trails of nail polish on the bathroom counter. But it's so worth it! If you show the slightest interest in their lives and well-being, those kids will become your biggest advocates. And you will have a ministry in their lives that will reap immeasurable reward!

When our oldest son was in high school, all his friends seemed to congregate at the Jaegers' house. The mom, Myrna, threw an impromptu party every time the kids came to visit. In fact, she dedicated one entire cupboard of her tiny kitchen for snacks for the kids. She'd ask each friend about their all-time favorite snack food. Then she'd be sure to stock that snack and write the kid's name in bold, black letters on the front of the box.

Myrna became everyone's mom. She cared about her children's friends, and they knew she cared. Hers was a home that was safe and warm and welcoming—and full! Of course, the fact that she had two beautiful daughters added to the draw.

Myrna simply modeled Galatians 6:10: "Therefore, as we have opportunity, let us do good to all people, especially those who belong to the family of believers." Every community needs a few Myrna Jaegers to throw open their home as a safe and fun place for teenagers to gather.

WISDOM, TO NAVIGATE THIS SEASON

During these teenage years, you are going to face decision after decision where there is no clear Bible verse telling you what to do!

At times you may feel like the proverbial deer caught in the headlights of an oncoming car, events and decisions coming at you so fast you feel frozen in place. The intensity of these years is entirely different from that of the toddler years, yet those same feelings of being overwhelmed will wash over you. You love your son or your daughter with such fierce devotion, yet you feel powerless to protect them from a freeway full of dangerous choices.

We know. We've been there. Although there were many more good times than bad, the fear, the worry, the dread of all that can go wrong is the worst part. Now we look back on that bleak cloud of worry that sometimes haunted our nights, and we feel nothing but humble thankfulness for the God who was with us in the midst of our fear. Not because He solved every dilemma seamlessly—He didn't—but because His comfort carried us as we turned to Him, and His Spirit taught us as we cried out to Him for the wisdom we did not have. We experienced the promise of James 1:5: "If any of you lacks wisdom, you should ask God, who gives generously to all without finding fault, and it will be given to you."

Time and time again, we lay in bed at night talking about the kids. In the quiet of our bedroom, after a long day of parenting in the midst of real life and all its pressures, we brought our teenage sons and daughters to God. We prayed specifically, and we prayed persistently, coming back again and again to the only One who had the answers that eluded us.

We prayed the prayer every parent of teenagers needs to know, taken right out of 2 Chronicles 20:12. An overwhelming-certain-to-be-doomed situation faced by God's people as they cried,

"We do not know what to do, but our eyes are on you." [6]

And we saw Him answer again and again! Praying at night, then getting up early the next morning to search the Scriptures for the wisdom we were certain He had waiting for us, we found answers—answers that worked.

In Proverbs chapter two, these words became our mantra:

"Tune your ears to wisdom, and concentrate on understanding. Cry out for insight, and ask for understanding. Search for them as you would for silver, seek them like hidden treasures. Then you will understand what it means to fear the LORD" (Proverbs 2:2–5 NLT), "and discover the knowledge of God. For the Lord gives wisdom!" (Proverbs 2:5,6 NASB 1973)"

For parents of teenagers, this way of actively seeking God in the Scriptures for wisdom is essential. There is no rulebook to follow. Every child, every home, every situation is just different enough to require insight and understanding which, apart from God, we simply aren't capable of. This season of your life must not be a period of lazy spirituality! You cannot afford to be negligent in prayer, personal devotions, or involvement in the community of your church.

During most of the times when we were reaching out for wisdom, God gave it to us in our early morning listening in the Word. He often gave us clarity in the middle of a Sunday sermon that had nothing to do with our dilemma, or in a passing comment from a wise, Spirit-filled friend. We sought counsel from people wiser and further ahead in child-raising than us, and their words often met the need immediately.

A.B Simpson's words are an apt reminder for every parent:

"God has hidden every precious thing in such a way that it is a reward to the diligent, but a disappointment to the slothful . . . All nature is arrayed against the lounger . . . The nut is hidden in its thorny case; the pearl is buried beneath the ocean waves; the gold is imprisoned in the rocks of the mountains; the gem is found only after you crush the rock which encloses it. So truth and God must be earnestly sought."[7]

When we asked for wisdom, God lavished it on us! He will do the same for you if you will ask Him, if you will search as for hidden treasure, if you will come to Him for what you need.

Our now-grown children are learning what we learned when we were raising them: Parenting is not an exact science with clear answers, but God holds all the wisdom we need in His hands, and He is more than willing to share.

Chapter 16

Three Secrets That Work

O ne of the most frustrating things about parenting teenagers is that near-constant feeling that you don't know what to do. While the early years are physically exhausting, the teenage years are emotionally wearing. So many surprising circumstances come up that parents are often left simply wondering, "Do I have this?"

This often leads to the question, "How do you do discipline during these years? They're too old to spank and too big to pick up and say, 'Look me in the eye!' but not nearly old enough to depend entirely on their own judgment. What should I do?"

Because the same questions haunted us when our kids were teenagers, we want to pass on to you three secrets to discipline in the teen years that worked wonders, making all the difference when our kids were in this stage. (Shh! Don't tell your teenager!)

SWITCH ROLES

The first secret to discipline in the teenage years that worked like magic for us is so simple anyone who is willing can do it: We switched roles.

When the children were younger, Diane actually implemented most of the discipline. Although Phil *did* discipline, the burden of training fell largely on Diane, as she was with the kids day and night while Phil was working to provide for our family of six.

During these teenage years, that needed to change. We noticed that as they got older, the kids began to push back more, often leaving their mom worn out and discouraged. Her desire to have peaceable, close relationships with her sons and daughters clashed with their need to push away. At the same time, their still-developing judgment required frequent correction and more supervision than they wanted. The tension was rising rapidly!

In a flash of insight, we realized that Diane's instinctively nurturing heart was easily defeated by this rising tension. Phil was better able to push back without becoming emotional about it. It was time for Phil to purposefully take over the primary disciplinary role so Diane could be set free to be the loving, relational mom our kids needed.

Phil became the bad guy. Not mean and grouchy, but firm and immovable, like a brick wall. He stood for godliness without excuse, for respectfulness and high standards. It was Phil who insisted our kids go to church whether they felt like it or not. Phil was the one who said, "No means no!" and stood firm when saying no was hard.

Diane got to be the good guy. After years of being the primary parent at home, the one doing most of the discipline, now she simply enforced Phil's rule of law. She was there to soften the no's, to explain Phil to the kids and explain the kids to Phil. It was her role to listen and empathize, to understand and cheer on the kids, helping them to deal with reasonable restrictions while fully honoring Phil's leadership.

It was Diane who helped the kids rephrase the way they said what they wanted to say so that it was respectful. We wanted our teenagers to be free to say anything to us, but they absolutely had to be willing to submit to our decisions whether they agreed or not. They had to be respectful. Sometimes—okay, *often*—our kids needed coaching on how to do that.

This is not a good time in your children's lives to suddenly draw a line in the sand. That works when they are younger, and in fact it is essential when your children are young. But now, the world in which our teenagers are being raised is a dangerous world. There are evil people lurking at bus stations, waiting for your runaway teenager. To kick out one of your sons or daughters for noncompliance in these times would be dangerously misapplied "tough love."

You will need to become a compelling leader in your home during these years, adjusting your tactics lest you alienate your kids. We worked on this together, encouraging and gently correcting each other when our internal response to the heated disagreement that sometimes followed a "no" tempted us to lose our cool.

These two approaches, firm standards combined with generous encouragement, took all the pressure off these years. What our kids didn't know was that it was most often Diane who told Phil behind closed doors that we needed to hold the line firmly!

As Phil loves to say, "The Bible says the husband is the head of the wife. But the wife is the neck. And we all know that it's the neck that turns the head!"

DIANE:

What worked so beautifully was that I didn't feel isolated and alone when our kids balked at our insistence that we remain more involved in their lives than they felt necessary. That tension between our children's need to grow up and become independent and our determination to stay close sometimes stretched our relationship with our kids to the breaking point. There are just so many judgment calls in these years and no clear rules to guarantee a good outcome.

When Phil said to our daughters, "You can't wear that to school today!" (because I told him to say it!) the girls would come crying to me, moaning that their dad was so old-fashioned and he couldn't possibly understand—that's when I would explain why.

"Honey, your dad is just watching out for you! He's not letting you wear that because he knows what the guys at school will be thinking as you walk down the hall. And that's the last thing you want! So can we just figure out how to wear that style without eliciting that kind of response?"

Or when Phil said, "No, you can't go there this Friday night!" I was the one who explained that he only wanted to keep them safe from a situation they couldn't control.

A word about friendships

Sometimes this means saying no to certain friends.

Scripture says, "Do not be misled: Bad company corrupts good character" (1 Corinthians 15:33) and "He who walks with wise men will be wise, but the companion of fools will suffer harm" (Proverbs 13:20 NASB).

You will need to gently teach this truth to your kids, using discerning filters as you speak about specific people. You do not want to be harshly judgmental of another's struggles, but filled with love and hope and the firm belief that God is the Redeemer who can and does change the hardest of hearts.

Both of us feel we crossed the line repeatedly in our fumbling attempts to keep our teenagers from getting swept into a crowd that could lead them into swampy waters. We operated too often out of fear. We may have been correct in our assessment about specific kids, but as a British friend of ours likes to say, "We may have been right, but we were dead right!"

Our perspective on people often needed to change. When it comes to teenagers, what they look like on the outside is often not who they are on the inside. They wear their hair funky and dress up in costumes as a means of self-defense—children are usually not yet tough enough for what can be a brutal world.

The quickest way to know the heart of a friend you're unsure about is to invite him or her into your home. Often, when the whole family scoots over to include this friend around the dinner table, you will discover a different side of the friend you were concerned about. Sometimes in the fun of our family circle, our kids' friends were able to take off their masks and let themselves be who they really were.

On the other hand, a few friends might not pass the "family circle test" no matter how hard you try to welcome them in. When a friend sat at our table and remained withdrawn or sullen, our teenagers could see in stark relief that this wasn't a friend to spend a lot of time with.

You need to be willing to discourage—even forbid—your teenager from cultivating certain friendships. If you see a friend having a negative influence on your child's attitude and choices, weakening their love for Jesus, you may need to intervene. It won't be easy, but remember what we said in chapter 15 about the four things parents will need during these teenage years? The first one was courage.

For parents with daughters at home, that courage may take the form of putting a moratorium on your son's friends spending the night. We have heard so many sad stories of sexual abuse by friends of siblings that we have to question the necessity of this social practice.

DIANE:

Our son had two school friends he was honestly hoping to help through some turbulent years. Neither of these kids was walking with the Lord, but they were intrigued by our son's genuine faith. He was not in any way being badly influenced by them, so when he asked if they could spend the night, I didn't know what to say, but I felt uneasy about these two boys.

Sometime in the middle of the night I woke up and realized why I was restless and uncomfortable—I was worried about the safety of our daughters. The rest of the night was pretty much sleepless, but the next morning I talked to my son about it. He didn't understand and was even a little offended. I knew I had to be gracious and yet courageous enough to stand firm. I trusted that someday he would get it.

And now? As a father of three children, he is more protective than I was. He's heard the same awful stories and has the courage to make the tough calls to ensure his kid's safety.

When Peter wrote to warn his people about friends who could entice them away from their faith, he reminded them of how Lot, "that righteous man, living among them day after day, was tormented in his righteous soul by the lawless deeds he saw and heard" (2 Peter 2:8).

He warned against friendships with "those who follow the corrupt desire of the flesh and despise authority" (2 Peter 2:10). Peter ended his second letter by saying, "be on your guard lest, being carried away by the error of unprincipled men, *you fall from your own steadfastness,* but grow in the grace and knowledge of our Lord and Savior, Jesus Christ" (2 Peter 3:17–18 NASB 1973).

Watching over your teenager's friendships may be one of the more challenging calls you have to make as a parent. But you do it for the love of your child. You don't want to see them fall away, you want them to be rooted and established in their faith.

ADJUST THE BOX

Remember The Box we talked about in the framing stage? Four sides which, when tightened simultaneously, create a secure frame around your child's life to enable your child to thrive and grow into the beautiful person God intended him or her to be.

What were the four sides of The Box?

1. Jesus: the undergirding foundation of every part of life
2. Discipline: using the tools of discipleship
3. Order: a structure that enables your child to thrive
4. Fun, affection, and affirmation: keeping your relationships strong and close

During the teenage years, there will be times when you need to tighten The Box. Although The Box is much bigger than when your teenager was a toddler, it's still there. The Box is still providing the framework every teenager needs as they stretch their independence muscles and move closer to the day when they will be fully responsible for themselves.

The teenage years can be an awkward season for your kids, especially in our culture. Lots and lots of kids your teenager knows will have few or no boundaries. Even Christian parents will often abandon their teenagers to pretty much rule themselves.

At the same time, most teenagers show—at least sometimes—a lack of good judgment. Their brains are still developing in the frontal lobe area, which controls decision-making, the ability to plan ahead, and impulse control. Your teenager is not yet fully capable of sorting through all the emotions and hormones and information that are coming at them faster than they can keep up.

Your teenager may say to you during these years, "Don't you trust me?" You will feel guilty, as if trusting your teenage son or daughter implicitly is the mark of a good parent. Tread carefully here—trust is earned, not entitled.

While distrust can crush a child and ruin a relationship, we would be foolish to unequivocally entrust our teenagers to rule themselves. Instead, say, "I trust *you*; I know your heart is gold. But I am hesitant to trust your judgment in some circumstances. Let's work together on that."

As you team up to allow time and open communication to build trust in your teenager's judgment, give him lots of encouragement. You don't want to be a belligerent parent sitting on the sidelines, waiting to pounce when your teenager messes up. Acting antagonistically is never wise and certainly will not foster mutual respect.

As you see her judgment maturing, you enlarge The Box, gladly inviting more of the freedom your teenager needs for growth. Instead of a tug-a-war, you are in this together, getting ready to launch your teenager into adulthood.

When your teenager makes a mistake—and he will—instead of stomping on him in anger or grounding her for the next six months, instead of using escalating anger and shame and rejection or some sort of off-the-charts "creative punishment," simply tighten The Box. Here's what that might look like:

First, you sit down with him and talk about what he did. No yelling, no dramatic sighing or eye rolling (uh-huh, we're talking to the parents here, not the teenager!), just a calm, shoulder-to-shoulder[1] conversation in private. Not at the dinner table, not in the car full of siblings!

Begin the conversation by asking good questions. Don't ask why he did what he did lest he blame his behavior on someone else. Instead, show that you care by asking, "What's going on?"

Let him know that even though it looks bad, you believe in him. You believe he is a good-hearted person. Show him that you're not mad, you're just helping him to grow, and you know growing up is sometimes hard. You're inviting him in; you're listening below the surface to learn what drove him to make the choice he did.

Next, bring Jesus into the conversation, not as judge but as your child's Redeemer, the One who bore our sins on His back lest we forever suffer the consequences. Remind your teenager that what Jesus wants is not perfection, but one whose heart is fully His.[2] Inspire him to remember that that's where joy and peace are found.

A conversation like this brings you together on a spiritual level, as fellow followers of Jesus. Here is where you may want to bring your own mess-ups into the conversation so that your teen can see that she is not alone and that you get it. You're in this together.

Then, if more than a verbal correction[3] is warranted, you can explain the reasonable restrictions on their freedom that you are about to temporarily impose. This isn't punishment, as in "You're bad and you deserve this." You are tightening The Box as, together, you work on maturing your teenager's judgment. This will most likely involve a loss of some privileges. You can give them a way of earning those privileges back by demonstrating a good attitude and a desire to do right. Don't make it too hard to be in your good graces lest your teenager lose heart.

Be sensitive to what the Spirit may be trying to tell you about your children. Only He knows all that is churning in their hearts. The wise parent depends on God to provide wisdom. There isn't a black-and-white twelve-steps-to-get-your-child-back-on-track. Instead, God invites us to ask Him for specific wisdom for specific situations and then He asks us to wait until He shows us what to do or say.

Next, it may be time to impose some order on your teenager's life—just until he is able to order his own world so that he can function efficiently and fulfill his responsibilities. This might mean a bedtime. Your teenager won't like that! Or maybe, if the problem is falling grades, you may need to step in and help him figure out why. Has he adopted an efficient approach to study? Maybe you need to show him how.

DIANE:

I really struggled with this as a teenager. I loved to read and writing was my strength, but I couldn't for the life of me manage a project. My parents, on the other hand, are the most organized, efficient people I know! They couldn't wrap their heads around a daughter who dropped the ball on big projects that required organization and long-range planning. I knew I wasn't being lazy, and I certainly wasn't unmotivated—I was just clueless about where to start.

I would have benefited from a checklist and a clear system for breaking down those high school projects into daily goals. But neither my parents nor I knew that then, so I floundered, and they were frustrated.

Now I advise parents to take a long look at their child's abilities and inabilities. They may well need your help in order to succeed at what you are asking of them.

Don't forget to put on the top of The Box! If you do, bitterness and rebellion may leak in. Remember the top? That's all the fun and affection and affirmation your child is craving.

Fun: Let's go shopping! Our daughters loved this, demonstrating that at least in these teenage years, shopping with either Dad or Mom was their primary love language!

Affection: Give plenty of hugs. Use fond names and reminders of their unique and valued contribution to the family. Being careful not to cross the line into hurtful teasing that teenagers are prone to take too seriously.

198 Raising Passionate Jesus Followers

Affirmation: This is the opposite of shame. You believe God is working in your teenager's life, and sometimes you have to believe *for* them. You need to point out to your teenager what God is doing and how He is changing them.

Kids can get beaten down by their peers at this stage of their lives, but also by adults who may treat them disrespectfully. And sometimes it's their own fault! But when their parents are walking close to God and choose to demonstrate compassion for and encouragement to their child, they have a power to propel them off that vicious cycle. Words of affirmation will strengthen your child as he gets back up to try again.

That's it—The Box. So simple! So much less stressful for the whole family than all the shouting and drama and fuming and sarcasm that characterizes too many families.

DIANE:

I wish I had understood this better when we were raising our first two teenagers. To my chagrin, I remember some of those punitive "creative disciplines" I used—mostly in frustrated anger when I didn't know what to do.

One that haunts me was aimed at our first son, John Mark. He was a godly teenager, really growing and following after Jesus in every area of his life. We were so proud of him, but he had that attitude—you know what I mean? That cocky, know-it-all superiority that is a thin veil over insecurity.

Phil was traveling a lot with his job, and I didn't know what to do with this man-child whose attitude pushed all my buttons. So I came up with what I thought was a clever cure: every time he used that cocky attitude with me I made him get on his hands and knees and mop the wood floor that covered a third of our downstairs.

I meant to teach my son to be humble. Now I know that all I was really teaching him was to resent me.

If I had understood The Box, I would have simply sat down and talked with my son. I would have asked questions. I would have prayed with him. I have no doubt, looking back, that John Mark would have responded with genuine humility.

The greatest part of this story came just a couple of years ago. We were teaching the Intentional conference for the first time, and John Mark, a young father himself now, was sitting in the back, listening. Afterward, when I asked him what he thought, he claimed complete amnesia regarding all those floor-scrubbing sessions.

"Mom," he insisted, "you made that up!"

What I was so certain was my worst parenting fail, he doesn't even remember! What a beautiful example of the goodness and grace of God.

Some kids will just get it easily. They will automatically adapt to the boundaries you put in place. But there are some kids who will insist on testing those boundaries to make sure that The Box is still there. For those kids to feel safe and secure, you are going to need to be incredibly consistent. Don't give up! Your teenager is worth the work.

Of course your teenager needs freedom to begin pulling away as they grow up. They will need to question things, and some will test you relentlessly, but you can still remain close. It will take maturity and effort on your part to make that happen. Even though your teen may not realize it, she still needs your guidance and discipline.

The Box is expanding, but it's still there!

Sometimes during these years, your teenager will try the time-honored technique to "divide and conquer." She will attempt to play the sympathy of one parent against the one who is holding to firm boundaries. "But Dad said it's okay with him!"

As much as this may anger you, the solution is not more discipline. The beautiful picture of unity between two very different parents will give your child a sense of security in the midst of their own turmoil. Remember the lamp and the light? You're working *together* to raise a godly son or daughter.

Jesus said, "And if a house is divided against itself, that house cannot stand" (Mark 3:25).

There will be times when two parents do not agree, but you need to speak with one voice. Rather than sweeping it under the carpet, talk to each other. Pray together, seek wise counsel from someone who knows you well, then listen to each other until you can come to a place of oneness about the situation.

This isn't about winning, but about loving your child enough to be unified. This is the ultimate goal of the lamp and the light,[4] distinctly different perspectives fused together to bring light to your son or daughter.

One last secret to managing these teenage years gracefully:

TEACH YOUR TEENAGER THE PROCESS AND POWER OF APPEAL

Two disconcerting changes occur when your child begins to step into adulthood, and if you're not prepared for those changes, you might miss their meaning.

The first is his need to question your authority. As a toddler, your child resisted your control. He may have even defied you. But you rose to the challenge and gave him the boundaries, the training, the correction, and the encouragement he needed in order to navigate his way into independence.

Now he's a teenager—no longer a toddler who can be placated with a hug and a snack. For years you have been his boss. You had control. He had to do what you wanted, when you wanted. That was right and good when he was younger, but now a seismic shift has occurred, and you need to prepare yourself for the changes.

Now all of a sudden he knows, without a smidgen of doubt, that you are not always right. In fact, he suspects you've been wrong a lot. And he's right, you know. Every parent is making constant judgment calls. Every parent has opinions and ways of doing things that made sense at one time, but that are wide open for scrutiny. In part, we form our rules out of our own fears and failures. Some of those rules are good. They keep us safe. But a lot are simply how we prefer to do life.

Now that your teenager is tentatively stepping into adulthood, he notices that your way of doing life is not infallible. In fact, he may be quick to point out just how wrong you are about anything and everything!

The second change that may catch you by surprise if you're not prepared (it did us!) is your emerging teen's need to be heard. Because they are often a mess of emotion at this stage of their lives, that legitimate need will often sound sassy or critical—even disrespectful. Your sweet little girl turned into your apparent enemy overnight!

A formula for disaster? Or the way to responsible independence?

The answer may have more to do with you as the parent than with your child. If we are willing to recognize and respond to these real, valid developmental needs, rather than react to the awkward and unfortunate way our teenagers express those needs, we can smooth the inevitable conflict rather than enflame it.

A simple, yet often overlooked biblical concept called an *appeal* is the third secret to discipline during the teenage years.

An appeal is a way of respectfully negotiating a change to an authority's decision. In our legal system, an appeal is often a means of correcting false assumptions in an initial court decision, a way of claiming that the first decision was either unfair or lacked pertinent information.

In our homes, an appeal is a way of honoring both the parents and the teenager by reopening a decision with new information or a different approach.

Permitting and even encouraging this process of appeal acknowledges a parent's God-given authority while preventing parents from becoming authoritarian. It is a humble recognition that we might just possibly be wrong!

To your teenager, an appeal is a legitimate means of being heard and respected, a platform for the peaceable working out of conflict between parent and child without having to pull out the "because I said so" mentality that so many of us resort to when we feel threatened. The apostle Paul wrote to Timothy about this tool of appeal. After encouraging his young protégé to teach truth with confident boldness, he said:

"Don't let anyone think less of you because you are young." (1 Timothy 4:12 NLT)

In a culture that highly valued the wisdom that comes with age, often to the point of disrespecting younger leaders, this was a pervasive problem. Paul tells Timothy how to overcome it:

"Be an example to all believers in what you teach, in the way you live, in your love, your faith, and your purity." (1 Timothy 4:12 NLT)

Sounds like a good word for parents! But let's read on:

"Never speak harshly to an older man, but appeal to him respectfully as you would to your own father." (1 Timothy 5:1 NLT)

Let's take a closer look at this verse. The term "speak harshly" can also be translated "reprimand" (1 Timothy 5:1 PHILLIPS) or "rebuke harshly" (NIV). So Paul is instructing Timothy to not answer his critics harshly but to appeal to them with the respect and love he would give to a good dad.

The word "appeal" (*parakaléō*) comes from the same word used of the Holy Spirit. It means to call on someone for help, or to invite someone to do something. An appeal is an invitation for help, a request for aid in some way. A humble ask.

If that sounds like the antithesis of the arguing and yelling and snide comments and slamming doors that our culture deems normal during the teenage years—you're right! It's the polar opposite.

Are you ready to understand how to implement this powerful tool? It's so simple yet so effective. This is how it works:

Your teenager brings home a new CD. She's blaring it loudly, singing along, when you hear some lyrics that alarm you. You forbid her from listening to such rebellious-sounding music. It's your right and both of you know it. You're the boss; this is your house.

At this point, conflict flares. She's insulted, even hurt by your assumption that she is somehow bad for enjoying this song. Just as your first response was to assert your authority, her first response is to resist, to argue. Because she feels disrespected, she speaks disrespectfully.

This is where an appeal comes in. She knows that she is allowed, even encouraged, to voice—reasonably and respectfully—her views on why this CD is fine for her to listen to. What does she do? She appeals to you.

First, she acknowledges your authority, your right to decide what music can be played in your home. She is letting you know (and reminding herself) that she is honoring her parents, and she is willing to do what you say.

Next, she asks in an appealing way if she can talk to you about your decision. "Can we take a minute to talk about this, Mom?"

This is your signal to get your reasonableness on. Take a deep breath, climb down from your moral high horse, and invite Jesus into the conversation. Look at your teenager for who she is: a little girl growing up into a beautiful woman right before your eyes. You're not mad at her or against her. You love this girl! So much so that you're willing to humble yourself and listen. You smile and say, "Sure, honey. What am I missing here?"

This allows her to relax. This is not a battle to be fought but a misunderstanding to be soothed. She has a voice, and she might even be right! Calmly, nicely, she reads the lyrics out loud to you. This is the whole story, the part you may have misinterpreted when you heard that offending snippet.

Now, one of two things happens. Either she's reading the lyrics and you realize that although you may not prefer the way the song-writer puts it, this is not really an evil song. It's just poetry expressing emotion in an intensely teenage-driven way. Or, while she's reading, she feels herself cringe at the words she thought were innocent. And because you're being humble and open-hearted, you've created an atmosphere that doesn't cause her to lose face.

Of course there is still the possibility that the two of you will disagree. If that happens, you have two choices. Either you assert your authority and let her know that she cannot play that CD at home, or you tell her you're still not comfortable with that song but you're going to get a second opinion before you forbid it.

That's an appeal. So simple! So reasonable and workable, humble and loving!

Your teenager's legitimate *need to question* your values and your opinions is respected, while you've satisfied her *need to be heard*.

And even though teenagers or mothers of teenagers are rarely as relaxed as that made-up conversation may sound, at least World War III has been averted. God has been honored, and love grows in leaps and bounds as both of you fumble your way to relational maturity.

Chapter 17

Three Things Your Teenager Will Need

Just as there are character qualities and skills you will need in order to navigate the teenage years wisely and well, there are also specific things your teenager will need from you—ways you can help them flourish rather than fumble through these years. Here are the three things that stood out to us; feel free to add your own!

TO DISCOVER WHAT THEY'RE GOOD AT

One of the most frequently quoted verses in the Bible that has to do with child raising is also one of the most misunderstood. You'll find it in the book of Proverbs:

> "Train up a child in the way he should go, Even when he is old he will not depart from it." (Proverbs 22:6 NASB)

Parents quote this verse when they're worried about the direction their child is heading, thinking it's a promise they can cling to. But as we stated earlier, a more accurate reading of this verse reveals that it is not so much a promise as an observation. Proverbs are poetically arranged sayings that make sense, observations about life and relationships and truth and culture.

When the writer of Proverbs (thought to be primarily Solomon) penned these words under the inspiration of the Holy Spirit, he was noticing something important. He did not mean that if a parent takes their child to church and youth group and Sunday school, he will automatically grow up to be the next Billy Graham.

As we said in chapter 8, what he does mean is this: Children who are trained over and over, day after day, week after week, year after year; and who are corrected, rebuked, encouraged, and patiently instructed in what it means to love God with passion and love people on purpose likely will not deviate from that training when they get older.

The phrase, "in the way he should go" can also be translated as "according to his own way" or "according to his own bent." While this verse has a spiritual application, it also has a practical one. This has to do with a person's individuality—how God has wired them. Every child is fearfully and wonderfully made by God, possessing a unique set of strengths.[1]

Wise parents understand that their children are not only to be molded but also unfolded.[2]

As you purposefully observe your children, noticing their differences and paying attention to their individual preferences, you will see their gifts emerge. Spiritual gifts,[3] such as mercy or teaching, and God-given abilities like writing, working with their hands, and creative artistry need to be identified and developed. By discovering what your child excels at in their teenage years, you will be better able to guide them into their college years.

Proverbs 22:29 says, "Do you see someone skilled in their work? They will serve before kings; they will not serve before officials of low rank." A parent who grasps this wisdom will work with their teenager to focus on what they are good at. For example, a boy who flunks algebra is probably not best suited to major in math in college. A girl who sells more Girl Scout cookies than anyone else in her troop might be directed towards marketing.

This is one of the best parts of parenting a teenager! You have been given this gift—a person who relies on you to notice the *imago dei*—the image of God—that is uniquely developing in them.

Our daughter Rebekah's middle name is Ruth, which means "compassionate, beautiful friend." Even as a very small child, she lived up to her name. She was irresistibly drawn to helping people, to giving comfort and taking charge of emergencies.

> ## PHIL:
>
> I saw this when Rebekah was as young as six. We were at the mall at Christmas time, juggling packages and trying to keep together in the crowd. Elizabeth was three, and we had her in the stroller with several heavy bags hanging off the back handle. I let go of the stroller for just a minute—just long enough for that added weight to pull Elizabeth down backwards.
>
> As she let out a terrified scream, Rebekah came rushing to the rescue! Before either of us could get to her, she'd righted the stroller and let us know that her little sister's head was bleeding. Diane just sort of panicked while I stood there, watching Rebekah jump into action.
>
> Ignoring her inept parents, Bekah proceeded to part the back of her sister's hair to see where the blood was flowing from. Then she started barking orders: "Mom, it's okay, it's just a little cut! Dad, get me some tissues! I've got this." She mopped up the blood and assured her sister that she'd be okay.
>
> It was no surprise that Rebekah went into the medical field!

On the other hand, Elizabeth hated hospitals like her dad does. She is like a prophetess, filled with wisdom and insight. Her balanced way of observing people and events and fitting facts together in logical sequence makes her the go-to person in our family when we just don't know what to do. Every one of us has gone to Elizabeth with our dilemmas and walked away with a plan that made sense.

She's also added her conviction that our bodies belong to God and are meant to be cared for to her passion for cooking, becoming a skilled teacher of healthy eating.

Our two sons, though alike in many ways, are very different.

┌─ **PHIL:** ──────────────────────────────────────┐

I'll never forget the time, one winter, when I couldn't take the dreary rain in Portland anymore, and Diane and I decided to drive south until we found some sun. The two oldest kids were teenagers and had responsibilities that kept them home, so we took Matt along and headed south, leaving John Mark in charge.

When we got to Southern Oregon, I called home with a list of reminders: *Remember, no movies tonight, you've all got to get up super early to serve at church tomorrow. Don't forget to make sure the girls do their chores. And will you be sure to have a family Bible time before everyone goes to bed?*

John Mark's response was a little annoyed: "Dad, I know all that! Chores are done, and we've already had Bible time. I know what to do!"

└──┘

We spotted our oldest son's gift for leadership and his anointing to teach when he was in high school. We witnessed his walk with God well before that. Combined with his compulsion to challenge the status quo and his immense love of learning, it has been no surprise to us to see him become a leader to his generation. Now we marvel as he teaches the Scriptures clearly and powerfully at the church he pastors in Portland, Oregon.[4]

Matthew's gift for bringing people together is part of his unique calling. He's like the Pied Piper. It's ingrained in his personality, part of what drives him—he loves people, and people love him. As far as Matthew is concerned, the more people the better.

When he was a teenager and asked us if he could have some friends over, we knew to expect a crowd. When Matt said, "Mom, Dad, I'm going to have a few people over for a game night," Phil would grab his keys and head out for pizzas because we knew that in an hour or so, twenty-five teenagers would be showing up at our house—and we loved it! We learned to be ready to support Matt's God-given gift for leadership and fun! Now he satisfies his love of bringing people together as a youth pastor in our church.

Both sons went on to become pastors, but with entirely different approaches to ministry. They learn from each other and they value each other's uniqueness.

Just like our kids, yours will be uniquely gifted to bring God's kingdom into our world. Help them to discover what they're good at, then spend the rest of your life relishing what you see.

TO GUARD THEIR PURITY

One of the most staggering realizations for a mother or father is that their child is a person—not just a kid, but a man or a woman in the making. You have been entrusted with molding a person who will in turn mold and affect other people.

Your son or daughter's humanness includes their sexuality. To be the one to introduce and influence our children's handling of their sexuality, as well as their honoring of the sexuality of others—this is a responsibility handed to us by God. What a privilege!

And He certainly hasn't been silent on the subject! In fact, the Bible is full of stories and specific verses—even an entire book detailing the beauty, romance, and dangers of our human sexuality.[5]

By this time you will hopefully have been talking to your child about his or her sexuality for several years. In fact, the earlier the better. Opening this awkward topic while your child is still a child with no developmental confusion or raging hormones disrupting their ability to think clearly is the wisest, easiest way to foster openness. But now, during these teenage years, your discussions about sex and sexuality move from the back burner to the front of the stove.

While we cannot present a thorough guide on how to handle teaching your child about their sexuality,[6] we do wish to open the door to your thinking by suggesting a three-prong approach.

First, talk to your teenager about sexual purity.

By the time your child is in his or her early teens, you should have established a normalness to conversations about sexuality. And although details are usually best left to the parent of the same sex as your child, both parents should be welcoming questions as well as initiating comfortable talks about sex and sexuality. If you wait too long, these discussions will feel one-sided, even invasive.

For followers of Jesus, this area of our lives must be about more than rules and cautionary tales. God created us as uniquely sexual beings, not mere animals with urges.

Giving dignity to a man's desires and beauty to a woman's physicality rather than giving in to the perversion that has lurked on the outskirts of sex for too long is a parent's privilege. We get to introduce our children to this wondrous way of a man and a woman.[7]

By being the first in your child's life to honor the gift of sexuality, you will be able to shape his or her attitude before this world has a chance to inform the way they will think and feel about the boundaries and purity of God-honoring sexuality.

Be aware that *not* talking about sex is also a form of communication. Every time you go the local shopping mall, you are confronted with highly sexual images. If you say nothing as you walk by a pornographic display, what does that communicate to your child? Or if you get in a huff and shame him for glancing in that direction, what are your attitudes saying? What is your child hearing in your silence?

If, on the other hand, you cultivate a respectful view of God's intention when He created the beauty of sex in the context of a lifetime of commitment between a husband and wife, you are setting up your son or daughter with a vision of what God has planned for them. To anticipate this gift may well be the best way to wrap it in the wonder it deserves.

To that end, be very careful about joking about sex. Put a quick stop to crude talk about women. Let your boys know that such talk will not be tolerated in your home. Talk about what it means to honor women, to value beauty that is God-created. Notice together how sex is used to sell cars and clothes, lipstick and the latest gadgets. Determine that you will honor God with how you talk about sex and sexuality.

Teach your teenager about sexual purity.

This should be an ongoing conversation, "when you walk by the way, when you rise up" (Deuteronomy 6:7). And yet there should also come a moment in your young teenager's life when the parent gives a thorough, detailed teaching about sex.

Yes, the sex talk!

For most of you, your parents said absolutely nothing to you because their parents said absolutely nothing to them! Most parents are fearful because they don't know *how* to talk to their sons and daughters about sex. But as we make disciples of our own children, we dare not leave them ignorant of the temptations that will be thrown in their path. If you have been creating an easy openness about sex and sexuality, this talk will be at least a *little* easier.

PHIL:

I did have a one-time talk with each of my sons. With one son it went awful, the other was grateful!

The one who thought it was awful later said to me, "Dad, you did it way too early and you did it all wrong!"

I told him, "Well, at least I did it!"

My dad never said a word to me about sex, and the truth is, if he had I would have listened. And I wish he had, because I messed up in this area and I have the scars to show for it.

With my other son, it was easy and he was grateful for my attempt. We took a walk on the beach and at one point he simply said to me, "Okay, Dad, I've heard enough. I get it. You don't need to say any more."

Author and teacher Jim Burns reminds parents that in a world where most kids do not receive much input at all from their parents, "something is better than nothing."[8]

Teach your teenager what the Scriptures say about sexuality: that it is intended to be a gluing of two hearts together forever. That it is worth waiting for so they won't carry a bunch of baggage into their marriage. Teach them that God Himself is the author of sexuality. He thought it up! And He set some beautiful boundaries around it. Inside these boundaries, sex is a gift from God for our pleasure.

Teach them that if they mess up, they can be fully forgiven, but it will hurt them deeply. There will be scars. Teach them that the safety and security of one man and one woman for a lifetime of faithfulness is the way God designed sex to be experienced. Anything else and anything less is a misuse of this gift God gave us.

If you messed up in this area, this is a great time to share your story with your son or daughter. You don't need to provide details; that wouldn't be appropriate. But rather than withdraw because of your own sense of guilt, use your mistakes to openly talk about how you were harmed by choices you made. They *will* listen!

Also, be sure to let your son or daughter know that sexual purity is something they will have to fight for their entire lives. Marriage does not end the need to guard our hearts when it comes to sexual purity![9] Some kids raised in Christian homes seem to miss this vital fact. As a parent, your tasteful transparency in this matter can give your child the courage he needs to keep fighting for sexual purity even when it may seem overwhelming.

Be detailed in your teaching about sexual purity with your teenager. Your child needs to know about the prevalence of oral sex, about masturbation, wet dreams, and the dangers of pornography. Our children are growing up in a culture saturated by promiscuity. They cannot afford to be ignorant.

Finally, protect their sexual purity.

Your teenager will not always understand why you impose the rules and restrictions you feel are for his or her best. They do not have to understand!

The statistics regarding teenagers' exposure to pornography are sobering: "Nearly half of young adults say they come across porn at least once a week—even when they aren't seeking it out."[10] How in the world are parents to protect their children from something so pervasive?

DIANE:

I talk to many young women in their twenties, and do you know what they tell me? They wish their parents had protected them.

They wonder why their parents never bothered to look at their browsing history. They wish their parents had asked more questions like, "Are you absolutely sure his parents are going to be home?" They wish their parents had taken an active role in making sure they didn't put themselves in a vulnerable position they couldn't handle.

Even though these girls acted like they didn't want their mom or dad to interfere at the time, they now wish their parents had cared enough to protect them.

The stakes are incredibly high. Right at the moment when your teenager is developing his or her theology of sexuality, pornography seeks to expose them to every perversion possible.

"Pornography viewing by teens disorients them during the developmental phase when they have to learn how to handle their sexuality and when they are most vulnerable to uncertainty about their sexual beliefs and moral values."[11]

Remember that your teenager will not always understand *why* you impose the rules and restrictions you feel are in their best interest.

That's okay; be brave. It is your job to watch over your child and guard their purity until they are able to do it for themselves.

On a practical level, here are some ways to protect your teenager's purity:

- Make sure your teenager is not alone or unsupervised in your home with a member of the opposite sex.
- If your teenager is invited to someone's house, make sure those parents are home and that they share your value of guarding their sons' and daughters' purity. You'll probably feel awkward initiating this sort of conversation, but your child is worth it.
- Keep phones and computers in the open, where they can be supervised by an adult. Your teenager's phone is not private. For that matter, *your* phone is not private. Live openly and transparently in the community that is your family. At the same time, be clear that internet history will be frequently checked—not because you are distrustful, but because you understand the pull of pornography.
- Stay involved in your teenager's dating relationships. It's up to you to *work with them*. Don't abdicate that responsibility just because your son or daughter objects—the stakes are entirely too high. Be kind, listen, be reasonable and open, but still be the parent!
- Help your daughters find a balance between modesty and stylishness. Let them know how God wired men to respond visually. Impress on them the need to respect young men enough to choose to dress and act modestly. But be careful here! You don't want to communicate to your daughters that they are at fault if men come on to them.
- Watch over your teenager's reading materials, magazines, movies, music, and TV shows. Are these materials promoting promiscuity? Ask them. Let them know that

watching and reading certain things affect *you* negatively, and then let them watch over you too!

When our daughter Elizabeth was dating Brook, the man she would eventually marry, she was still living at home. We asked them to wait for us on the front porch if we weren't home yet. Both of them tell us now how much that helped them to keep their relationship pure, and Brook is convinced it even helped him harness his thoughts. It was awkward for all of us at times, but well worth it.

When your son or daughter talks to you about their battle for purity, keep your responses gentle and grace-filled. If they are afraid of your reaction, they will likely go underground where you cannot be a part of their reasoning process. And you need to be part of that process, even if it makes you uncomfortable at times.

Friends of ours had twin sons. As they were struggling to avoid the ever-present temptation of viewing pornography, they talked with their parents and together came up with one solution that helped. Whenever either of the boys was in the bathroom—a place that was a temptation for them when alone with the internet—they had to leave their iPhone on the floor outside the door. Their mom would smile and then remember to pray for her boys as she walked past that cell phone on the floor.

Today those young men serve on the same ship in the Navy, and they're still spurring each other on in their commitment to purity.

PHIL:

I strongly believe that a dad needs to protect his daughter's purity and stay involved in her dating life. When Elizabeth started dating Brook, a drummer, I joked with him that if I heard of him touching her inappropriately, I'd break his hands, and he'd never drum again.

It was all said light-heartedly, but he got the point! I wanted him to know I was watching. I wanted him to understand that it was a privilege to date my daughter, and I was allowing him limited access to her while he proved to me he would honor her.

Although Elizabeth was somewhat mortified by my involvement, now Brook and Elizabeth are married, and Brook has told us that he'll be at least as tough, if not more so, when their daughters are teenagers. My words to him as a teenager hit home. He valued my daughter more because he recognized the high price required to be with her.

Oh, and by the way, Brook and I were and still are great friends!

YOUR TEENAGER NEEDS YOU

Your teenager needs *you*. He may not know it. She may never admit it. But don't let that fool you! Your active, involved, interested, and protective presence in their lives is crucial.

We have identified five ways your teenager needs you.

Your Teenager Needs Your Presence

PHIL:

I was thirteen when a friend of mine came to me and said, "Let's start a rock band!" I said, "All I play is the trumpet." He said, "Well, I don't play anything!" So I picked the drums, he chose the guitar, and for the next nine years, that band was my life.

Here's the amazing thing: Instead of rolling their eyes and complaining about this loud new music, my parents invited us to practice in their family room.

My mom fed us her homemade fudge, while Dad gave his unabashed approval of how hard we worked to make our band successful. When we played at local high school dances, Dad came. He'd stand in the back and tell us we were great—on our way to stardom!

> Many years later, after saying "yes" to Jesus and "good-bye" to my band, I preached my first sermon. There was my dad in the back, tears in his eyes, his heart full of pride.
>
> My dad went out of his way to show interest in my life. Whatever I was into, he was too. I now know that this kind of support is rare. Too rare. Without a lot of words, my dad gave me *himself*: his interest, his time, and his presence. In short, he believed in me! Every son needs a dad who believes in him.

When your child enters the later teenage years, it is tempting to slip into the thinking that she no longer needs you like she once did. Your teenager is independent; he is capable and smart, no longer hanging on your every word, no longer needing or wanting your constant supervision. She has her own ideas and sometimes isn't all that diplomatic in the way she expresses her changing opinions.

These behaviors tempt parents to pull away, to put a safe distance of indifference between themselves and their teenage son or daughter. But listen to the findings of a new study:

"The Holy Grail for helping youth remain religiously active as young adults has been at home all along: parents! Mothers and fathers who practice what they preach and preach what they practice are far and away the major influence related to adolescents keeping the faith into their 20's."[12]

Dads, keep in mind that the early part of this stage and the latter part of the last stage (the upper elementary years) are excellent times to bring your kids along with you as you do life. Why? Because in those years they actually want to spend quality time with you! They think you can do no wrong and that you know everything! Take advantage of that season, because the later teenage years are coming when they'll suddenly think you don't know anything! Hence the saying, "Hire a teenager while he still knows everything."

Spend time intentionally with your teenager. Go out of your way to be a part of the things that interest him or her and include them in all aspects of your own life.

DIANE:

When our oldest kids were teenagers, I was shocked by some of their friends' hairstyles! Stiff, spikey hair that made them look like modern-day dinosaurs—I was sure that kids like that must be rebels! But Rebekah patiently showed me a different side of the story. She compelled me to see that what that wild-looking kid was really saying was that he was unique. Instead of following the preppy crowd—those I saw as clean-cut and entirely acceptable—he was determined to be his own man.

At the same time, both my teenagers let me know what was often going on behind that preppy look I preferred: drunken parties, immorality, and a lifestyle that was anything but clean.

No, my kids were not always sweet and nice about the way they corrected me. Sometimes my judgmental tendencies irritated my teenagers. But God used them to change the way I saw a generation of individualists, and I will be forever grateful to my kids for forcing me to see what they were really saying.

Serve Together

This is how Jesus trained His disciples: by working and living and laughing and talking together *a lot!* The disciples (some of whom may have been teenagers) watched, wide-eyed, as Jesus responded to his critics. They saw him forgive the unforgiveable. They looked on as he poured mercy on people who needed him. They listened as He prayed to His Father.

All that watching and living and being part of His life created a bond that caused them to fall in love with the Father.

PHIL:

While I was traveling with international evangelist Luis Palau, my daughter Rebekah came with me as a personal assistant from the time she was fifteen until she was twenty-three. She got to see much of the US and travel to England, witnessing thousands of people give their lives to Jesus.

Those years of traveling and serving shaped Rebekah, giving her confidence and igniting her love of travel. And we establishd a camaraderie that we still share, stories that are just ours, father/daughter memories of good times. Now, when I run into associates I worked with, they inevitably want to know all about what Bekah is up to.

Then, when we planted a church in Portland, my daughter Elizabeth sang on the worship team while I led worship. We loved those years of ministry together.

Our younger son, who was twelve at the time, taught four-year-olds their Bible lesson. Every Saturday after I finished my sermon preparations, I helped Matt with his lesson. We went over the story together and talked about what he would teach and how.

Finally, when Diane and I planted a church alongside John Mark, we got to experience the thrill of seeing God move powerfully. On Friday nights, he led a worship night called The Way, which grew to well over 1000 kids. We stood in the back and marveled at what God was doing through our son.

Cultivate Fellowship Together

Something nearly magical begins to happen during the early teenage years, and if you catch it and are careful with it, you will benefit from it for the rest of your life.

Your child begins to grow in spiritual wisdom and insight, and he or she spills that fresh insight onto you. A situation comes up, and she grabs your hand to pray with you about it because she knows you're worried, and she knows the best antidote to anxiety is prayer. Or you don't know what to do, so your son gives you wisdom straight from the Word—and it makes sense!

No one ever told us about this incredible facet of parenting teenagers. We just heard horror stories of rebellion and disrespect, as if that was what we should expect. But as each of our teenage children grew in their own relationship with God, they became our closest brothers and sisters. In fact, they still are! They remind us of what is true and right and of real value. They exhort us and sometimes correct us when our thinking is off. They pray with us and for us, and they offer real wisdom right when we need it.

They need your presence for sure, but they need more.

YOUR TEENAGER NEEDS YOUR ENCOURAGEMENT

We noticed a cycle during this stage of our teenager's lives. After a correction of any sort—reproving, rebuking, a restriction—they would deflate.

When they were younger, they would just bounce right back, but as teenagers they couldn't snap out of it so easily. With all the raging hormones and the constant peer pressure and all the rudeness that goes on in school, when we corrected them, they *sank*. Their attitudes would sink with them, which led to more rebuking and more deflating.

That's when we discovered afresh the power of encouragement. Encouragement is simply *giving courage*. In giving courage and lending our strength, they felt our belief in them when their belief in themselves faltered.

In statistics gathered in 2015, about three million teens ages twelve to seventeen had at least one major depressive episode in the past year. More than two million reported experiencing depression that impaired their daily ability to function. About 6.3 million teens have had an anxiety disorder.[13] These statistics seem to indicate that saying your teen needs your encouragement is a gross understatement!

Heaping encouragement onto your deflated teenager is the surest way for you to build up their courage so they can get up and keep going.

YOUR TEENAGER NEEDS YOUR AFFECTION

Yes, your teenager needs your protection and your discipline, and for sure they need your encouragement. But more than anything else, they need your *affection*. Give them tons of hugs, even if they stiffen up or back away.

A study by psychotherapist Virginia Satir concluded that people need at least twelve hugs every day in order to grow and thrive. Eight hugs a day are needed to maintain a stable level of emotional health, and a minimum of four hugs a day are considered necessary for survival.

Physical affection greatly increases our sense of happiness. "A hug, a pat on the back, and even a friendly handshake are processed by the reward center in the central nervous system, which is why they can have a powerful impact on the human psyche, making us feel happiness and joy."[14]

It is natural and normal for your teenager to pull away from you, but parents shouldn't pull away from their teenage sons or daughters. Teens need the assurance and sense of security your physical and verbal affection provides, and they need you to be the one to initiate affection that asks for nothing in return. Your affection assures your teenager that you like them when sometimes it seems to them that *no one does*—when they do not even like themselves very much.

Be careful about that sarcastic sense of humor that brought laughs from your grade-school children. In these teenage years, that kind of humor is rarely appreciated and can do subtle damage to your teen's already fragile emotions.

Is your teenager oversensitive? Yes, probably. But their oversensitivity is only a symptom. He or she may be showing you that attacks from the world they live in, the craziness of their changing body, and a general sense of not being good enough are conspiring to bring them to a low place. When you assure your teenager with fond words and warm affection, you may well be rescuing him from a place of dangerous vulnerability.

This is another time when the concept of the lamp and the light come to your aid. By working together and listening to each other, we were able to be more aware of our teenager's emotional needs. It was often Diane who saw through the façade hiding the fragile emotions of our teenage children. On the other hand, when she was growing up, it was most often her father who saw Diane's need for gentleness and tender affection. John Eldredge was right when he said that every boy is asking the question, *Do I have what it takes?* and every girl is asking, *Am I lovely?*

Dads, you hold the answers to both of those questions. Your sons and daughters are looking to you, in all their vulnerability, to shout a resounding "Yes!" If you fail to give them that affirmation, they may look for it elsewhere. Sadly, that elsewhere can end up leaving damaging scars.

Phil had one of those rare chances to open a door for our daughter Elizabeth when she was in high school. A vulnerable moment that could have led to resentment instead led her to courageous faith.

PHIL:

We were living in southern Oregon when it became clear to Diane and me that the Lord was calling us north to Portland to plant a church. The day came when we had to sit down and tell our daughter Elizabeth that we were moving.

She was sixteen and about to begin her senior year of high school. Everything was going well in her life. She had great friends, was doing well in school, and was enthusiastically involved in a great church. She was thriving in every way.

When I sat her down to give her the news, she said, "Dad, can you give me a few minutes?" She went into her room and closed the door. Ten minutes later she came out, and with a tear rolling down her cheek, said, "We're supposed to go. Dad, will you sing me a worship song?"

I picked up my guitar and began to sing a song we both knew from church. With tears now streaming down both cheeks, she began singing with me. When I asked her where she learned to sing like that, she said, "I don't know." But I saw in that moment that she had a great voice and could even sing harmony parts! Without realizing it, she'd learned how to sing during the worship services at the church we were part of. I told her that when we planted this church, I wanted her to sing with me on the worship team.

When she protested, saying, "Dad, I could never do that!" I told her I knew she could; she had the voice, and she had the relationship with God.

"You can do this," I said. "I know you can."

Thus began a new adventure for all of us, and for several beautiful years a father and a daughter got to serve the Lord side by side in ministry together. And guess who was behind us playing the drums? You guessed it! Brook, the young man who would later become her husband.

You'll hear people say, "Never move your kids during high school." In most cases, I'd agree. But there's one exception: Move if the Lord is moving you! When He is leading, and we follow by faith, He causes all things to work out according to His purposes.

When we delivered the news that day, my daughter didn't kick and scream and say, "How could you do this to me? How could you take me away from my friends right before my senior year?" She was able to go into her room and spend a few minutes with Jesus, surrendering to His plan for her, then walk out and say, "We're supposed to move."

> Elizabeth was able to do this because she had become "rooted and established" in her own very real faith. We pray that you will be able to experience something similar one day with your teenage son or daughter. There's nothing like it!

It will take an immense amount of time for you to navigate these teenage years wisely and well. As writer, teacher, and parent Charles Swindoll said, "Don't be fooled by the 'quality time' myth. Quantity time is what will be required of you as a parent—your primary role in life over the next several years. It takes time to know someone else deeply. Lots of time. Time you don't think you have but must find. Time to stop, look, listen, encourage, and love. Time, looking back, you'll never regret."[15]

Well said.

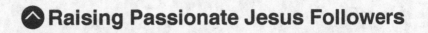Raising Passionate Jesus Followers

Installing the Functional Systems
(13 to 17 yrs.)

The aim is to help your child develop a heart of *godliness*. In this stage, you want to see their faith become their own.

Nearing the end of this stage, your child...

☐ Understands the why and the how of dealing with temptation.

☐ Establishes a personal commitment to purity.

☐ Knows what he / she is good at.

☐ Is hard working.

☐ Is involved in the community of the church.

☐ Loves hanging out with their family.

☐ Has developed a consistent personal time with God.

☐ Chooses friends wisely.

4 THINGS YOU WILL NEED ...

1. *COURAGE* to stand against the tide (Josh 1v9).

2. *PERSEVERANCE* to keep the training going (Heb 5v14; 1 Tim 4v8).

3. *DETERMINATION* to keep your family close.

4. *WISDOM* to navigate through this season (James 1v5; 2 Chr 20v12).

3 THINGS YOUR TEENAGER WILL NEED ...

1. *DISCOVER* what they're good at (Prov 22v6; 22v29).

2. *GUARD* their purity (Prov 4v23).

3. *YOU* ...
   - your presence
   - your encouragement
   - your affection

3 SECRETS TO DISCIPLINE DURING THE TEENAGE YEARS ...

1. *THE BOX*

2. *SWITCH ROLES*

3. *THE PROCESS AND POWER* OF APPEAL

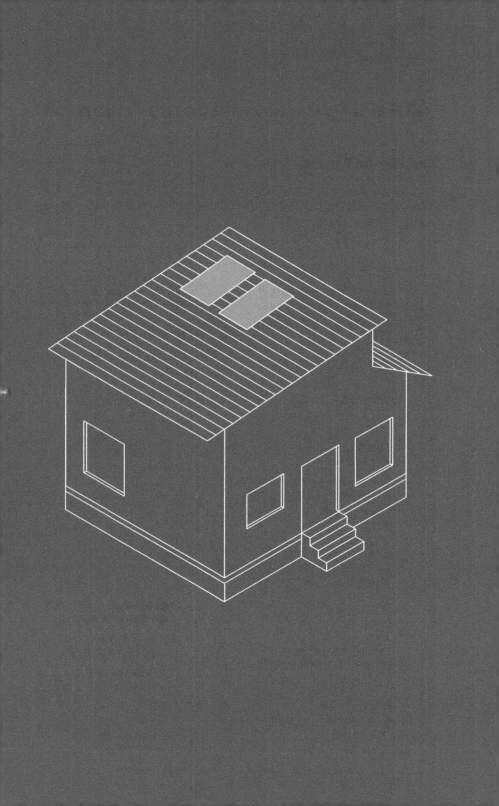

Part 5

Completing the Finish Work

Ages 18–22

Thus Solomon finished the house of the LORD
and the King's palace, and successfully completed
all that he had planned on doing in the house
of the LORD and in his palace.

2 CHRONICLES 7:11 NASB

Chapter 18

The Box Now

The final stage of building a house is called the finish work. Plywood counters are overlaid with tile or honed stone. Thick carpet and stained wood cover the floors. Molding wraps the rooms in elegance while the fireplace boasts a finely crafted mantle.

Your home is now complete!

After months of work, you step back and smile with satisfaction at the vision in front of you. Your dreams and plans have come to fruition, and your house looks like home.

Both times we built houses, when we came to this finish stage of construction, we ran out of money! This is so frustrating, because this is where all the beauty of design comes together. We learned the hard way that the budget doesn't really cover everything. Because we ran out of money, we couldn't finish our finish work!

May we urge you, in these last couple of years of raising your sons and daughters, don't run out of "money!" Keep at it a little longer; you're not done yet. Whoever decided to tell parents that their job is done when their child reaches eighteen had it all wrong. There is still essential work to be done.

Finishing well is an oft-repeated refrain in Scripture. The Bible says, "And so Moses finished the work" (Exodus 40:33).

Paul declared, "I have fought the good fight, I have finished the race, I have kept the faith" (2 Timothy 4:7).

Paul urged the Corinthians, "Now finish the work, so that your eager willingness to do it may be matched by your completion of it, according to your means" (2 Corinthians 8:11).

Moses finished his work, Paul finished his work, and Paul admonished the Corinthians to finish their work.

Above all, *Jesus* finished *His* work. He said to the Father, "I have brought you glory on earth by finishing the work you gave me to do" (John 17:4).

You started out eighteen years ago, working hard to lay a strong foundation. You managed to survive both the toddler and teenage years! Don't quit now. Finish! Finish! Finish!

Remember The Box? The bottom is Jesus, one side is discipline, the other side is order, and the much-needed top of The Box is the affection, affirmation, and fun our kids crave. In this final stage, The Box is still there, but its shape has changed dramatically. It looks like this:

Jesus is still there; your conversations still revolve around Him. He will always be the foundation of your relationship with your children. And affection, affirmation, and fun are more important than ever.

This is when you get to be friends! You have so much in common now, and your sons and daughters need your encouragement to get through what experts warn us can be the most confusing and anxiety-prone stage of their lives.[1] But the ordering of their everyday lives is no longer your primary responsibility, and the discipline you used in order to train them and shape their character is now minimal and rare.

During these finishing years, you will want to remember an important principle: *don't overcorrect!* Don't nitpick your son or daughter at this stage of their growth. Maybe there is something you tried to teach them, but they're still not doing it to your satisfaction.

You don't want to defeat your son or squelch your daughter as they make their first attempts at independent adulthood. That's not how God deals with His children. Billy Graham wisely observed, "God does not discipline us to subdue us, but to condition us for a life of usefulness and blessedness."[2]

Your son or daughter is already stepping (albeit imperfectly) into a life of usefulness. Give them your approval for the things they are doing right. Build them up and spur them on in their relationship with Jesus.

As Bob Goff says, "God isn't an editor, He's a creator; He's not looking for typos in our lives, He's looking for the beauty in them."[3] May we be the kind of parents who see the beauty in our children's lives!

If you have been doing the work of training your kids to be Jesus followers for many years, by this stage you are simply guiding them, reminding them, and refining them—making minor tweaks as you hand them more and more responsibility for their own lives.

This is the stage of their lives when you want to practice respecting your differences as you recognize that God desires your son or daughter to live out their own unique calling.

GOALS AND VALUES

At the beginning of this book, we talked about the difference between goals and values. Your one, overarching goal is that your child will grow up to love the Lord their God with all their strength, mind, and heart, and to love people on purpose.

As for that list of values, those ways of doing life that you really hoped they'd adopt as their own, but just haven't—well, at this stage you simply have to let it go. We're not talking about moral values, here, but about everyday ways of living. You tried your best, and your son just doesn't get why a perfectly ordered, color-coordinated closet is such a big deal! Or why keeping his elbows off the table when he's eating is so important.

Just let it go!

You may not have been able to teach them manners, but now it's his problem, not yours. Eventually, it will be his wife's problem! His boss, friends, and coworkers will all be weighing in with whatever annoys them. Now is the time for you to back off and just give him that rare, unconditional love every one of us longs for.

Do not destroy your relationship with your nearly adult kids by insisting they adhere to your particular values. If you push your children to adopt every one of your values as they grow into adulthood, you will alienate them. Sensing disapproval from you, they will back away. So instead of pushing your son or daughter to comply with the way you prefer to do life, be thankful that he or she is heading towards the goal of following Jesus. What could be better than that?

Thousands of years ago, through the prophet Isaiah, God warned about a people whose "worship of Me is nothing but man-made rules learned by rote" (Isaiah 29:13 NLT). That's the last thing we want for our kids! We must be careful not to dilute our children's passion for God by imposing our own "man-made rules" as they become adults.

Remember, Mom and Dad, that even though your job is *nearing* completion, God is far from done! The Father will never stop doing His work in both you and your child. Paul describes this beautifully in Philippians 1:6:

"For I *am* confident of this very thing, that He who began a good work in you will continue His work until it is finally finished on the day when Christ Jesus returns."[4]

Chapter 19

The List

The countdown has begun. In just a few months, your eighteen-to twenty-two-year-old will be completely on their own. Ready or not, it will be time for you to launch your son or daughter into the world. Your primary job will be done.

Some kids will be ready and raring to go. Others will lag behind a little, loving the freedom but reluctant to take on the responsibilities that come with adulthood. In fact, in 2015 the "new word of the year" was a verb: *adulting*. Webster's tongue-in-cheek description:

> "If you haven't heard it (or don't use it) already, you'll hear it soon: adult as a verb, as in 'Someone please teach me how to adult.'"

If your son or daughter is finding *adulting* a little daunting, don't despair! Instead, adopt the patient outlook of Paul, who spent years instructing and teaching God's people how to live out their God-centered values in real life, yet found they continued to need more:

> "As for other matters, brothers and sisters, we instructed you how to live in order to please God, as in fact you are living. Now we ask you and urge you in the Lord Jesus to do this more and more." (1 Thessalonians 4:1)

Many, if not most, young adults need *more* of your patient instruction and training during this stage. You have this one last opportunity, before your son or daughter leaves the shelter of your influence, to fill in the gaps. Remember, your highest priority is to raise kids who don't just *profess* a faith, but who actually *possess* a real faith, kids who love God with all their heart, soul, mind, and strength—and who love people on purpose.

TEN THINGS YOU'VE GOT TO TEACH YOUR KIDS

A few years ago, Phil was invited to a lunch with pastors in the Portland area featuring Francis Chan as the speaker. Instead of talking about church growth, or how to preach great messages, or any of the likely topics for a gathering of pastors, Francis spoke personally to the room full of leaders about what was on his own heart as his daughter entered her last year of high school.

"My daughter will be leaving for college soon," he said. "I only have one year left with her under my roof, and there are so many things I want to know she understands—things I want to be sure have become part of her life."

Every pastor in the room leaned forward as Chan rattled off a list of ten things he felt compelled to impress on his daughter before she left home for college. Since our last son, Matthew, was living at home while attending a nearby college, Phil couldn't take notes fast enough!

We talked late into the night about Chan's list, his sense of urgency rubbing off on us. Then we made a list of our own, specific things we'd been talking and instructing our son about that we needed to urge him into, as Paul said, more and more.

We encourage you to do the same. Make a list—your own list—of what your son or daughter still needs. Even better, begin that list early in your child's life.

Together, come up with the top ten (or twenty!) things you know your son or daughter needs in order to function as a fully devoted follower of Jesus.

These are not things you begin working on at age eighteen. They are the values that you will teach to your children for years—starting when they are very young—with the aim, the hope, and the prayer that they will become firm personal convictions in the life of your son or daughter. Then, by the process of reverse engineering, you decide when and how to teach and train your child in each of your top ten things. You want your child to not just understand *how to*, but actually *be able to* put these values into practice.

To Stand Firm

Our young adult children need to be consciously developing their own convictions by this age, convictions about how to live and who to befriend, about honesty and healthy relationships. They need to have an understanding of their own values—the values that drive them—accompanied by an inward determination to live by those convictions.

In Ephesians 6:10–11, Paul used a battle metaphor to help his people understand what is involved in learning to stand strong against the barrage of persuasive temptation each of us face. He warns us not to simply assimilate the beliefs and values of the world around us:

> "Finally, be strong in the Lord and in the strength of His might.
> Put on the full armor of God, so that you will be able to stand
> firm against the schemes of the devil. For our struggle is not
> against flesh and blood, but against the rulers, against the
> powers, against the world forces of this darkness, against the
> spiritual *forces* of wickedness in the heavenly *places*. Therefore,
> take up the full armor of God, so that you will be able to resist in
> the evil day, and having done everything, to stand firm." (NASB)

Paul attaches a list to his exhortation to stand strong in the face of opposition, a list of specific ways to shield and strengthen ourselves so that we will stand rather than fall in the "day of evil". Keep in mind that the Greek word translated "evil" in this passage (*ponērós*) is not speaking of haunted houses and horror flicks. The word refers to "evil in a moral or spiritual sense . . . evil which corrupts others, is malignant."[1]

You want your son or daughter to be so strong in the Lord, so firm in their convictions that they will not be swayed by peer pressure. If they find themselves in a situation they shouldn't be, with friends pushing them to do things they shouldn't do—no problem! They will know when to speak up and when to flee.

We do well to teach our children how to exercise their willful determination to stick with what they believe. By acknowledging that peer pressure and people-pleasing are powerful forces that can derail our determination to stay true to our beliefs, we stand alongside our kids to give them the courage to stand strong in their own convictions. We teach them to make intentional decisions based not on what they feel in the moment but on the convictions they have made their own.

Then, and only then, will they have what Jesus promised when he said, "The thief comes only to steal, kill, and destroy; I have come that they might have life, and have it to the full" (John 10:10).

To Stay Sexually Pure

Paul says in 1 Thessalonians 4:3–6:

> "It is God's will that you should be sanctified; that you should avoid sexual immorality; that each of you should learn to control your own body in a way that is holy and honorable, not in passionate lust like the pagans, who do not know God; and that in this matter no one should wrong or take advantage of a brother or sister."

Never stop talking about sexual purity! Keep the conversation going. "How are you doing with internet temptations, son?" "Have you come to an agreement with your boyfriend about physical boundaries, honey?" These conversations need to be happening "when you sit at home and when you walk along the road, when you lie down and when you get up" (Deuteronomy 6:7).

This is not just about their virginity, as beautiful and important as that is for your unmarried children to maintain. It is about sexual *purity*, which also involves reining in lust, knowing what to do about temptation, what kinds of standards to maintain in dating, what movies or places might trigger temptation, and how to express affection without crossing the line to passion. Both mothers and fathers need to be actively and openly teaching their sons and daughters why and how to guard their own purity for the rest of their lives.

More than anything, your kids need to understand that guarding their purity is a life-long quest. We are in this together, honoring God with our sexuality. We know it's hard; we all encounter failures along the way, but we bring those mess-ups to the Father for forgiveness and strength to go on.

PHIL:

After college and two hospital jobs in her hometown of Portland, Oregon, my daughter Rebekah took a temporary job in the Los Angeles area as a respiratory therapist. She said, "Dad, I think I'll take this travel job for three to six months or so. I'm ready for a fun adventure!"

Just before she was planning on coming home, Rebekah met Steve, who eventually became her husband. Not knowing Steve at all, but knowing they were growing serious about each other, I hopped on a plane and flew down to meet him.

I took him out for coffee, which made Rebekah really nervous.

"Your daughter is so beautiful in every way," Steve said to me over our coffees.

"I know she is." I looked him in the eye then and said, "I've been guarding Rebekah's purity all her life, and I am asking you to do the same."

Years earlier, I had given Rebekah a small diamond ring to wear as a "promise ring," a sign of her covenant with the Lord to keep herself pure until her wedding day. What I didn't know until just before their wedding was that Steve's dad, a pastor in Canada, had done the same thing with his son!

One day, shortly before the wedding, my phone rang. It was Bekah.

"Dad, you're going to be doing our vows and handing us our rings. We want you to tell our friends that Steve and I saved ourselves for each other, and that we melted our promise rings into his wedding ring."

I could hardly hold back the tears as I held those rings for a few short moments before Steve and Rebekah placed them on each other's fingers. I will never forget it.

While this may not be everyone's story—it wasn't mine—why not pray that your sons and daughters will remain sexually pure and enter marriage as virgins? That is God's plan, and it's a beautiful one!

To Know How to Choose a Husband or Wife

When our sons were in this stage of early adulthood, each of them approached Diane with the same question: *How will I know who I should marry? What should I be looking for in a wife?* Both times, Diane, being a writer, wrote a series of letters to her sons to answer that question.

She called her letters to John Mark, "In Search of Eve," and sent them off by snail mail every few weeks during his first year of college. As John Mark read those letters, he began to get a growing sense that his "Eve" was emerging right before his eyes. His best friend's sister, Tammy, seemed to exhibit the very character traits Diane was articulating week after week. Plus, he thought she was gorgeous!

As he observed the gentle way she related to her family and friends, her beauty, and her servant-hearted life, he began to allow his heart to fall in love with her. She was the kind of woman he wanted to spend the rest of his life with: a co-laborer who would be sympathetic to his calling, the kind of woman who would help raise their children with shared values, and a partner with whom he could join to discover their mission together.

By the time Matt asked the same question, Diane had begun writing a blog. With his permission, she posted each of her letters to him as part of a series named "Letters to My Son"[2] as a means of teaching both men and women about who they should strive to be, as well as what to look for in a life partner.

As Matt read each post, he was given insight into what to watch for, what to avoid, and how to be himself while dating. While he was reading his mom's advice, so were hundreds of other young people, many of whom are now married.

Later, John Mark wrote a book titled *Loveology*.[3] In it he laid out a biblical theology of love, sex, and marriage for a generation of young people who grew up with a highly fantasized, fairy-tale view of love and romance. We strongly advise you to pick up this book and read it with your son or daughter. You will gain a clear picture of God's purpose and plan for marriage and dating.

Don't leave this most important of decisions to chance. Guide your son or daughter, giving them helpful insights into what you know about them. One of the saddest stories we've heard repeatedly is of good Christian parents who don't think it's their place to "interfere."

After a friend's husband left her for another woman, her parents told her, "We were concerned about this when you were dating. We hoped and prayed that you wouldn't marry him." This dear woman raised her two daughters alone, struggling to forgive her parents for not speaking up before the wedding. Her respect for her parents was so great that she's sure she would have listened to them.

You need to ask God for the courage to speak up—in gentleness and humility—when you sense things that concern you. Although the conversation may be difficult, over the long haul you'll be glad you did.

To Know How to Handle Money

Before your son or daughter begins to be responsible for their own support, make sure they know basic biblical and practical concepts about the stewardship of finances: how to make a budget, how to stick to a budget, how to stay out of debilitating debt, what to do with credit and debit card offers, and why paying bills on time matters.

Do this vigilantly, because if you don't, and they get into financial trouble, do you know who they'll call first? You!

Help your adult children to make a conscious choice about the lifestyle they wish to live and how much it will cost. Before choosing a college major or a career, make sure they are realistic about financial earnings and the demands their chosen profession will require of them.

Teach them the joy of generosity and the faith involved in tithing (giving 10% of their income) right off the top.[4] The earlier they learn the joy and discipline of tithing, the better. If they learn to tithe when they are earning one hundred dollars per week, it will be easy to keep it up one day when they earn one thousand dollars a week. Those who say, "Someday, when I'm making more money, I'll start tithing" are fooling themselves. It works in reverse. As we are faithful over little, God provides more.[5] Show them that consistently setting aside savings from an early age compounds interest and provides for their future.

More than anything, teach your children that every part of their lives belongs to God, that they are stewards of every penny in their pockets, that allowing God to guide and guard their spending will ensure a life of adventure and faith.

To Have a Consistent Time with God

Both of us came to know Jesus in early adulthood. The church that embraced and taught us emphasized the importance of developing a personal morning time set aside for Bible reading. Publications were made available to those who had the discipline to read through the Bible in a year, and both of us rose to the challenge. Thus began a rhythm of early morning devotions in which we fed on God's Word.

Spending time in God's Word morning by morning is a spiritual discipline that your kids have hopefully been watching you consistently engage in for years, a habit that, by now, you cannot imagine missing. It is also, you hope, a habit your kids can't imagine missing for themselves. "Holy habits are that: disciplines, routines by which we stay alive and focused on Him. At first we choose them and carry them out; after a while they are part of who we are. And they carry us."[6]

DIANE:

For all the years I have known him, Phil has read through the entire Bible every year. In January he starts in Genesis, reading two chapters in the Old Testament, one chapter of Proverbs, a Psalm, and one chapter in the New Testament. Every morning he gets up, brews a strong cup of coffee, sits in his favorite chair and opens his Bible. He reads his assigned chapters and checks off the corresponding box. Every morning! No wonder I call him my walking concordance! I'll ask him where that verse is that says (fill in the blank), and he'll know, if not the exact chapter and verse, at least which book of the Bible, and approximately where it is, or on what side of the page.[7]

I followed Phil's example for many years, walking my way from beginning to end, filling up on the wisdom in every story, on every page. Eventually, the habit became for me a difficult must-do, a chore. I read my Bible because I felt I ought to, because being disciplined is important, because I knew I should. Then, a few years ago, I began to pray about whether this method was the best one for me. As I quieted my "ought-tos," I realized that the method that worked so well for Phil wasn't working for me anymore.

Every day when I read my Bible, I had a gazillion questions that begged for answers, for study, for research and further thought—I grew more and more frustrated as those same questions snagged my curiosity, going unanswered year after year.

I decided to slow it down, to read and study and open commentaries and mull over passages over and over. I loved it! I felt fed and satisfied. I began to get up earlier in order to have longer to feast on God's Word. It no longer felt like a discipline, because my heart craved more and more!

Those early morning times of listening to God as I slowly chew on His Words have become my favorite time of day. He speaks to me through His Word, walking with me at my naturally slow pace, storing up wisdom I need for the days ahead.

Two different people, with two different methods, resulting in the same reward. Neither one of us would ever consider skipping that time alone with God in the Scriptures. We have each found a method that is well-suited to who we are.

By this early adulthood stage, your children need to have discovered not only the importance of developing their own consistent time with God, but also their own way of engaging His Word, the way that works best for who they are and the stage of life they are in.

Your aim and prayer is that by the time they leave home they will consistently rise *early* to sit at the feet of Jesus—just as Mary did—with their Bible and a pen in hand. Luke observed that, "Jesus often withdrew to lonely places and prayed" (Luke 5:16).

They need to have an understanding of their purpose in reading their Bibles every morning: to feast on God Himself, to gather wisdom, to listen and to learn what the Spirit wants to talk to them about. This is so much more than a rigid discipline! Brushing your teeth is a discipline—curling up with your Bible to listen to and learn from God is a delight!

To Know Where to Find Key Passages in Scripture for Life's Challenges

Our kids need to know where to turn when life throws them a hardball or a curveball. For those inevitable times when they've blown it and they feel the shame of their guilt—is there a Scripture or a story for that?

Or when worry is keeping them uptight and touchy—is there a way to peace, a word in God's Word that will alleviate their fretfulness before it becomes full-blown anxiety?

How about when sexual temptation seems overwhelming? Is there a place to go in the Scriptures to gain a deeper understanding of what it's about and what they can do about it?

As parents, we cannot afford to be ignorant! If you, in your twenties, thirties, forties, or beyond, still do not know where to search for answers to real-life dilemmas, your young adult children are liable to dismiss the Bible as irrelevant, even archaic. After all, if Dad's done fine without knowing where to look in the Scriptures, it's obviously not all that important!

PHIL:

When John Mark was 9, he came to me and asked, "Dad, where in the Bible does it talk about sticking with things?" Then, the next day, "Where is the story of the Good Samaritan?" We need to know how to find those answers as we guide our kids into the truth!

By the way, it's okay to say, "I don't know, but let's go find out together!"

A word of advice: keep track of your own discoveries as you come across Scriptures that help you go through times of hardship or temptation. Write them in the margins of your Bible or in a journal kept for that purpose. Then, when your teenage son comes to you with a problem, you'll know right where to point him. You will have your own story of how you came upon this passage and how it helped. If you do this, you'll be passing on a rich legacy!

John G. Mitchell, who founded Multnomah University, used to humorously prod his students into knowing the Word of God by asking, "Where's this verse?" and when no one could answer, he'd say, "Don't you folks ever read your Bibles?" He had much of the Bible memorized from decades of reading through the Bible over and over again. Today, a plaque greets visitors to the campus library with Dr. Mitchell's words.

To be wise parents, we need to delve deeply into the Scriptures ourselves and then encourage our kids to develop the same practice.

To Live Missionally

What does living missionally mean? That our purpose in life is not to build a nice, tight, Christian safe place, but to go about our everyday lives serving and loving and bringing Jesus into every corner.

When our children were young, the hot topic in many churches was evangelism: how to share your faith and bring someone to a saving knowledge of the Savior. Leading someone to Jesus usually meant a brief explanation of the gospel and a repeat-after-me prayer to receive Christ. Nothing wrong with that!

Now a new generation of preachers is showing us a way of living in authentic community, a way of doing life together that is so genuinely appealing that the people around us want to know more about who God is. Instead of just inviting them to church, we bring the church to them.

Thus, the church has become more of a serving place, and not just a place to serve. We serve each other, and we serve our communities. Outreach is about giving, loving, making other people's lives good, meeting real needs. Then we can share the hope we have in Jesus, introducing those who are ready to the One who compels us to love.

Our time belongs to Jesus, and we are called to use it to make this world a better place. Our home belongs to Him, so we invite our neighbors in for a meal, sharing our bounty and our love with them. And while we are loving and serving our neighbors, we are praying for an open door to share the Good News.

As Christians make themselves servants to the world around them instead of retreating into a carefully sanitized bubble, the world notices and responds to our message of redemption for all. What a respectful and Jesus-honoring way to live with our neighbors!

It is when we are living missionally, not perfectly, that we get to answer people's queries about the love of God that is shining through us.

To Love the Church

Make it your quest to be sure your kids understand the importance of being part of a Bible-teaching, Jesus-focused, Spirit-led church—a church where He is at the center, on the throne, and clearly lifted up in every way. It is within this kind of church that your kids will grow to "love Jesus, learn the way of Jesus, and live on the mission of Jesus."[8]

It is in close community with God's people that our children will learn and grow and flourish in following after Jesus. As Jan Johnson writes, "I have become convinced that we learn about God best through relationship with each other. There are certain things about God we don't grasp until we see them in another person . . . community enables transformation because spiritual disciplines are as much caught as taught."[9]

Your nearly adult children need to know that church is not "just that place I go to, but something I'm part of." You want them to understand that the church is actually the family of God, and they are an integral part of it.

You want to raise your kids so firmly in this conviction that when they move away, the first thing they will do is find a good church, and they wouldn't even think about not going to the gathering on Sunday and being part of the community.

PHIL:

It always blesses me when one of the young people in our church sends me an email or comes up to me and says, "I'm moving to Seattle . . . or L.A . . . or Boise. Do you know of a good church there?" It tells me they know this is vital to their walk with Jesus. That they've already decided that they are going to need to gather with God's people.

To Learn to Listen to the Spirit

We continue to be surprised and dismayed by the reality that the vast majority of men and women in our churches have yet to learn to listen to God.

Bible study and Bible reading are wonderful and wise, but as we miss learning to listen to God speaking to each of us individually, we miss out on the intimacy we were created to crave. Every one of us has a longing for that close connection with the One who loves us like no other.

Jesus devoted His last conversations with His disciples almost entirely to this essential skill:

"All this I have spoken while still with you. But the Advocate, the Holy Spirit, whom the Father will send in my name, will teach you all things and will remind you of everything I have said to you. Peace I leave with you; my peace I give you. I do not give to you as the world gives. Do not let your hearts be troubled and do not be afraid." (John 14:25–27)

"I have much more to say to you, more than you can now bear. But when he, the Spirit of truth, comes, he will guide you into all the truth." (John 16:12–13)

"He calls his own sheep by name and leads them out. When he has brought out all his own, he goes on ahead of them, and his sheep follow him because they know his voice . . . I am the good shepherd; I know my sheep and my sheep know me—just as the Father knows me and I know the Father . . . My sheep listen to my voice; I know them and they follow me." (John 10:3–4, 14–15, 27)

God has spoken and God is still speaking.

"In the past God spoke to our ancestors through the prophets at many times and in various ways, but in these last days he has spoken to us by his Son, whom he appointed heir of all things, and through whom also he made the universe." (Hebrews 1:1–2)

When we read the red-lettered words of Jesus, God the Son is speaking. And remember that God speaks primarily through the Scriptures:

"All Scripture is God-breathed and is useful for teaching, for rebuking, correcting and training in righteousness, so that the servant of God may be thoroughly equipped for every good work." (2 Timothy 3:16–17)

Take note that in the verse preceding this passage, Paul is reminding young Timothy of his godly heritage:

"But as for you, continue in what you have learned and have become convinced of, because you know those from whom you learned it, and how from infancy you have known the Holy Scriptures . . ." (2 Timothy 3:14–15)

This is a truth every parent, as well as every Jesus-following grandparent, can stand strong on!

But God speaks in other ways too. Through creation, for one:

"The heavens proclaim the glory of God. The skies display his craftsmanship. Day after day they continue to speak; night after night they make him known. They speak without a sound or word, their voice is never heard. Yet their message has gone throughout the earth, and their words to all the world . . ." (Psalm 19:1–4 NLT)

God has been known to speak to individuals through dreams and visions,[10] through prophets and people in the church,[11] through those with whom we are in close community, as well as through imagery.[12]

God's words to us are primarily felt, an impression that doesn't sound like the way we talk to ourselves, a sense that He is leading, that He has things to show us if we will only pay attention. King David learned this skill over a lifetime of worshiping and listening:

"Show me your ways, LORD, teach me your paths. Guide me in your truth and teach me, for you are God my Savior, and my hope is in you all day long." (Psalm 25:4–5)

As we sit before the Lord, Bibles open, hearts eager to obey, He shows us His ways! He encourages us, he reproves us, and sometimes He rebukes us. But His rebukes feel like salve to our souls. Often, He gives us the specific wisdom we ask for, helping us to know how to navigate the ups and downs of life. When it comes to parenting, He is especially generous in giving us great doses of insight into our children!

Once a man, woman, or child learns to love and recognize the voice of God, to lean in and listen to what He is saying to them individually, that's when they become all-in, fully devoted followers of Jesus.

Without that knowing, that close connection, our faith can become simply a complex set of moral codes to live by. We run the risk of becoming what Dallas Willard called, "very proper spiritual corpses filling our pews."[13]

In Diane's book, *He Speaks in the Silence*, she tells her own story of learning to listen to God and how that listening led her into the intimacy with God her soul longed for.[14]

To Have a Theology of Suffering

DIANE:

When I was twenty-six, I was diagnosed with a progressive hearing loss—I was going deaf. Doctors gave me little hope for a cure, instead urging me to get fitted for hearing aids and warning me that at the current rate of loss, I would be completely deaf within just a few years.

I had three young children, a godly husband, and a custom-created pop theology that could not support the concept that God would allow me to lose my hearing.

My faith began to disintegrate as rapidly as my hearing. I was so angry at God, doubting His goodness, questioning His character, viciously lashing out at God about how He was being unfaithful and unfair to me. I felt abandoned and misused by a God I had committed my life to serving.

I fell into a deep, dark depression that I could not climb out of—all because I had a faulty theology of suffering. It was basically this:

God loves me and has a wonderful plan for my life. Therefore, of course God wants to heal me! Because if I was God, I would heal me.

When He didn't, I went into a tailspin of self-pity and despair, and Satan's age-old lie crept in just like when he tempted Eve. It sounds something like this:

I know God could heal me if He wanted to. It doesn't take much faith to believe that the One who made my ears can fix them. So why won't He?

My conclusion? God must not be good, or He wouldn't allow this to happen to me.

This is exactly what some of your children may conclude when they encounter suffering in their own lives. We have seen it over and over, enough to see a dangerous pattern that we feel compelled to warn parents about: young people from really good, godly, Jesus-centered homes who wind up rejecting Jesus—not in a slow drift of disinterest but in a terrible burst of disillusionment and anger. And when you start to dig a little into their stories, it often comes back to this: a weak Biblical understanding of suffering. Like Diane, they thought following Jesus meant everything would go well in their lives.

What nearly shipwrecked Diane's faith might well destroy your son or daughter's trust in God. As parents, we have the privilege and the real-life opportunities to teach our children a solidly Scriptural theology of suffering.

Jesus told His followers that they would suffer. He said, "I have told you these things, so that in me you may have peace. In this world you will have trouble. But take heart! I have overcome the world" (John 16:33). And the apostle Paul prayed, "that I may know Him and the power of His resurrection and the fellowship of His sufferings" (Philippians 3:10 NASB). Bad things do happen to good people—even God's people! This doesn't mean that God causes the suffering, but He is gracious and loving enough to make it count—He will use our suffering for our good.

DIANE:

Fortunately, my story doesn't end with my angry rejection of God. At Phil's urging I went to the elders of my church to ask them to anoint me with oil and pray for healing. What followed was an experience with God that was so intimate and surprising that it changed my entire life! God brought healing that day in the back room of a church in Santa Cruz, California—a healing I didn't even know I needed—a healing of my heart. Soon after, He gave me Psalm 40 as the song I will sing for the rest of my life.

Psalm 40:6 (KJV) says,

"Mine ears hast thou opened . . ."

Or, as the New Living Translation reveals,

"Now that you have made me listen, I finally understand . . ."

He set me on a quest to know and experience His love and all the beautiful intimacy with the Savior I had not even known was possible.

He didn't heal my ears, but He did heal *me*.

Diane is deaf now—completely, irrevocably deaf. In the endorsement he wrote for his mom's book about her journey into deafness, John Mark penned these words:

"When I think back to my childhood, one memory sticks out over all the noise; every morning I would walk down the stairs and find my mom sitting in her chair, Bible open, pen in hand, eyes focused but distant. She was hearing the one voice that could bypass her deafness. My mom taught me how to listen to God . . ."

DIANE:

Now I see what I couldn't possibly grasp all those years ago; that in allowing my ears to fail, God was giving me the greatest gift I could ever ask for: a way for my children to experience God with me, every day of their lives.

They knew I depended on Him just to survive the silence that shrouded my days and limited my world. They saw me fill up with His love every morning as I drank Him in through the pages of Scripture.

My children had a front-row seat to my suffering and the realness and at times rawness of my pain led each of them, one by one, into their own intimate love for the Savior.

These are the Ten Things we wanted to be sure our children had a handle on before they left our home. You will have your own Ten Things, your own list of ideas and ideals you want your children to thoroughly grasp and know how to live out. As we said, we encourage you to write them down, think them through. Feel free to add to and expand on our list as you prepare your nearly adult kids to launch out into the world on their own.

Chapter 20

Putting the Roof On

We cannot end this section without an emphasis on prayer. How else, really, could any of us hope to raise a child who passionately and persistently follows after God? And to continue the analogy of building a spiritual house, we have come to recognize, after hours and years of praying for our kids, sometimes wrestling in prayer for our children, that *prayer is like putting on the roof.* As we pray for our kids, we are actually protecting them from the attacks that will come their way.

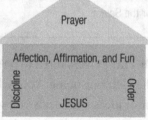

While we were rummaging through the years of material we had saved with the idea of one day writing this book, we came across a notebook Diane made when our kids were growing up. Those pages are a reminder of all God has done for our family, of all those times we cried out to Him for wisdom, for knowing, for help. And now, all these years later, seeing how specifically He answered—we stopped and worshiped right there!

The journal is filled with Scriptures Diane prayed for our children. Verses like Jeremiah 32:40:

"I will put a desire in their hearts to worship me, and they will never leave me." (NLT)

That is what we asked God—over and over—to do in our children's hearts. We knew full well that children are born with a choice to follow God or not. God will not force your child to love Him! But we also had no doubt that He hears our cries for help and that He sends His Spirit to allure our children to Himself.

Hosea's story became our prayer for the work of God's Spirit:

"Therefore I am now going to allure her; I will lead her into the wilderness and speak tenderly to her." (Hosea 2:14)

Diane asked the Father to allure our children to Himself. Using Romans 10:1 as a guide, she prayed that each of our children would be saved at a young age: "Brethren, my heart's desire and my prayer to God for them is for *their* salvation" (NASB).[1]

We prayed that each of our children would see their very real need for the Lord, and that at the same time they would have eyes to see and ears to hear His very real love for them. Since their infancy, Diane prayed Ephesians 3:19 over them: "May you *experience* the love of Christ, though it is too great to understand fully. Then you will be made complete with all the fullness of life and power that comes from God" (NLT, emphasis ours).

DIANE:

Once, when I complained to a wise older woman who was mentoring me about being so tired because my baby would not sleep through the night, she challenged me to spend that time praying for him.

So I did. I prayed over every possible scenario and stage of his life.

I prayed for his future wife, that God would protect her and watch over her, keeping her from horrors that could affect their marriage. I prayed for career choice, for godly friends, for health and happiness.

For a while I prayed that he'd even get good grades—until the unease in my spirit as I prayed changed my perspective.

Eventually, I began praying that each of my children would grow into men and women with a deep love of learning.

When I was pregnant, I learned to pray instead of complain, latching on to Isaiah 46:3–4:

"I have cared for you since you were born. Yes, I carried you before you were born. I will be your God throughout your lifetime—until your hair is white with age. I made you, and I will care for you. I will carry you along and save you." (NLT)

My kids grew up knowing I was praying for them. That's the one thing I knew I could do. I wouldn't always be patient, and I wouldn't always memorize Scripture with them like I knew I ought to—but I could pray.

We prayed *with* our children as well as *for* them. It's so easy to say, "I'll be praying for you," but sometimes it seems like a struggle to actually stop right then and there and pray with them.

If your child says, "Mom, pray for me. I have a big test in Algebra this afternoon," stop and pray right then and there! Put your hand on your child's shoulder before he walks out the front door and pray, even if it feels awkward at first!

Now our grown children do this for us, enveloping us in their faith, hemming us in with their affection. We love it!

A three-by-five card we found in a box of memories recently had Colossians 1:9–12 written on it in Diane's handwriting:

"So we have not stopped praying for you since we first heard about you. We asked God to give you complete knowledge of his will and to give you spiritual wisdom and understanding. Then the way you live will always honor and please the Lord, and your lives will produce every kind of good fruit. All the while, you will grow as you learn to know God better and better. We also pray that you will be strengthened with all his glorious power so you will have all the endurance and patience you need. May you be filled with joy, always thanking the Father." (NLT)

Diane walked the hills surrounding our neighborhood as she prayed for our daughter, who had been offered a job in L.A. and would be on her own for the first time. We wondered and worried if she was strong enough to stand with Jesus, if her faith had developed the kind of fortitude we knew she would need.

Instead of continuing to deplete her confidence by warning her ourselves, we decided to set aside "Fasting Fridays" just for this girl we loved so much. And she did stand strong, learning to wear her faith in her own way, developing her own God-given values and convictions.

Another prayer came from Luke 22:32, the same prayer Jesus prayed for His boy, Simon Peter: "I have pleaded in prayer for you, Simon, that your faith should not fail" (NLT). Insert your child's name in place of Peter's, and pray with confidence that God is listening.

There are also times when we plead for our kids in prayer.

One mother told Diane with a fierceness that belied her petite frame, "I saw what was happening to my daughter at school, and one day when I was praying, I just stomped my foot and raised my fist at Satan and told him in no uncertain terms, "Not with my daughter! She belongs to the LORD!" That daughter is now a confident woman, intentionally raising her own passionate Jesus followers.

When our children were teenagers, Diane prayed specifically for the spouses our children would someday meet. Catching herself falling into the nasty habit of worrying through their dating years, she watched and prayed as each of our children were beginning to figure out what kind of person they needed and wanted to marry.

When our first son met his future wife, Tammy, all the pieces of Diane's prayers seemed to come together. Tammy was seventeen years old when they met, already a godly woman from a rich heritage of faith. By the time John Mark asked for her hand in marriage, Diane had a confident sense that Tammy was the very woman she had prayed for all those years. Diane experienced a joyful recognition, a heart connection that continues to this day.

It happened again many years later when our youngest, Matthew, started dating the woman he would marry. There is no doubt whatsoever that Simona is an answer to many hours of prayer—her gentle beauty adds richness to our family.

Ephesians 3:14–19 has become the prayer of our hearts for the next generation of Comers who will take over where we leave off:

"When I think of all this, I fall to my knees and pray to the Father, the Creator of everything in heaven and on earth. I pray that from his glorious, unlimited resources he will empower you with inner strength through his Spirit. Then Christ will make his home in your hearts as you trust in him. Your roots will grow down into God's love and keep you strong. And may you have the power to understand, as all God's people should, how wide, how long, how high, and how deep his love is. May you experience the love of Christ, though it is too great to understand fully. Then you will be made complete with all the fullness of life and power that comes from God" (NLT).

We began this section, Completing the Finish Work, with 2 Chronicles 7:11:

"Thus Solomon finished the house of the LORD . . . and successfully completed all that he had planned on doing . . ." (NASB)

Now read the next verse!

"Then the Lord appeared to Solomon at night and said to him, 'I have heard your prayer and have chosen this place for Myself as a house of sacrifice.'" (2 Chronicles 7:12 NASB, emphasis ours)

God hears the prayers of a mother for her sons and daughters. And dads, your prayers are just as powerful. Both of us fully believe that in addition to God's grace *towards* our children, it is the prayers we prayed *for* our children that had the most impact in seeing each one of them become passionate Jesus followers.

E.M. Bounds once said, "Talking to men for God is a great thing, but talking to God for men is greater still."[2]

Begin your own prayer lists and cards with Scriptures you find. Take those truths with you to pray and clear space for God to work in your children's lives. Remember, prayer is like putting on the roof to protect our children from the rains we know are coming.

⬆ Raising Passionate Jesus Followers

Completing the Finish Work
(18 to 21 yrs.)

The aim is to help your children develop a heart of *maturity*. Don't quit after the teenage years. Finish what you started.

Nearing the end of this stage, your nearly-adult child...

☐ Has the ability to stand alone.

☐ Consistently protects their own sexual purity.

☐ Understands how to choose a husband or wife.

☐ Knows how to handle money wisely.

☐ Has consistent personal time with God.

☐ Knows how to find key Scripture passages for life's challenges.

☐ Is learning to listen to the Spirit.

☐ Lives missionally and loves the Church.

☐ Understands a Biblical theology of suffering.

Affection, Affirmation, and Fun

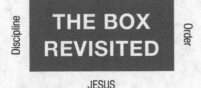

Discipline | THE BOX REVISITED | Order

JESUS

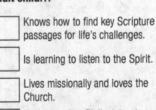

1. The box is still there in this stage, but it changes shape dramatically. Remember not to over-discipline, over-structure, or over-correct.

2. In this stage, remind yourself to distinguish between the One GOAL and your personal Values—your goal is still the same for your children, that they would love Jesus and love others as their own values continue to develop.

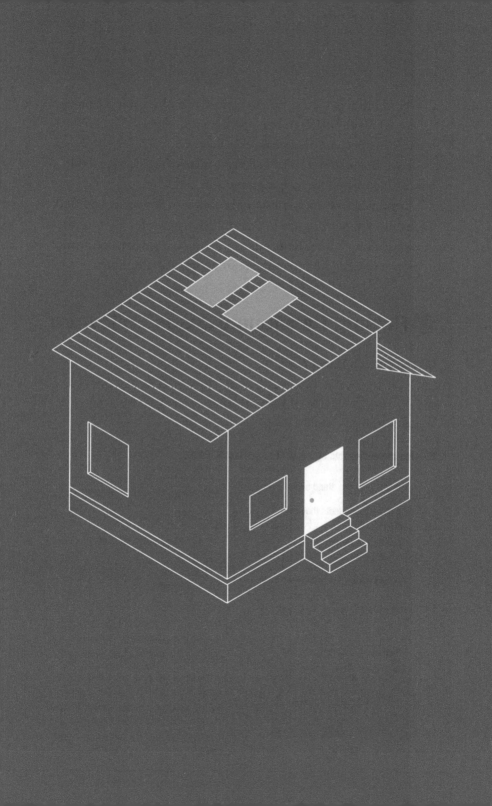

Part 6

Opening the Front Door

"May the God before whom my grandfather
Abraham and my father, Isaac, walked—the God
who has been my shepherd all my life, to this
very day, the Angel who has redeemed me from
all harm—may he bless these boys. May they
preserve my name and the names of Abraham
and Isaac. And may their descendants
multiply greatly throughout the earth."

~ JACOB, GENESIS 48:15–16 NLT

Chapter 21

The Blessing, The Box, and the Key

The day your house is finally completed and ready to become your home is the best of all days! This is what you have been working toward so diligently. Finally, it's come to fruition; it's time to move in.

The last thing your contractor does, once your home is complete, is put on your permanent front door. Until now there's been a cheap, generic door in place—a construction door—in order to keep the door you've picked out from getting nicked and scratched during all the coming and going of the construction crews. Now it's time to replace that fill-in with the dramatic impact of your own carefully chosen front door.

Through this door your family and friends will enter and enjoy the home you have created. This is the moment. After writing your contractor that final check (ouch!), he hands you the keys to your house.

In this final chapter, we want to leave you with detailed instructions about how to let go—and let go *well*—of your son or daughter. The time has come to hand them the keys, to officially launch them into the world.

We have seen repeatedly the tension created when good parents fumble in these last moments of active parenting. The hurt and misunderstanding on both sides all too often overshadows years of intentional, Jesus-centered parenting. It is often the really good Christian parents who, reluctant to hand over the baton, hang on a little bit too long, causing unnecessary tension and conflict. It doesn't have to be this way! We want to get you thinking and planning for that hand-off as early as possible.

While you will always be their mom or dad, your role will change—*must* change—in order to hand over the responsibility for their own lives to your now-grown children.

What you've heard a million times is true: your children will grow up faster than you can possibly imagine. Before you blink, the toddler you spent endless hours training, the teenager you were certain would never grow up, will be driving away with a truckload of memories. A monumental shift in your role *must* occur if you want to continue to have the incredible influence wise and godly parents can have on their adult children. If you miss this, your children will miss out on the rich treasures they need as they begin to build their own homes.

Is it possible to avoid the tension so many intentional, godly, well-meaning parents face as their children fly the coop? Yes! It is!

Is an empty nest so terribly depressing? No, it can be a blast!

Why does letting go have to be so hard, so fraught with misunderstanding and conflict? These are the questions we hear from other parents our age, and these are the questions young parents are asking us.

Come along as we show you a different way: the kingdom way of letting go, an approach that inevitably brings your children back, no longer as responsibilities under your authority but as friends and partners in a legacy. We want to share three insights with you that have helped us tremendously in this letting go process: the Blessing, The Box, and the Key.

THE BLESSING

In the patriarchal families of the Old Testament, we discover the God-ordained beauty of the Blessing. Jacob blessed Joseph and his sons when he said, "May the God before whom my grandfather Abraham and my father, Isaac, walked—the God who has been my shepherd all my life, to this very day, the Angel who has redeemed me from all harm—may he bless these boys. May they preserve my name and the names of Abraham and Isaac. And may their descendants multiply greatly throughout the earth" (Genesis 48:15–16 NLT).

Here are four ways you can pass on the Blessing to your children:

Bless your grown children by believing in them

Before our kids can become confidently responsible for themselves, they need our approval and affirmation, a symbolic letting go. Not because we have to, nor because their birthdate demands we do it, but because we acknowledge their readiness to run their own lives.

We give our kids an enormous amount of courage when we say, "We see your character, your competence, and your calling—*we believe in you*. We know you the best and we believe in you the most."

The truth is, your child will never be ready to make infallible life decisions. They are not ready for perfection, nor are they going to live exactly according to your values. What they are being launched into is life under the direction and protection of God. Your position is changing, but the Father's place in their lives will take on even greater prominence as their need to depend on Him grows. Remember, He who began a good work in your children right in your very own home, will carry it on to completion.[1]

Bless your adult children by choosing not to criticize them

The Blessing is more than simply affirming them; we also need to include a clear punctuation mark to end our deeply ingrained auto-response of training and correcting our kids. It was our right and our responsibility when they were younger, but now the time has come when we no longer correct our children, when we *choose not to criticize* our kids! *Ever*. When we do not allow ourselves to poke or comment or talk about how they could have and should have done something differently. When their misjudgments and mistakes are no longer ours to evaluate. When not so much as a hint of glowering disapproval is allowed a place in our hearts. And when, even between husband and wife, we do not allow ourselves to voice picky negativity about the way our grown kids are doing life.

Now, all of a sudden, you've let go so completely that your kids are more like friends—close, intimate, precious friends. Would you give your friends unsolicited advice about how to spend their money or manage their time? Would you expect your friends to adjust their vacations and celebrations to accommodate your preferences? Of course not!

Bless your adult children by listening to them instead of judging them

---
DIANE: ────────────────────────────

Remember when I said that neither of my daughters would have considered me their best friend when they were fifteen? Now we are friends, real friends—best friends! My daughters tell me what is on their hearts without having to worry that I'll disapprove or tell them how wrong they are. My sons understand that I am the one who knows everything about them—and yet I still think they're perfect.

I am so much better at this than I was at being a disciplinarian. Even I like myself better in this role!

As we were working on this section, the phone rang. It was one of our daughters calling to ask Diane for advice. A few minutes after she hung up, one of our sons called and said, "I just need to talk to Mom for a minute." Two of our grown kids called because they wanted Diane's wisdom and perspective on how to best handle situations they were facing.

Parents, that's a right to be earned!

You earn this close relationship with your son or daughter by accepting them instead of disapproving of them, by listening to them instead of judging them. Give your opinion when they ask you for it, and then try your best to couch your words in the most supportive way you can find. Allow them the freedom to learn the hard way sometimes, just like you did. Unless they're doing something truly awful or illegal, don't say, "I could have told you not to do that!" Instead say, "We made a bunch of dumb decisions too, but God was with us, and He saw us through!"

Bless your adult children by praying for them

At this stage of your child's life, your *authority* and *responsibility* gets replaced with *influence* and *intercession*. If you will affirm and accept and appreciate *who they are becoming*, you will have an enormous amount of influence. And if you'll become a committed and dependable pray-er on their behalf, you'll have the delight of seeing God fathering your children in the decades ahead.

This is why we take a walk every morning. As we walk, we pray out loud for each of our kids, their spouses, our grandkids—all by name. Knowing this, our kids call or text, asking us to pray specifically for things they are concerned about.

Just this week we prayed our son-in-law through a tense phone call, asking God to pour out wisdom, discernment, and love on the person he would be talking to. Because he knew we would be praying, he asked Phil for some advice, which Phil gladly gave. When it didn't go as well as our son-in-law had hoped, we blessed him by viewing him through the lens of a mother-in-law and father-in-law who respect him deeply.

If your son or daughter is not walking with Jesus as you enter this stage, the most effective thing you can do is pray. Prayer changes things! Persistent prayer moves the hand of God in ways we can hardly comprehend. The prophet Samuel said,

> "Moreover, as for me, far be it from me that I should sin against the LORD by ceasing to pray for you." (1 Samuel 12:23 NASB)

As we pray for our children now, we get the unique perspective the Spirit gives to those who are intentional about intercession. He shows us things, whispers wisdom, taps us on the shoulder to partner with Him and His plans for our children. It's uncanny! Somehow He melds our hearts with His, and we see our adult children through His eyes. Our respect for them grows as we pray them through hard times. Our compassion for them swells as we bear the burden of life's realities with them.

Recently, our daughter and son-in-law were walking through an especially frightening time. Their seven-month-old daughter started having seizures, which led to a diagnosis of infantile spasms. This is a terrible, debilitating form of epilepsy. The treatment was brutal, involving daily intermuscular injections, causing off-the-charts high blood pressure. Added to that were sleepless nights and long hospitalizations. Fear for their daughter's future was never far from their minds.

As we have walked and prayed for Brook and Elizabeth, our respect for both of them has grown enormously. In his helplessness to fix this, Brook has become a man of the truest kind of faith, a champion. His faith is grounded in truth, in the reality that sometimes life is hard and doesn't make sense, but God is good—always. He is leading his family in this rock-solid theology.

Our daughter Elizabeth is showing remarkable inner strength as she lives a story no mother wants for her child. On the way to the hospital, she sensed God's hand on her shoulder and heard Him whisper, "I am with you in this, Elizabeth. I am with you." All throughout this ordeal, she has clung to God's assurance—not that He will do what she wants, nor that He guarantees a great outcome, but that He is present and real and all she needs.

This is the truest kind of faith. We didn't put that kind of faithfulness into our kids—their Father in heaven did. And we get the privilege and joy of partnering with Him by praying for them.

Blessing You Back

Not only do you get to give your kids a blessing, they will turn around and bless you! We got to experience something that is every parent's dream.

DIANE:

On the morning our youngest son, Matthew, was leaving for his last year of college, we were stuffing the car with all the things he'd need to live on his own. We'd had a delightful summer together, every moment weighted with the realization that these would be our last memories of actively parenting our last child. As Matt slammed the trunk door, he turned to us and said, "I need to talk to you."

I, of course, started to worry right away, my mind reeling with possible problems!

Matt led us into the kitchen, placed his hands on my shoulders and started to talk, pouring words of blessing and approval all over me. Tears ran down my face as my son recognized the years I had given to raising and training and caring for him. All the guilty shame of my own failures, all those times I'd blown it as a mom, all my genuine regrets were erased in his fluent soliloquy of blessing to me.

Then Matt turned to Phil, and as he did I grabbed my phone to record his words to his father. This is what he said:

"Dad, I just want to say how much I love you, and that I appreciate you so much as a father. In the last year, I've realized how much you've done for me and how I didn't notice that through high school. I love you so much, but you know it's hard to notice those things. I know how much you care for me. I'm thankful for everything you've done for me—how you've raised me, how you've disciplined me, and how you've wanted me to be a good man. I know that sometimes you've been tough on me, but I know that's good. I want you to know how much I care about you and how much I respect you. If you weren't the man you are, I don't think

I'd be walking with Jesus. Everything you preach, you do, and I respect that. You're one of my greatest friends. I love watching movies with you and hanging out, and I'm going to miss you."

There are no words to describe the holiness of that moment or the way our hearts were humbled by our son's grace-filled perspective of our stumbling attempts at intentional parenting. But Phil managed to gather his thoughts into words back to his son, saying,

"Well, I'm going to miss you more. You are a good man and you're going to be a great man. I'm very proud of you. I loved you when you were a little boy, and I love you as a young man. I will love you as an older man, if God lets me live. I'm going to miss you, but I'm happy for you. I fully bless you going."

All those years you spend pouring into your kids—it's worth it! Hang on to the hope that there is a day coming when your children will bless you back, when they will see you through eyes of grace.

Nothing and no one can come back to bless you like those children you call your own. All that disciplining and fixing, the trips to the E.R., the endless loads of laundry, the meals and bedtimes, scuffed walls and messes—*every moment is worth it.*

There is no higher calling in this life. No greater privilege. This is the best possible use of your time!

WHAT ABOUT THE BOX?

The Box is now gone!

The moment you begin raising your children, you are preparing them to leave home. Now it's time to turn over responsibility for their life completely to them. You are no longer in authority over your son or daughter. Now you walk alongside them.

It is no longer your job to discipline them or to impose order on their lives. Now your job is to cheer them on and encourage them.

You are available for counsel, to give input, to share wisdom, to answer questions—to help them when they want you to.

The Box is gone, but the foundation remains.

Jesus will always be the bedrock of your relationship with your kids. He is the solid rock upon which both you and your children stand. If they are following Jesus by this time, you are not just parent and child, you are brothers and sisters in Christ. He is the one who will give you opportunities to grow together in wonder at who God is and how He works in your lives.

As you launch your adult children into the world, stepping back from your role of authority, you get the joy of watching them use the skills they learned in your home as they live on mission to a world that needs Jesus.

THE KEY

On the day you take ownership of your house, your contractor hands you a shiny, new key. His work is done. For twenty years, you've been partnering with God as He has been building a spiritual house in the life of your son or daughter. Now your work is complete, and it's time for you to hand them the key to their own house.

What does it mean to hand over the Key to your son or daughter?

When our adult children left home, we gave each of them a key to our house in a semi-ceremonial act of assurance, telling them, "You are welcome to come over anytime; we don't even have to be there. Our house is your house!"

But we didn't ask for, nor would we accept, a key to theirs. This was on purpose and symbolic. The last thing your kids want or need is to wonder if their mom or dad might just drop by anytime! Their house is not your house!

We wanted our grown children and their spouses to know that we get that, and that we respect their need to build their own houses, to have their own families apart from their parents.

On their wedding days, we took each of our children aside and told them, "Your first year of marriage is foundational to the rest of your lives together. We aren't going to put any pressure on you, or guilt-trip you to come to our house because we want to see more of you. We want to see as much of you as you desire, but we aren't going to whine, 'We never see you anymore!'"

The truth is, some of your kids are going to start out so poor that they will *ask* to come over for dinner. We did, every week! Both of our moms always made sure to send us off with leftovers to tide us over until the following week.

But we wanted our children to see their need to cleave to their own emerging families, to give their spouse the best of their time and attention. This is God's plan, as expressed in Genesis 2:24: "For this reason a man shall leave his father and his mother, and be joined to his wife; and they shall become one flesh" (NASB).

For this to happen without a lot of stress and drama, moms and dads need to intentionally let go. Your children need your permission and approval in the letting-go process. It's not healthy for us to need our kids on into adulthood. We are to stand together, strong and satisfied in Jesus, giving our children freedom to launch into adult life strong.

Someday it will be just the two of you again, and you're going to have a blast! Give them your Blessing, dismantle The Box, and hand them the Key to your house. Tell them this:

"You're going to be building your own house now, raising the next generation of passionate Jesus followers. You'll be formulating your own plans, laying your own foundation, doing your own framing, installing your own functional systems, doing your own finish work, and one day, handing your kids their own key."

Regrets

Be aware of this: when you build a house, every time you walk through that door, you'll wish you'd done some things differently. The kitchen nook is too small; you should have put a sink in the laundry room; why, oh why, didn't we put a window there?

When it comes to raising children, you'll have regrets—every parent does. No mom or dad looks back and says, "I did it perfectly!" You'll remember the times you reacted out of fear instead of wisdom. You'll wish you had known what you didn't—things that look so clear in the rearview mirror. If you had it to do all over again, of course you'd make some adjustments! Some of those mistakes may well become fodder for hilarious family lore, while others may find you apologizing many years after the fact. Go in the grace of humility, and you will forever be deeply grateful for the mercy your kids extend towards those missteps.

When it comes to building godly men and women, remember: your goal is not to raise perfect sons and daughters! Your goal is to raise passionate followers of Jesus who will then turn around and raise the *next* generation of passionate Jesus followers.

Just as the Psalmist described in Psalm 78:

O my people, listen to my instructions.
Open your ears to what I am saying,
for I will speak to you in a parable.
I will teach you hidden lessons from our past—
stories we have heard and known,
stories our ancestors handed down to us.
We will not hide these truths from our children;
we will tell the next generation
about the glorious deeds of the Lord,
about his power and his mighty wonders.
For he issued his laws to Jacob;
he gave his instructions to Israel.
He commanded our ancestors
to teach them to their children,
so the next generation might know them—

even the children not yet born—
and they in turn will teach their own children.
So each generation should set its hope anew on God,
not forgetting his glorious miracles
and obeying his commands. (Psalm 78:1–7 NLT)

May you have the privilege of raising sons and daughters who love God with passion and who love people on purpose, who set their hope on Jesus Christ, the solid rock.

And may the kingdom of God come crashing down into your home and family, bringing His beauty and glory to every corner of the earth.

Amen.

⌃ Raising Passionate Jesus Followers

Opening the Front Door

 + +

BLESSING
Bless your kids by believing in them, choosing not to criticize them, listening to them instead of judging them, and praying for them

BOX
The box is now gone, but the foundation of Jesus remains. You are no longer *over* them. You are now *alongside* them.

KEY
Hand them a key to your house to let them know that you will always be there for them. Respect their need to build their own house—differently than yours

Appendix A

Retrofitting

> "Your people will rebuild the ancient ruins
> and will raise up the age-old foundations;
> you will be called Repairer of Broken Walls,
> Restorer of Streets with Dwellings."
>
> ISAIAH 58:12

Right around the time our last child was finishing college, we looked around at our big empty house on a hill overlooking the city of Portland, and decided it was time to move. We no longer needed all those bedrooms and bathrooms and extra space—or the mortgage that went with it.

Our friend Bob happened to mention that there was a house that might be coming up for sale in the neighborhood in which he was remodeling a house for resale. The house was in a forested enclave, quiet and yet close to a delightful area of cottages and shops—a European-like town nestled right up against the city. We hurried over to take a look.

My heart fell when I saw the house for the first time. It was ugly! Built in 1969, it was a squatty little ranch-style home that had never been cute. I'd been imagining a lovely cottage just waiting for me to come and restore it to its former coziness. Instead, the garage smelled of cat urine, and the house was cramped, stinky, and mildewed—pathetic.

We bought it.

Thus began a restoration and rebuilding project that we're still working on. Turning a shoddily built house into a beautiful home where we live and love and laugh and where all Comers (sixteen now and counting!) come together to celebrate. With help from brilliant builders, framers, designers, and craftsmen, we are slowly watching Firwood Cottage turn into a place we love.

Some of you know what we're talking about. You've come late to this quest of raising sons and daughters to be full-on, passionate followers of Jesus. When you had your children, you either weren't following Jesus yourself, or you just didn't know what to do, so how could you train your kids?

In Psalm 11, David asks, "If the foundations are destroyed, what can the righteous do?"[1]

The answer is this: Rebuild the foundations.

You're asking the same question David asked: *What can I do now? Is there hope for my grown kids? For my teenager? For that son or daughter who wants nothing to do with Jesus?*

Yes! In fact, God specializes in turning squatty fixer-uppers into showcases of His glory. And He particularly loves prodigals and rebels—just look at the disciples Jesus chose!

Although this is not the story you wish for your son or daughter, we would urge you to throw off the ensnaring chains of shame. Guilt is one of Satan's favorite arrows to fling our way—he seems to find it especially useful on parents. Sometimes the better the parent, the worse the guilt!

The writer of Hebrews cast a little light on this when he wrote,

". . . we had earthly fathers to discipline us, and we respected them . . . for they disciplined us for a short time as seemed best to them, but He *disciplines us* for our *good*, that we may share His holiness." (Hebrews 12:9–10 NASB)

Just because you have not done all you wish you had, or your children have not responded as you'd hoped, doesn't mean He hasn't been at work all along. In fact, God often calls other men and women alongside to step in and do the spiritual parenting we are not able to do. The apostle Paul makes a fleeting mention of a woman who impacted his life when he says in Romans, "Greet Rufus, chosen in the Lord, and his mother who has been a mother to me, too" (Romans 16:13). Someone other than his mom contributed to Paul's nurturing needs.

Paul also saw himself as a sort of surrogate father to Timothy, affectionately calling him, "my dear son" (2 Timothy 2:1) as he offered wise advice for living.

All that said, don't give up yet. There's work to be done, and it's never—*ever*—too late.

We'll use our verse in Isaiah as a template for the rebuilding of your spiritual home. Note the verbs—the how-tos of the process: *Rebuild. Raise up. Repair. Restore.*

Rebuild

The books of Ezra and Nehemiah are historic and spiritual records of the rebuilding of the temple in Jerusalem. The city that was the center of worship had fallen and been almost entirely destroyed in 587 B.C. with the invasion of the Babylonians. God raised up Ezra and Nehemiah to initiate and complete the work of restoring the temple and the city as a place for God's people to once again live in freedom in the presence of God. Ezra challenged the people by saying, "Whoever there is among you of all His people, may his God be with him! Let him . . . rebuild the house of the LORD" (Ezra 1:3 NASB). Isn't this an apt challenge for parents who are facing the challenge of "rebuilding" a heart for God in their children?

Ezra's cry resulted in key leaders who took up the challenge: "then Zerubbabel the son of Shealtiel and Jeshua the son of Jozadak *arose* and began to *rebuild* the house of God which is in Jerusalem; and the prophets of God were with them supporting them" (Ezra 5:2 NASB, emphasis ours).

See what they did first? They *arose*. They decided to do what needed to be done no matter how fearsome the work appeared. That's the kind of determination you're going to need as well. Rebuilding is much more difficult than starting from scratch.

After retirement, Diane's parents built their dream home high in the Sierras of California. A beautiful log home to showcase their antiques, it was perched on a ridge overlooking the mountains they loved. They relished their home for ten years, opening their doors wide to welcome friends and family, as well as traveling missionaries and anyone who needed a respite.

One night while they were sleeping, a fire erupted. They woke up to flames in every direction, barely escaping with their lives. Then they watched as their beautiful home burned to the ground. They lost nearly everything they owned, but worse than that, they lost the dog they loved dearly.

Within a week of their catastrophic loss, Jack and Sue were preparing to rebuild. When someone broached the idea of moving down the mountain to a retirement community, they glanced at each other and said, "Not a chance! We love our life here."

To their relief, the foundation, although badly damaged, was still intact, needing shoring up and repairs but otherwise usable.

Rebuilding your family's *spiritual* house starts with you. It starts with your humble acknowledgement that Jesus has not been the rock-solid foundation of your home. God "shows favor[2] to the humble" (1 Peter 5:5).

How might this look? Maybe it will involve you apologizing to your kids. You might say, "I regret that I have not followed God closely, that I haven't brought Him in as the center of our home. Now, with His help, things around here are going to change. I want this to be a home where God's love permeates everything we do and say, and I know I have a lot of work to do." It may feel awkward at first, but that's okay.

Then you've got to get to it, just like the people in the book of Ezra did. Just like Diane's parents painstakingly rebuilt their dream home, spending hours and hours getting it right, so you, too, can dedicate yourself to rebuilding your family's spiritual home.

Raise Up

The first inclination of many parents, upon waking up to their spiritual responsibility to their kids, is to set up a long list of rules. Behaviors need changing. Attitudes need a major adjustment. A massive house cleaning is in order! You know *what* you want to do, but you aren't sure *how* to go about it.

First things first. Remember what we said way back in chapter 11? Jesus is the foundation. Not church, not the Christian way of living, not AWANA or any sort of program—just Jesus. We noted that Paul prayed that the Ephesians would "know the love of Christ" (Ephesians 3:19 NASB).

So raise up Jesus! Just start with Him. He Himself is the "cornerstone" (Ephesians 2:20). Ask Him for wisdom. Pray for boldness tempered with gentle persuasion as you open your heart to your kids. He will be eager to answer your prayers!

Jesus is the foundation. His *love* is what we need—what our children need. The lifestyle changes come out of the change Jesus works in our hearts. That's the way the gospel works—pretty counterintuitive in our "get it done!" culture. As we fall more deeply in love with Jesus, *He* gets it done in us.

On His way to the cross where He would pour out His life out of love for us, Jesus said, ". . . now the prince of this world will be driven out. And I, when I am lifted up from the earth, will draw all people to myself" (John 12:31–32).

You are driving the "prince of the world" out of your home and lifting Jesus up. Talking about His grace, His mercy. Telling the story of what He's doing in your heart. Show your kids the love you're experiencing from Him. Be generous and kind, overlooking irritations that normally set you off. Ask forgiveness when you blow it. Show your joy. Your kids will see that peace and marvel!

Yes, some things will need to go, but it will be your new love for Jesus that informs which activities, movies, magazines—things you once thought were fine—now feel embarrassingly out of place with Jesus in your life and home.

Repair

Without the love of Jesus at the center of your home you've undoubtedly allowed things to be said and done that are the antithesis of Jesus' love. Attitudes have taken root, behaviors—on both your part and the kids'—may not line up with the kingdom way of doing life. Relationships may need some major repair.

DIANE:

When I was seventeen, my mom apologized to me. All of us were new believers, having stumbled on a church that brought Jesus to us in a way we had never heard before. Although I was beginning to follow Jesus, my relationship with my mom was tense.

She'd grown up with an angry, abusive father, and she was ill-equipped to deal with the rage that sometimes seemed to burst involuntarily from her insides. I was mad at her for being angry with me for reasons I couldn't understand. When she sat me down and humbly asked my forgiveness, telling me she'd realized at a women's retreat that her anger towards me was wrong, I was astounded into silence.

All my cocky teenager attitude just hung there, suspended between us. I couldn't believe my ears. My mom was telling me she was sorry?

That day marked a change in our relationship which enabled us to become friends. My own adversarial stance slowly softened as I saw Jesus, the Redeemer, at work in my mom's life. She didn't become perfectly patient overnight, but she purposely began to repair what was broken between us. In the process, I fell more deeply in love with a Savior who can change even my mom. Without needing me to fess up and apologize too, my mother showed me the way of grace and beckoned me to follow.

Years later I learned the meaning of the word *mercy*. Mercy is when we don't give people what they deserve, but instead, we choose to forgive as we've been forgiven.

When a parent apologizes, mercy is displayed with an extravagance that even a teenager cannot ignore!

Restore

It is the Good Shepherd who restores our souls, and He does it with infinite gentleness.[3] The word *restore* means to turn, or to turn back towards.

After you rebuild your foundation, raise up Jesus, and repair broken relationships, now comes the long process of restoring.

The last two verses of the Old Testament say:

"Behold, I am going to send you Elijah the prophet before the coming of the great and terrible day of the LORD. He will restore the hearts of the fathers to *their* children and the hearts of the children to their fathers, so that I will not come and smite the land with a curse." (Malachi 4:5–6 NASB)

It's God's heart to restore or turn back the hearts of fathers and mothers towards their children. This is what restoration is all about.

When a father turns away from whatever is keeping him from radically loving and leading his kids, and instead turns his focus *towards* his son or daughter, that's when restoration happens. When mom turns away from her phone or her career or her church activities or her anger, and focuses her love and attention on her child, that's when restoration happens.

This is the way God wants to use you to bring your home under His alignment. He will use you to display His soul-saving grace as He changes you right before your children's eyes. What could be greater proof of His power than that?

But it won't be all smooth sailing. There's one more point we'd be remiss to leave out.

Expect resistance

DIANE:

By the time my dad decided to attempt to lead us in family devotions, all three of us were cocky teenagers. Yes, we were all finding our way towards Jesus, but we had not yet learned the concept of honoring our parents—far from it!

Dad called us all into the rarely used living room, where we sat in stiff-backed chairs, wondering what in the world was wrong. I thought for sure we were in some kind of trouble, so when he explained that we were going to read the Bible and talk about it as a family, I burst out in an awkward giggle. Undeterred, Dad cleared his throat, put on his most official voice, and began by reading from the book of Matthew. After a few verses, he passed the Bible to Mom. She read for a while, and then passed the Bible to my brother, who immediately started to snicker and snort his way through his verses. Then it was my turn. I took the Bible in my hands, genuinely trying to comply, but I couldn't help it—I started laughing so hard I couldn't read a word.

Poor Dad. I look back now and see that what he did was nothing short of courageous. And yet our mocking attitudes (even though we were all enthusiastically embracing the way of Jesus) were too much for him. It wasn't until many years later that our family was able to laugh together about those first, awkward attempts at bringing Jesus into the center of our home.

May I just encourage you? Although that day didn't go smoothly, talking about spiritual things—even praying together—eventually became a natural and delightful part of our times together as a family.

Take note of an event in the story of the rebuilding of Jerusalem. Things are going well when, in spite of intense opposition, Nehemiah wrote:

"So we rebuilt the wall till all of it reached half its height, for the people worked with all their heart.

But when Sanballat, Tobiah, the Arabs, the Ammonites and the people of Ashdod heard that the repairs to Jerusalem's walls had gone ahead and that the gaps were being closed, they were very angry. They all plotted together to come and fight against [it]." (Nehemiah 4:6–8)

Then follows a laundry list of troubles that threatened to defeat the wall builders. But Nehemiah came up with a plan:

"Those who were rebuilding the wall and those who carried burdens took *their* load with one hand doing the work and the other holding a weapon." (Nehemiah 4:17 NASB)

Resistance is not a sign that it's time to back off and give up! Rather, it is often a direct consequence of walking in God's will. Just like the wall builders, parents who do the hard work of rebuilding their homes to more beautifully reflect the way of Jesus will find obstacles strewn across the way. So we do the work with one hand, and with the other hand we hold on tight to our weapons!

What are our weapons? Find a list in Ephesians 6:10, 18:

"A final word: Be strong in the Lord and in his mighty power . . . pray in the Spirit at all times and on every occasion. Stay alert and be persistent in your prayers for all believers everywhere." (NLT)

As you rebuild, raise up, repair, and restore, you'll see your family slowly transformed right before your eyes. May God give you the grace, wisdom, understanding, and determination you will need to rebuild your home into a place that is a showcase of His amazing grace!

Appendix B

Leading Your Child to Jesus

After she attended one of our parenting conferences in Glasgow, Scotland, a motivated mom went home and asked her eight-year-old daughter if she had ever invited Jesus to be her Savior. She said, "No, mommy, I haven't." When Lynne asked her if she would like to, she said, "Yes, I would."

After talking about it, sleeping on it, and praying about it, Lynne led her daughter to faith in Jesus. We will never forget the joy on that mom's face when we saw her the next morning!

We've noticed recently that some young parents who love Jesus seem to be shying away or shrinking back from sitting down with their son or daughter and clearly presenting the good news of salvation to them.

Fearing their child might "pray a prayer" which might not be genuine, parents can sometimes be reluctant to come right out and *ask* their kids if they would like to commit their lives to Jesus.

1 John 4:18 says, "There is no fear in love; but perfect love casts out fear." (NASB)

Because we love our kids, we need to lay aside our fears, and step out and talk to them about Jesus!

Many who serve in children's ministry today are talking about the "4–14 Window." Children are most open to the gospel and to receiving Jesus between the ages of four and fourteen.

Jesus said: "Let the little children come to me, and do not hinder them, for the kingdom of heaven belongs to such as these" (Matthew 19:14). As parents, we can't afford to neglect sharing the good news with our kids when they are young.

Maybe you're thinking, *Of course, I get that. I just don't know how.*

In this appendix, we offer eight guidelines we pray will be helpful to you as you seek to lead your child to a saving faith in Jesus, and then make disciples of your own kids. Here they are:

Rejoice

Rejoice that you have the privilege of sharing Jesus with your children. It's not just a duty to discharge; it's a fun calling to carry out.

In Luke 15:10 Jesus said: "There is rejoicing in the presence of the angels of God over one sinner who repents."

The angels in heaven rejoice when one person is saved. And Jesus Himself rejoices when names are "written in heaven" (Luke 10:20).

Should not moms and dads rejoice both at the privilege they have of sharing Jesus with their kids as well as in sharing that moment when their son or daughter receives Jesus as Savior and Lord? Absolutely yes!

Read

Read the Scriptures to them regularly! Read John 3:16 to them and talk about how much God loves them. Tell them God loves them so much, He sent his one and only Son on a mission that they might be saved. Tell them Jesus literally gave His life on the cross for them.

Recite

Recite key verses to them.

Deuteronomy 6:7 tells parents they are to talk to their kids about the Lord "when you sit in your house and when you walk by the way and when you lie down and when you rise up" (NASB).

Some verses to share and talk about with your son or daughter might be: John 8:12; 10:10; 14:6, Romans 3:23; 6:23; 5:8; 10:9–10.

Request

Request wisdom from God about *when* and *how* to talk to your kids about making a decision to receive Jesus as Savior.

The good news is, when we ask God for wisdom, He's eager to give it to us! James 1:5 says, "If any of you lacks wisdom, he should ask God, who gives generously to all without finding fault, and it will be given to you."

Jesus said, "Ask and it will be given to you; seek and you will find; knock and the door will be opened to you. For everyone who asks receives; the one who seeks finds; and to the one who knocks, the door will be opened" (Matthew 7:7–8).

Jesus also said, "No one can come to me unless the father who sent me draws them; and I will raise them up at the last day" (John 6:44).

Since this is true, of course we want to pray and ask the Father to open the heart of our son or daughter to receive the good news of salvation! He is the one who opens hearts, and He is the one who can soften hard hearts!

Jeremiah 32:40 says, "I will put a desire in their hearts to worship me, and they will never leave me." (NLT) Diane prayed this verse over and over again for our four kids, and we watched in awe as it came to pass!

Receive

Receive Jesus as Savior and Lord.

It's one thing to "believe" that God exists. The Bible says even demons, who hate God, know He exists (James 2:19). It's another thing to "receive" Jesus into your life as Savior and Lord, committing yourself to follow Him and walk in His ways.

A good verse to help explain this to your kids is John 1:12: "Yet to all who did receive him, to those who believed in his name, he gave the right to become children of God."

After modeling for your kids what it looks like to follow Jesus; and after praying and talking to them about making a decision to follow the way of Jesus; when you feel the time is right, be bold and ask them if they would like to receive Jesus as their Savior and Lord!

Remind

Remind them over and over (once they have received the Lord) of the decision they made to give their life to Jesus Christ.

If they are really young, it's important to periodically remind them repeatedly of where they were when they prayed and surrendered their life to Jesus.

One Sunday afternoon after church, we were driving to a friend's house for lunch. Our oldest son, John Mark, who was just four-and-a-half years old at the time, was in the car with us. He'd just heard a clear presentation of the good news in his children's class at church and, as we were driving, he blurted out: "I want to give my life to Jesus right now!"

We pulled the car over next to a strip mall on a busy boulevard and led him in a prayer to receive Jesus as his Savior and Lord. Right there, in that moment, he was saved!

But because he was only four-and-a-half years old, in the years that followed, whenever we drove by that spot, we stopped the car, and asked, "John Mark, what happened right there?" He knew, and he would tell us: "I received Jesus as my Savior!"

The apostle Peter said, "I consider it right . . . to stir you up by way of reminder" (2 Peter 1:13 NASB).

It's so important that we both remind our kids of the decision they made to follow Jesus, and reinforce the reality of that decision as they continue to grow and mature into young adults.

A good friend of ours told us that from the time he was a young boy, all the way through high school, his parents continually reminded him that he had told them, "When I grow up, I want to serve Jesus as an evangelist." Today, Jose Zayas is in his forties and travels all over the world sharing the good news as an international evangelist!

Remember

You want your child to remember the life-changing decision they made, so talk about the place, the time, the night, and who was there when they gave their life to the Lord. Anything to help them remember their decision as they grow older.

What about baptism?

While the Bible does not give an age that someone should be baptized at, we have found that in the case of a young child, it is best if this happens later, not before age seven to ten. This is only a guideline, though. The key is to be sensitive to what is going on in your child's heart.

By waiting until they are a little older to follow Jesus in baptism, they will be more likely to remember this event which, biblically, is a one-time event.

With our daughter Elizabeth, we waited until she was ten years old before we considered allowing her to be baptized. Before that, she would bring it up occasionally, but then drift off into talking about something else. But when she turned ten, she strongly insisted, "I want to get baptized." We were able to have a long, serious conversation with her, so we knew she was ready and that it was the right time for her to follow Jesus in baptism.

Have someone take photos of your child being baptized. Invite friends to witness this beautiful event. Make a photo album your child can look at in the years that follow to help them remember it.

Rejoice Again

Finally, rejoice again! First, you rejoice that you get the privilege of talking to your kids about Jesus. But once they've actually received him as their Savior, you get to really rejoice, because their names are written in the book of life (Revelation 3:5, 20:15).

Jesus told his disciples: "Rejoice that your names are recorded in heaven" (Luke 10:20 NASB). So, mom and dad, lead your child to Jesus! Let your children come to him!

Rejoice, read, recite, request, receive, remind, remember, and then rejoice again, because there is nothing more important than this. Everything else pales in comparison to the joy you will feel, knowing that you and your child will experience the new heaven and the new earth, eternity with Jesus, together forever!

Appendix C

Recommended Reading

Love & Respect in the Family by Dr. Emerson Eggerichs

Parenting: 14 Gospel Principles That Can Radically Change Your Family by Paul David Tripp

Age of Opportunity: A Biblical Guide to Parenting Teens by Paul David Tripp

Parenting: From Surviving to Thriving by Charles R. Swindoll

Loveology: God. Love. Marriage. Sex. And the Never-Ending Story of Male and Female by John Mark Comer

Garden City: Work, Rest, and the Art of Being Human by John Mark Comer

Never Say No: Raising Big-Picture Kids by Mark and Jan Foreman

Peacemaking for Families: A Biblical Guide to Managing Conflict in Your Home by Kenn Sande

The Young Peacemaker by Corlette Sande

When Sorry Isn't Enough: Making Things Right with Those You Love by Gary Chapman and Jennifer Thomas

Anger: Taming a Powerful Emotion by Gary Chapman

The Heart of Anger: Practical Help for the Prevention and Cure of Anger in Children by Lou Priolo

Effective Parenting in a Defective World: How to Raise Kids Who Stand Out from the Crowd by Chip Ingram

Hands Free Mama: A Guide to Putting Down the Phone, Burning the To-Do List, and Letting Go of Perfection to Grasp What Really Matters! by Rachel Macy Stafford

Why Wait? What You Need to Know About the Teen Sexuality Crisis
    by Josh McDowell and Dick Day

**Resources that help you to understand the unique personality
and gifts of your child:**

Children Are Wet Cement by Anne Ortlund
The Road Back to You by Ian Morgan Cron and Suzanne Stabile
*Dad, Here's What I Really Need from You: A Guide for Connecting
    with Your Daughter's Heart* by Michelle Watson
*Understanding How Others Misunderstand You: A Unique and
    Proven Plan for Strengthening Personal Relationships* by Ken
    Voges and Ron Braund
*Are My Kids on Track? The 12 Emotional, Social, and Spiritual
    Milestones Your Child Needs to Reach* by Sissy Goff, David
    Thomas, and Melissa Trevathan

Notes

Author Note

1. See Mark 2:15–17.

Chapter 1: Our Story

1. Elisabeth D. Dodds, *Marriage to a Difficult Man* (Philadelphia: The Westminster Press, 1971).

Chapter 2: The Cost

1. See 2 Corinthians 5:17.
2. J. Warner Wallace, "Are Young People Really Leaving Christianity?" *Cold-Case Christianity*, Oct. 20, 2017, http://coldcasechristianity.com/2017/are-young-people-really-leaving-christianity/.
3. Ibid.
4. A.W. Tozer, *The Pursuit of God* (Chicago: Moody Publishers, 2015), 1.
5. "Spiritual champions" is Barna's term for what we call "passionate Jesus followers," what Bill Hybels termed, "fully devoted followers of Christ."
6. George Barna, *Revolutionary Parenting* (Wheaton, IL: Tyndale House Publishers, 2007), 30.
7. Ibid.
8. Matthew 6:33 NLT

Chapter 3: Your Story

1. Don Devine, "How Long Is a Generation?" Ancestry.com Learning Centre, accessed Dec. 13, 2017, http://www.ancestry.ca/learn/learningcenters/default.aspx?section=lib_Generation.
2. Ruth Bell Graham, *Prodigals and Those Who Love Them* (Colorado Springs: Focus on the Family Publishing, 1991), xiii.

Chapter 4: The Great Shema

1. See 1 Corinthians 6:19
2. Wayne Rice, *Generation to Generation: Practical and Creative Ideas for Raising Kids to Know and Love God* (Cincinnati: Standard Publishing, 2004), 11.
3. Barna, 29.

4. Mark and Jan Foreman are the parents of John and Tim Foreman of the band Switchfoot.

5. Mark and Jan Foreman, *Never Say No: Raising Big Picture Kids* (Colorado Springs: David C. Cook, 2015), 125.

6. General William Booth, "Training Your Children for Christ," *The Last Days Magazine*, Vol.8 No.5, 44–45.

7. Dallas Willard, *The Divine Conspiracy* (San Francisco: HarperCollins, 1998).

8. Charles Spurgeon, *The Treasury of David*, Vol. 2 (McLean, VA: McDonald Publishing Co., 1982), 331.

Chapter 5: The Lamp and the Light

1. Dr. Gerry Breshears, Professor of Theology at Western Seminary in Portland, Oregon wisely points out that this is Hebrew parallelism, meaning that the commandment of the father and the teaching of the mother are referring to the same thing. Thus, the point the writer of Proverbs is making here is that children do well to listen to the teaching of *both* their mother and their father. The point we are making is that *both* the mother and the father's teaching are of vital importance.

2. See Ezra 7:6.

3. An American television series which aired from 1957 to 1963 depicting the "perfect" family living in an idyllic age.

4. See John 10:10.

Chapter 6: Goals versus Values

1. John and Charles Wesley were the founders of the Methodist Movement.

2. Emerson and Sarah Eggerichs conduct the best conference on marriage we have ever attended. See also their books: *Love and Respect* and *Love and Respect in the Family*. Remarkably insightful, biblical teaching on the family.

Chapter 7: A Heart of Obedience

1. Andrew Murray, *How to Raise Your Children for Christ* (Minneapolis: Bethany Fellowship, 1975), 167 (emphasis ours).

Chapter 8: Tools for Discipline

1. This is a great story! Read it and talk about it with your children to highlight a godly strategy for decision making.

2. Robert E. Larzelere, Robert B. Cox, Jr., and Jelani Mandara, *Responding to Misbehavior in Young Children: How Authoritative Parents Enhance Reasoning with Firm Control* (Washington, D.C.: APA Books, 2013), 211.

3. St. Theophan, *Raising Them Right: A Saint's Advice on Raising Children* (Ben Loman, CA: Conciliar Press, 1989), 44.

4. Adam Grant, *Originals: How Non-Conformists Move the World* (New York: Penguin, 2016), 163.

5. Emerson Eggerichs writes on loveandresprect.com, "This begs the question: What does striking a child with a rod mean? On the one hand we read that

the child 'will not die' but does that mean a parent can do whatever just short of killing the child? Certainly the rod can kill according to Exodus 21:30 . . . take the most conservative interpretation of 'shebet' (the rod) for disciplining, which would mean a small branch or offshoot that stings but disallows bodily injury or deadly harm. In other words, striking a child with such a branch will not kill him. It can't. 'He will not die.' This interpretation of 'shebet' is a safe, conservative, and valid interpretation, and our state codes reflect this conservative, common-sense approach."

6. This quote is taken from Proverbs 3:11–12.

7. W. E. Vine, *The Expanded Vine's Expository Dictionary of New Testament Words*, (Minneapolis: Bethany House Publishers, 1984), 1000.

8. *New American Standard Exhaustive Concordance of The Bible*, (Nashville, TN: Holman Bible Publishers, 1981), 1665.

9. "God's chastisement of us includes not only His 'whipping' us, as it were, for specific transgressions (with remedial not retributive intent), but also the entire range of trial and tribulations which He providentially ordains and which work to mortify sin and nurture faith." *The Complete Word Study Dictionary New Testament*, (Chattanooga, TN: AMG Publishers, 1993), 948.

10. Larzelere, Cox, Jr., and Mandara. "Non-abusive spanking led to more compliance or less aggression in 2-to 6-year-old children than 10 of 13 other alternative tactics when used for defiant responses to milder disciplinary tactics, such as time out or reasoning."

11. Larzelere, Cox, Jr., and Mandara. "Child outcomes were more adverse for physical punishment than for alternative tactics only when it was overly severe or the primary discipline method."

12. James C. Dobson, *The New Dare to Discipline* (Wheaton, IL: Tyndale Momentum, 1992), 118.

13. Karyn B. Purvis, Ph.D, David R. Cross, Ph.D., Wendy Lyons Sunshine, *The Connected Child* (New York: McGraw Hill, 2007), 102.

14. Spiros Zodhiates, Th.d. *The Complete Word Study Dictionary, New Testament* (Chattanooga: AMG Publishers, 1992), 1088. Zodhiates says that *discipline* is used of "activity directed toward the moral and spiritual nurture and training of the child, to influence conscious will and action. It is educative discipline; to chastise for the purpose of educating someone to conform to divine truth."

15. Ibid.

16. This is the same Hebrew word used in the phrase *rod of discipline*.

17. Some examples of what else might be going on in the heart of your child that looks like defiant disobedience but might not be include: fear, confusion, grief, problems at school that are wearing the child down to an emotional low, lack of confidence, problems with attention. This is why we study our children and ask God to help us look into their hearts as we train them in His ways.

Chapter 9: A Heart of Self-Control

1. Dr. James Dobson, *Temper Your Child's Tantrums* (Wheaton, IL: Tyndale House Publishers, 1986), 19.

2. For more specifics on dealing with temper tantrums, see Part 3.

3. Dobson, 19.

4. See James 4:8, John 15:5.

5. J. Oswald Sanders, *Spiritual Leadership, Revised Edition* (Chicago: Moody Publishers, 1980), 141–145.

Chapter 10: Bring Them Up

1. Barna, 42.

2. Foreman and Foreman, 109.

3. Rachel Macy Stafford, *Hands Free Mama: A Guide to Putting Down the Phone, Burning the To-Do List, and Letting Go of Perfection, to Grasp What Truly Matters* (Grand Rapids: Zondervan, 2013), 212.

4. The New American Standard Bible translates *training* as *discipline*.

5. See Ephesians 2:10.

6. Steven M. Southwick, M.D. and Dennis S. Charney, M.D., *Resilience: The Science of Mastering Life's Greatest Challenges* (Cambridge, UK: Cambridge University Press, 2012), 13.

Chapter 11: The Box

1. See Ephesians 3:19 NLT, "May you experience the love of Christ, though it is too great to understand fully."

2. See intentionalparenting.org for three reasons we used the rod of discipline (spanking).

3. Dave Stone, *Building Family Ties with Faith, Love and Laughter,* (Nashville, TN: Thomas Nelson, 2012), 61.

Chapter 12: Character Development

1. The focus of our experience, training, and education has to do with biblical studies and pastoral care, not child development. We urge parents to be alert to biological and/or neurological symptoms that may make it all but impossible for your child to respond to discipline and training as other children do.

There are learning disorders and physical difficulties such as ADHD, fetal alcohol syndrome, sensory issues, and food intolerances that sometimes disguise themselves as behavior or character problems. Be aware and seek professional help as needed when problems arise that do not make sense.

2. Thank you, Emerson and Sarah Eggerichs, for this simple, yet profound insight.

3. See Matthew 21:12–13

4. David Powlison, *Angry Children: Understanding and Helping Your Child Regain Control* (Greensboro, NC: New Growth Press, 2008), 5.

5. Proverbs 22:15 (NASB) states the problem of foolishness that we are all born with. Rather than acting appalled when your child acts foolishly, be proactive in guiding your son or daughter into social and emotional confidence.

6. One of the best things Phil did with both our sons was to take on a paper route *together*. He made it so fun that they grew up with fond memories of

those early morning hours of delivering newspapers. After paying for gas (there were no bike routes available), the kids got to keep their money and learn how to tithe, save, be generous, and enjoy the rest.

7. Dr. Gerry Breshears notes: "This is one of those really big words in the Old Testament. It is commonly translated 'blameless,' healthy, complete, perfect. It is similar to the 'without reproach' of elders in 1 Timothy 3. See Zechariah in Luke 1 and others."

8. See also Ecclesiastes 9:10.

Chapter 13: Relationship Building

1. See Ephesians 1:7–8.
2. Jon Courson is the pastor of Applegate Christian Fellowship in Jacksonville, OR. This is how he explains John 15:5.
3. Dr. Dobson's Family Talk Facebook page, Jan. 21, 2017, https://www .facebook.com/DrJamesDobsonsFamilyTalk/posts/10153943269166735.
4. Read the story of Adam and Eve's sons, Cain and Abel, in Genesis 4.
5. Read Philippians 2:1–11 for the whole beautiful context.
6. For an excellent and thorough explanation of an effective way to make things right, we highly recommend *When Sorry Isn't Enough* by Gary Chapman (author of *The Five Love Languages*) and Jennifer Thomas.

Chapter 14: Spiritual Training

1. See intentionalparents.org for resources.
2. See intentionalparents.org for the Bibles we recommend for kids in this stage.
3. Barna, 31.
4. Thank you, Glenn Miller, for the wise and balanced teaching you poured into us in those early years.
5. Mark Buchanan, *Your God Is Too Safe* (Colorado Springs: Multnomah, 2001), 131.
6. It took me many more years of learning to listen to realize I didn't need to come to church all dressed in my finest. You can read that story in my book, *He Speaks in the Silence* (Grand Rapids: Zondervan, 2015).
7. See https://en.wiktionary.org/wiki/kindergarchy.
8. See John 15:1–5.
9. John Lawrence, *Seven Laws of the Harvest* (Grand Rapids, MI: Kregel Publishing, 1975), 92.

Chapter 15: Four Things You Will Need

1. Mark Twain, *The Wit and Wisdom of Mark Twain: A Book of Quotations* (Mineola, NY: Dover Publications, 1998), 120.
2. Barna, 43.
3. Joshua McDowell and Dick Day, *Why Wait? What You Need to Know About the Teen Sexuality Crisis* (San Bernardino, CA: Here's Life Publishers, Inc., 1987), 178.
4. Jim Burns, "The Power of Bring There," HomeWord, Jan. 5, 2015, https:// homeword.com/articles/the-power-of-being-there/#.WjFueVWnGM8.
5. Shauna Niequist, *Bread and Wine* (Grand Rapids, MI: Zondervan, 2015), 258.

6. Read the whole story in 2 Chronicles 20.
7. Gary W. Smith, *Life-Changing Thoughts* (Bloomington, IN: AuthorHouse, 2009), 482.

Chapter 16: Three Secrets that Work

1. In Emerson Eggerich's excellent book, *Love & Respect in the Family*, he explains why—especially for men—this kind of side-by-side conversation is better than an intense "look me in the eye!" confrontation.
2. See 2 Chronicles 16:9.
3. For a full explanation of the meaning of the tool of *correction*, see chapter 10.
4. See chapter 6.

Chapter 17: Three Things Your Teenager Will Need

1. See Psalm 139:14.
2. Thanks to Pastor Jon Courson of the Applegate Christian Fellowship for this insight.
3. For more on spiritual gifts, see Romans 12:4–8, 1 Corinthians 12:4–11, 28.
4. John Mark is the pastor of a great church in urban Portland. Check out the website at http://bridgetown.church.
5. See Song of Songs.
6. Recommended materials can be found at intentionalparents.org.
7. See Proverbs 30:19.
8. Jim Burns, *Five Keys for Teaching Kids Healthy Sexuality* (Bloomington, MN: Bethany House, 2008).
9. See Proverbs 4:23 NASB, "What over your heart with all diligence, for from it flow the springs of life."
10. "Internet pornography by the numbers; a significant threat to society," Webroot, visited Dec. 13, 2017, https://www.webroot.com/us/en/home/resources/tips/digital-family-life/internet-pornography-by-the-numbers
11. Ibid.
12. David Briggs, "The No. 1 Reason Teens Keeps the Faith as Young Adults," *Huffington Post*, Dec. 29, 2014, http://www.huffingtonpost.com/david-briggs/the-no-1-reason-teens-kee_b_6067838.html#.
13. Susanna Schrobsdorff, "The Kids Are Not All Right" *TIME*, Vol.188, No.19, 47.
14. Shekar Raman, MD, quoted by Diana Spechler in "The Power of Touch: How Physical Contact Can Improve Your Health," *Huffington Post*, May 14, 2013, https://www.huffingtonpost.com/2013/05/14/the-power-of-touch-physical-contact-health_n_3253987.html.
15. Charles R. Swindoll, *Parenting: From Surviving to Thriving* (Nashville: Thomas Nelson, 2008), 20.

Chapter 18: The Box Now

1. Sharon Jayson, "Who's feeling stressed? Young adults, new survey shows." *USA Today*, Feb. 7, 2013. http://www.usatoday.com/story/news/nation/2013/02/06/stress-psychology-millennials-depression/1878295/.

2. Franklin Graham and Donna Lee Toney, *Billy Graham in Quotes* (Nashville: Thomas Nelson, 2011), 118.
3. Bob Goff, Twitter, May 30, 2017.
4. We've woven the NASB and NLT translations of Philippians 1:6 together here.

Chapter 19: The List

1. Zodhiates, 1198.
2. These "Letters to My Son" can be found in the archives of Diane's blog, hespeaksinthesilence.com.
3. John Mark Comer, *Loveology: God. Love. Marriage. Sex. And the Never-Ending Story of Male and Female* (Grand Rapids, MI: Zondervan, 2014).
4. Though some dismiss tithing as an Old Testament concept, Jesus affirmed the practice in Matthew 23:23. We believe that tithing is a great place to *begin* a life of generosity. See also Malachi 3:8–11 and 2 Corinthians 9:6–11.
5. See Luke 16:10–12, Matthew 25:21.
6. Buchanan, 131.
7. Visit https://www.intentionalparents.org for a free copy of Phil's Scripture reading plan.
8. This is the mission statement of Westside: a Jesus church in Portland, Oregon.
9. Jan Johnson, "Spiritual Formation as Abiding," Jan Johnson, 2015, http://janjohnson.org/pdf/Contagious.pdf.
10. Ananias and Paul in Acts 9, Cornelius and Peter in Acts 10.
11. See Acts 21:8–14.
12. See Jeremiah 17:8, James 3:6, Psalm 42:1.
13. Dallas Willard, *Hearing God, Updated and Expanded Edition* (Downers Grove, IL: IVP books, 2012), 143.
14. Diane Comer, *He Speaks in the Silence: Finding Intimacy with God by Learning to Listen* (Grand Rapids, MI: Zondervan, 2015).

Chapter 20: Putting the Roof On

1. Also see Appendix B: Leading Your Child to Jesus.
2. Edward M. Bounds, *Power through Prayer* (Grand Rapids, MI.: Baker Book House, 1972), 31.

Chapter 21: The Blessing, The Box, and the Key

1. "And I am convinced and sure of this very thing, that He Who began a good work in you will continue until the day of Jesus Christ [right up to the time of His return], developing [that good work] and perfecting and bringing it to full completion in you" (Philippians 2:6 AMP).

Appendix A: Retrofitting

1. Psalm 11:3 NASB
2. Also translated *grace*.
3. See Psalm 23:3.

Acknowledgments

This book has been in process for nearly forty years—thus a complete list of people who poured into and added to the material is probably futile. Yet here are a few who stand out:

First and foremost, we thank the God who rescued us, cleaned off the muck we'd accumulated in our years of living apart from Him, and then poured undeserved riches first into our souls, and then into our home.

To our kids: John Mark, Bekah, Elizabeth, and Matt. You've seen the worst of us and have chosen to rewrite history through eyes of grace. We will spend the rest of our lives attempting to live up to your loyal, merciful love.

To Tammy, Simona, Steve, and Brook, for all the grace you give us. You married into a family with such strong opinions, yet instead of rolling your eyes at us, you joined right in by adding your own wisdom to the conversations. We love each of you like our own kids!

Simo, your tender care of Diane's mom in her last days gave us the freedom to finish.

To our parents, who learned to follow Jesus later in life, thank you. You modeled humility while demonstrating the power of the Spirit to change lives. We miss you terribly.

To Bill and Laurie Keyes, who spent endless hours mentoring, teaching, exhorting, explaining, and describing what a family who follows Jesus looks like. Much of what we applied and now teach is pure plagiarism. We copied you then, and we hope to keep copying you through the next stages of our lives.

To the elders of our church, who had the vision to let us set aside six months to get it all down in teaching form: Steve Marshman, Todd Newell, Peter Quint, Matt Norman, and Tony Viducich. And our son, John Mark Comer, who led the charge.

Thanks go to several people who tirelessly helped us with research: Daniel Golder (Greek and Hebrew spellings), Richard Tamburro (theological review), Sunny Grover (those charts!), Tyler Hanns (for the house diagrams), Melody and Alex Graeber (statistics, articles, quotes, sources, books), and Kathie Taggart (you are the quote queen!)

Thank you to Dr. Gerry Breshears, Professor of Theology at Western Seminary, for making sure we correctly interpret the Scriptures we use in our teaching and writing. You are a godly, grace-oriented man with seemingly endless patience. Our respect for who you are, as well as for what you know, keeps growing.

To pastor and author Chuck Bomar, for showing us that building a good marriage is like putting rebar in the foundation of our homes. Brilliant.

To Cyndi and Alex Guidry, who believe in us and let us know over and over. Together, you're the finest blended family we know. Cyndi, you deserve a Ph.D. in the Language of Encouragement. And to Jay and Michelle Fordice who advised us, believed in us, and helped us get this ministry going—watching you intentionally raise up three men-in-the-making gives us hope for the next generation.

To the host of friends who offered godly input that has influenced both the way we parented our kids and what we teach parents now: Glen and Patty Miller, Stan and Cindy Campbell, Todd and Danita Newell, Jan Bisenius, and Mary Courson. And to Jodi Hughes, whose wisdom and insight enabled us to understand the specific concerns of single parents.

To the Intentional Parents International board: Tim and Brittany McDonald, and Tony and Beth Viducich. You are some of the most intentional parents we know, as well as our closest partners in ministry.

Thank you for giving endless hours of prayer, support, advice, structure, wisdom, and friendship.

Diane wishes to thank her Sistas: Julie Kohl, Melody Dobson, Mary Kay Taylor, Jodi Stilp, and Ann Menke. You prayed me through, invited (ok, pressured) me to come out and play, and encouraged me to keep writing when I thought I couldn't. You are the friends—my closest community—who give more than you take, more than I'll ever deserve. I love you.

Phil wants to thank lead pastor Dominic Doan and the current elders of Westside, A Jesus Church for giving us the freedom to continue to carry out our calling to bring hope and help to parents while still serving Jesus as part of the pastor/elder team.

To Michael and Rhonda Cotton, who invited us to enjoy their beautiful beach house, giving us the gift of a quiet place to write where the only distraction was the breathtaking view. Thank you for your generous hearts.

To Bill Jensen, literary agent extraordinaire. Someone forgot to tell you that once we signed the contract, your job was done. Instead you advised, coached, encouraged, and added content, lugging your computer into lunch at Jefe's too many times to count.

Carolyn McCready, how can we begin to thank you? You've opened doors for us while being a true friend and a tireless encourager. How is it that you never run out of energy, never complain, and always have time?

Mick Silva, you edited out the less-than-grace-filled parts, challenging us to rethink and rewrite until we said what we meant. You are an incredibly gifted editor and a gentle critic, as well as a fine man. May your girls grow up to know how rare a father they have.

Harmony Harkema, you are the best! Your laborious work of smoothing out awkward sentences and making sure every quote was sourced correctly, along with your enthusiastic support and kind words, gave us the energy we needed to complete the task.

To the rest of the Zondervan team: Kait Lamphere, and Curt

Diepenhorst for creating a beautiful book; Bridgette Brooks, Jennifer Verhage, and Tom Dean, for patiently guiding us through this project.

Finally, we want to thank the hundreds of parents who have come to our Intentional Parents conferences, both in the US and around the world. Your eagerness to listen and learn, to take notes and ask questions, to tell us your stories and open up your hearts—you are the riches we treasure.

To learn more about Intentional Parents or how to host
a conference, go to www.intentionalparents.org.

For more inspirational content for parents, subscribe and
follow our blog at www.intentionalparents.org/blog.

To stay connected with the Intentional Parents
ministry, follow us on social media:

Instagram: @intentional_parents

Twitter: @intparents

He Speaks in the Silence

Finding Intimacy with God by Learning to Listen

Diane Comer

Diane Comer was a young pastor's wife, a mother with a family and a future. Her life appeared charmed, *perfect.* Yet just beneath the surface, a vastly different story was unfolding.

Disappointed with all she had been told was supposed to fulfill her, Diane begged God in desperation to give her more.

And he did.

But first he took her through a trial so debilitating it almost destroyed what little faith she had.

He allowed her to go deaf.

The wonderful life Dian thought she had signed up for was shattered. The fact she knew God could heal her and yet chose not to, despite all her desperate pleas and prayers, shook Diane's faith to its very foundation.

Yet in her brokenness and grief, in the midst of deep doubt and raging anger, she heard God's voice as clearly as if he were speaking in her ear. He showed her a way out of her despair, out of her performance-driven life, a way into a tender, intimate relationship with him.

Using vivid parallels between her deafness and every woman's struggle to hear God, *He Speaks in the Silence* will lead you on your own journey to learn to listen to God, finding intimacy with the Savior and the soul-deep satisfaction we all long for.

Available in stores and online!

ZONDERVAN®
.com